PENGUIN LIFE

TALK WITH HER

Kimberly Wolf, M.Ed., is an educator, speaker, and educational consultant with an undergraduate degree in gender studies from Brown University and a master's degree in human development and psychology from the Harvard Graduate School of Education. Her experiences growing up in Los Angeles and attending an all-girls school sparked her passion for equipping girls with the wisdom and skills they need to succeed in all areas of life during the school years and beyond. Fifteen years into her career, through conversations with friends, colleagues, and collaborators who were fathers of daughters, Wolf realized she was in a unique position to demystify girlhood for dads, helping them communicate better with their daughters, maximize their parental impact, and inspire young women to reach their potential. In addition to being an expert in her field, she is also a daughter with a deep personal belief in the transformative power of strong father-daughter relationships. *Talk with Her* is her first book.

TALK WITH HER

A Dad's Essential Guide to Raising Healthy, Confident, and Capable Daughters

KIMBERLY WOLF

life

For all the boys and men who have lit the way,
especially Dad, Alex, Max, and Leo

PENGUIN BOOKS

An imprint of Penguin Random House LLC
penguinrandomhouse.com

A Penguin Life Book

"A Guide to Being an Ally to Transgender and Nonbinary Youth" and "Glossary" used with
permission from The Trevor Project.

LIBRARY OF CONGRESS CATALOGING-IN-PUBLICATION DATA
Names: Wolf, Kimberly, author.
Title: Talk with her : a dad's essential guide to raising healthy, confident,
and capable daughters / Kimberly Wolf.
Description: First edition. | New York : Penguin Books, [2022] |
Includes bibliographical references and index.
Identifiers: LCCN 2021014084 (print) | LCCN 2021014085 (ebook) |
ISBN 9780143135272 (paperback) | ISBN 9780525506942 (ebook)
Subjects: LCSH: Daughters. | Fathers and daughters. | Girls—Psychology. |
Girls—Conduct of life. | Parenting.
Classification: LCC HQ777 .W656 2022 (print) |
LCC HQ777 (ebook) | DDC 649/.133—dc23
LC record available at https://lccn.loc.gov/2021014084
LC ebook record available at https://lccn.loc.gov/2021014085

Printed in the United States of America
2nd Printing

Set in Baskerville MT Std
Designed by Cassandra Garruzzo

CONTENTS

The Girls' Empowerment Movement Needs Its Dads

K immy, the waterfalls are the fullest they've been in years. We have to go see them!"

Yosemite is my dad's idea of paradise. He loves national parks and waterfalls, and Yosemite checks both of those boxes in grand fashion. Growing up in rural Illinois, it was one of the first places in California he ever visited, and he remains captivated by its majesty. One of my favorite memories of all time was this father-daughter road trip we took there together.

We left LA and headed up the 5 toward the mountains. My dad staked out Dairy Queens on the route, a childhood ritual of his. We listened to the Beach Boys and a bunch of nineties one-hit wonders, the soundtrack to many of our special times together. We chatted, and I sang along with the playlist while he listened.

We started to see signs for the outlet stores, and my dad had another idea.

"Kimmy, what if we stop at the Polo outlet"—also one of his favorite places—"and get matching outfits? Then we can take matching pictures all over the Valley floor!"

I looked at him. "That would be awesome, Dad. I would love

that!" So we took the exit. He bought us matching mint-green pull-over sweatshirts. Then he got carried away and bought us matching baseball hats in one of the gift shops at the park, and we spent three glorious days in Yosemite hiking around, marveling at the waterfalls, having father-daughter dinners in the old lodges, and finding kind strangers to take pictures of us in our coordinated gear.

I was thirty-three years old.

I would never have gone along with this as a teenager—I was way too cool. However, I've come to realize that it was all the groundwork my dad laid when I was younger, it was his powering through some challenging adolescent years with me, keeping our talks going and building our connection, that facilitated this memorable trip years later.

I grew up in Los Angeles, where I went to an all-girls' high school. During that time, I became acutely aware of the cultural forces contributing to my sense of self, my body confidence, romantic relationship ideals, and overall well-being. In the spotlight of Hollywood, societal expectations and media's influence over my life were unquestionable.

Adolescence was an exciting and also rough-and-tumble phase for me and my friends, as it has been for all girls since the beginning of time. I weathered my own struggles and witnessed others around me wading through their own challenges. Even the most supportive parents and watchful teachers couldn't have full visibility into our complex inner lives, the pressures we faced, and the obstacles we were surmounting on our journeys to womanhood. Sometimes we couldn't articulate our experiences. More often, we didn't want to bring them up. I started to think we all needed a lot more help navigating the real world than we were getting.

It was the early 2000s. I looked to magazines and books and the Internet for information, but I couldn't find resources that felt reliable and relevant on topics like relationships and mental health. As a freshman in college, I already knew I wanted a career in girlhood, to be a guiding presence for young women so that they could struggle less and achieve more in all areas of their lives.

I have spent my academic and professional career studying, advocating for, and teaching adolescent girls. As a gender studies major at Brown University, I wrote my senior thesis on the impact of *Seventeen* magazine on girls' health. At Harvard, while studying for a master's degree in human development and psychology, I further immersed myself in the study of girlhood. I've written articles, developed curricula, spoken at conferences, and given interviews about girls. As a national speaker, school wellness counselor, and writer I have reached thousands of girls and answered countless questions about the habits and strategies that can boost their mental, physical, emotional, and relational health. I've designed courses in positive psychology, media literacy, and healthy relationships, all with the goal of supporting teenagers' personal development. I'm also an educational entrepreneur who has launched my own companies and advised other businesses and nonprofits driving positive change for young women around the globe.

I never expected men to be at the center of my work. But something happened a few years ago that shifted my focus.

I was standing outside an LA coffee shop with a potential investor for a girls' health platform I was launching. As we were saying goodbye, he said he had one more question. I was ready with another sound bite from my plan, but then he said, "I just got divorced. Can I start dating again? Or will that hurt my daughter?"

I had an answer, but I was caught off guard by the fact that in the middle of his workday on a Tuesday, this man was worried about how to be a better dad to his daughter. Of course he was. But this was a revelation to me.

It was only the first of many conversations I would have with men who sought me out for real advice about their girls. I had similar experiences in other business meetings, in conversations with the administrators at schools where I was presenting, and with parents of girls I was teaching and mentoring. Over and over again, I encountered fathers of daughters who felt concerned, lost, and out-of-touch when it came to guiding their girls. They all had worries and questions. They confessed to feeling as if they were losing ground to their wives, their daughters' friends, and popular media and culture. They wondered if they should just sit on the sidelines until their daughters "grew out of it." They had questions like:

- She complains about her weight a lot. What do I say to her?

- She texts with her friends until 2:00 a.m. most nights. Can I do anything to stop it?

- My wife thinks it's too early for her to date, but I think it's fine. Is it okay?

I asked my own dad if it was harder for him to raise me through my adolescent years than my brother, and he replied without hesitation, "Absolutely."

Realizing that this need I had stumbled upon was very widespread, I thought, *I can help with this.*

As I immersed myself in the research about fatherhood, in search of more data to offer the dads I was encountering, I realized something else: for a very long time, like so many daughters before me, I had taken the positive potential of father-daughter communication and relationships for granted.

I wrote this book as an insider when it comes to teenage girls. I was, of course, once a teenage girl myself, and with years of professional experience, I have a knowledge base you can tap into. I'm also a daughter who is really close to my dad, and I can connect much of what he taught me and the conversations we had to my drive and my confidence—and the skills that have helped me build a fulfilling life and achieve my greatest accomplishments.

What I am sure of is that you have vast potential to influence your daughter's life for the better. Research ties strong father-daughter relationships to multiple positive outcomes for young women, from better health to increased confidence to long-term professional success. Your presence in your daughter's life can inspire her to eat better,[1] reduce the chance that she becomes sexually active before she's ready,[2] and boost her career ambitions.[3]

Some of the most powerful training girls can get for the adult world is through the interactions and conversations they have at home with their dads. How you treat your daughter and talk with her will shape her expectations for future personal and professional relationships. You can help your daughter recognize positive relationships and learn how to self-advocate in the face of damaging or dangerous power dynamics. Guiding her in thoughtful parent-child conversations and negotiations, you can help her develop an essential comfort level interacting with men in positions of power. Making her feel heard and respected, you can boost your daughter's confidence, inspiring her to discover her potential to make unique contributions to the world.

Moms feel somewhat prepared for their girls' adolescence, no doubt because they've been through it themselves, and also because generations of women before them have passed down their secrets to raising girls. I've noticed that men ask me different questions than women—questions characterized by a lot more fear and a lot less confidence. By nature of not having been young women themselves, men lack a baseline of knowledge. It's so simple, but something not often enough addressed. As a result, the questions men ask me suggest they are worried about doing a bad job when really, most of the time, they are doing a lot right.

This book won't just show you how to avoid mistakes; it will reveal the positive effect you are already having. You will learn that "communicating" doesn't mean having "big" conversations all the time. You'll see how creating even the smallest moments of connection can build bonds. And you'll discover that if your daughter shuts you down, that means you are right where you need to be: present in her life. It may seem like she's not listening to you, but she can hear you, and that's what matters most.

I wrote this book to answer the questions that are top of mind for fathers, to help you support your daughter but also so that you can spend more time feeling successful and less time feeling worried, helpless, and confused. Teenage girls may seem scary, until you have a basic understanding of what they are going through. This book will broaden your perspective, reminding you that girls are just evolving humans, and they really need their dads to step up.

I'm not always going to tell you exactly what rules to make, when to give her a cell phone, whether her bedroom door should be opened or closed, when she can date, whether you should spy on her social media, or when she should be grounded. These decisions should account for your family's values, your daughter's age and maturity, her social context, and your relationship with her. But I will give you advice, tools, and guidelines to help you in the process.

This book is informed by years of research and hundreds of conversations I've had with girls and their dads. I have also rounded up the latest research on girls' well-being and behavior, and I've called on other leading experts in girls' development to give you the information, strategies, and inspiration you need to be successful. We will look at sensitive topics up close and think about what exactly you might do and say . . . and a few things you'll want to avoid doing and saying. This book is about finding your own father-daughter communication style. It's about realizing that, at one time or another, every dad feels the same dread you feel and experiences similar moments of weakness. It's about shaking off the fear that you are going to mess her up and instead tapping into your own inherent wisdom, the kind that is going to make your daughter an empowered woman.

I recommend first reading this book cover to cover because it's going to make you feel more confident and in control at a time when you are conditioned to feel the opposite. Then, you'll be able to refer back to these pages to help you navigate conversations or conflicts as they arise.

In chapter 1, "You Are Important, Even When You Feel Irrelevant: The Essential Role You Play in Her Life," I talk about the cornerstones of your daughter's adolescence and outline the natural and acceptable reasons you sometimes feel out of touch and at a loss for what to do and say. This chapter will explain where your daughter is coming from, the evolving roles of fathers, and your impact on your daughter's development, even when it seems like you can't do anything right.

In chapter 2, "'The Talk' Is Dead: Thirty Ways to Level Up Your Father-Daughter Communication," you'll discover the ways you can make a difference in your daughter's life, from setting the tone for your relationship with her to having sit-down conversations to simply being present watching TV, a concert, or sporting event with her.

Chapter 3, "Maximizing Your Impact: Information and Inspiration for Key Conversations," highlights the nineteen fundamental topics defining your daughter's life. You will find the information you need to address them with care and confidence. Categorized under Boost Her Well-Being, Strengthen Her Relationships, or Broaden Her Horizons, you will find briefs on topics ranging from clothing choices to substance use to love and career. You can read this chapter from start to finish, or you can skip to those sections most relevant to you in the moment. Think of each section in chapter 3 as a guide within the guide.

For each topic within chapter 3, you will find the following subsections to build your background knowledge, help you plan your approach, and point you in the direction of more information and support:

Some Background includes cutting-edge research, expert perspectives, terminology reviews, and anecdotes to help bring broad-ranging and often overwhelming topics into focus. I have done the research for you so that you can begin any conversation with an essential baseline of knowledge.

Your Goal describes your ideal impact. No, your overarching goals do not include things like "get my daughter to wear longer shorts" or "prevent her from dating forever." Tempting, I know. (Also, good luck.) Instead, these goals will help you focus on deeper, more lasting impacts than effectively policing your daughter's everyday actions. Examples include supporting your daughter in developing her personal style as part of healthy self-expression ("Clothing Choices") or helping your daughter recognize healthy romantic relationships and her power to shape them ("Love").

Rule #1 points to a common trap that you want to avoid for your daughter's well-being, your own peace of mind, or both. For instance, when it comes to friendship, don't tell your daughter she "needs to be friends with everyone." That message can translate to a lot of pressure and spur people-pleasing habits.

Talking Points are "ins" for conversations. They incorporate ideas from the research and expert contributions in *Some Background* as well as additional insights that will help you meet your daughter where she is developmentally to have a meaningful interaction. In "Mental Health" (page 76), for example, talking points include "A Mental Health Condition Is Nothing to be Ashamed Of" and "Symptoms Can Feel Permanent, but They Are Often Temporary."

How It's Done provides specifics on what to say and what not to say. Words are powerful, and this section will sharpen your ability to say the right thing more often. For instance, if your daughter says, "Dad, let's go on a diet together!" Don't say, "Great idea, honey!" A better response would be to ask a question such as "That's an interesting suggestion. What makes you want to change your eating habits?"

Beyond the Conversation reveals the numerous ways you can reinforce important messages for your daughter, whether by setting a positive example or seeking additional support for her or yourself.

Chapter 4, "Building Your Support Team: Who and How to Call for Help," highlights that it's okay not to have all the answers. Crisis situations and parent burnout can be relieved with the help of outside counselors and health-care providers. This section will present common scenarios and tell you who to call and what questions to ask them.

In chapter 5, "FAQs: Fathers Asking Questions," I answer questions men ask me that speak to their struggles balancing fatherhood with their other responsibilities, relationships, and personal needs.

Chapter 6, "You've Got This: You and Your Daughter in the Long Game," will show you how the foundational relationship you strengthen during your daughter's adolescent years will serve both of you for decades to come.

Once you've read this book through, you will have a sense of the communication strategies that feel right for you. I suggest that you pair them with key topics, which you can review in the chapters as they come up for you and your daughter.

You don't have to do everything all at once. Making a lifelong impact happens one conversation at a time. And, if you put in the time with your daughter now, it is likely to pay off. Whether or not matching outfits are your thing, maybe one day your daughter will happily go along with your crazy ideas, so you can continue having a positive impact on her life and making memories for years to come.

You Are Important, Even When You Feel Irrelevant

The Essential Role You Play in Her Life

When little girls are born, it's as if they come with built-in warnings for parents, especially dads: "Just wait until she's a teenager."

Teenage girls have quite the reputation in our society, and it's not a reputation that parenting dreams are made of. From the time of the gender reveal, most parents are conditioned to brace for the middle and high school years, expecting their girls to become moody, self-centered, difficult, rebellious versions of their former selves.

I will say that much of what you have heard (and dreaded) about teenage girls will probably turn out to be true of your daughter at one time or another: She will be less affectionate, trading snuggles for side-hugs. She won't gush about how much you mean to her. She'll fail to thank you for a lot of the little things and won't understand the significance of your grand gestures. She will complain to you. She'll discount your advice. She will make you feel as though everyone else—literally *everyone* else—knows more than you do. She'll get angry at you and stay mad for extended periods. She will tell you that you're embarrassing. She will bury herself in her phone when you're excited to see and talk to her, and she will make it known that she would rather hang out with her friends than with you. She will give you attitude, make decisions you don't understand, hang out with friends who concern you, and date people you don't like. She will confuse you, and she will make you worry.

Raising a teenage daughter is a process practically engineered to make you feel useless and ineffective much of the time. It can feel deeply personal and emotional for fathers, and if you have moments characterized by deep sadness, defeat, frustration, or even the sense that you're now managing one more "complicated" relationship with a woman in your life, you aren't alone.

But what's important to know is that the teenage years are also a time of wonder for your daughter, a time for new experiences, expanding knowledge, self-exploration, and deep interpersonal connection. A lot of what may strike you as hurtful, bewildering, annoying, or disrespectful—and a lot of what might feel especially unfamiliar or scary for most men who haven't experienced girlhood firsthand—are often age-appropriate markers of healthy development and the natural individuation process that begins in adolescence.

Some Cornerstones of Her Experience

Through the pages of this book, you will learn about the intricacies of "girl world" and how you can help make the adolescent years go more smoothly for your daughter. But before we get there, here are some overarching themes of your daughter's physical, emotional, intellectual, and social development that can help explain some of the hurtful, concerning behaviors you might observe or find yourself on the receiving end of.

PUBERTY WILL CHALLENGE HER

While experts are a bit at odds about the endpoint of adolescence, puberty is the agreed-upon starting point, typically beginning for girls between the ages of eight and thirteen. Hair in new places, breakouts, breasts, weight gain, curves, hips, new sexual sensations, growth spurts, and new body odors are all part of the process and take some getting used to.[1] Even the most confident girls will feel clumsy and self-conscious.

It's hard to put into words the impact that having monthly periods has on girls and women, and getting accustomed to them is a serious adjustment.[2] It's surprising for some girls who have gotten their first periods to learn that they're still expected to go to school when they're menstruating. *"Really? I'm embarrassed. I'm bleeding, I feel sick. I just want to take a nap. And I have to show up for class?"* And it's not uncommon for girls who tell me about their stressful days to add, "And can you believe I also got my period?!" For some girls, as I will discuss later in "Body Positivity" (see page 35), the impacts of the menstrual cycle can be so severe that they require medical attention.

The physical transition of adolescence would be hard enough if it were a solo journey, but it's not. Girls wonder if people can see their bras through their clothes. They notice whether other girls are shaving their legs. They are aware when classmates notice their breasts. And there's always a grandparent or aunt who makes a comment about "blossoming" that would make anyone in the room want to crawl under a table. You probably have or will pick up on this awkwardness at some point. The physical changes of adolescence are one of the main forces that can pull fathers and daughters apart. Girls don't always want to be as affectionate as they adjust to their new bodies, and, simultaneously, a lot of dads find themselves feeling like they should give their girls physical space. While this separation can help both girls and their dads feel more comfortable in ways, it can translate to emotional distance.

SHE'LL START FINDING HERSELF

Identity work is a major task of adolescence, as you'll see under multiple headings in the following pages. You may notice your daughter trying new hairstyles and clothing styles. She may ask you to call her by chosen pronouns or nicknames. She'll have more independence to choose classes, clubs, and activities to pursue. She will look toward her friends for support and connection as she naturally gains freedom to experience the world independently of your family unit. In the name of fitting in and being accepted by peers, she may take some distance from you, which can come in the form of telling you how embarrassing you are. The changes as you experience them can be downright startling, especially the ones that fly in the face of your most deeply held beliefs. But don't worry too hard or too fast. While some aspects of her emerging identity will stick, others will fall by the wayside.

SHE'LL MAKE SOME QUESTIONABLE DECISIONS

In Professor Laurence Steinberg's lab at Temple University, he and his team study adolescent behavior. Dr. Steinberg explains that there are two brain functions at work simultaneously in adolescence.[3] The first involves the prefrontal cortex, which contributes to advanced thinking, impulse control, and self-regulation. This system isn't fully developed until adolescents' early twenties, leaving them relatively ill-equipped to control themselves. The second brain function, involving the limbic system, contributes to processing emotions, social information, and information related to punishment and rewards. Surging hormones cause the limbic system to become easily aroused in early adolescence.

"Adolescents are just more likely to get excited about things, in both positive and negative ways, and they have more difficulty controlling those emotions," Dr. Steinberg told me. "It's like having the accelerator pressed to the floor before there's a good braking system in place."[4]

Because adolescents are programmed to get caught up in the moment, they are less likely than adults to be thoughtful about the future and the potential consequences of their actions.[5] In addition, right and wrong aren't always immediately obvious to adolescents, because they're having a lot of new experiences. Their lives are marked by much trial and error as they try to reconcile what they've been taught is "right" with what friends, popular culture, and media suggest is expected and acceptable behavior.

Adolescents can make questionable decisions related to experimenting with drugs and alcohol, texting and driving, testing the boundaries of academic integrity, sexting, and engaging in unsafe sexual behaviors. Developing good judgment is a gradual, imperfect, two-steps-forward-and-one-step-back kind of process for adolescents. Even the most capable, "mature" girls will make decisions that will leave you scratching your head—or furious.

SHE'LL FEEL THE PRESSURE

Today's adolescents are under more pressure than any other generation in history.[6] A 2014 American Psychological Association study of 1,018 teens revealed that their stress levels rivaled those of their parents and that these stress levels are surpassing what even teens believe is healthy for them.[7] Girls have a lot to do, and a lot of expectations to live up to, all while managing the physical demands of adolescence with brains that are works in progress. School is a lot of work. Applying to college is a long, competitive, high-stakes process. Social lives and drama take up time and energy. Social media adds complexity, offering sophisticated tools for quantifying friends and praise, while delivering a constant stream of curated, polished images of what girls and their lives "should be." There are endless opportunities to compare and despair and to conclude (falsely) that they don't measure up and maybe never will. Young adults, with easy access to the news, are also aware of what can be very frightening local, national, and international developments. They live in an era when lockdown drills are the norm. They are affected by the political tensions dominating our national discourse, with girls reporting more stress than boys in regards to the topic.[8] And they lived through the COVID-19 pandemic, an international crisis the likes of which is entirely unprecedented and has the potential to stoke long-term mental health issues across large swaths of the global population.

As adults, it's easy to think that girls' lives are less complicated than ours, that the problems they face are less significant. It's easy to think, "What does she have to worry about? She just has to go to school. I am paying all of her bills." But to girls, the stress they experience is real, intense, and even frightening at times. It can affect their mental health, physical health, performance (academic and extracurricular), and relationships, just as it can our own. And the stress they feel isn't just from their own experiences. If there is stress in your family, if there is tension in your household from an unhealthy relationship with your spouse, financial woes, a chronically ill family member, or the death of a loved one (which we'll delve into more in "Grief and Tragedy" on page 113), your daughter is feeling it, too. As Dr. Steinberg mentioned, adolescents are likely to get more excited about things in both positive and negative ways. The hormonal surges of adolescence mean that your daughter's emotional experiences will be in Technicolor. So if there are times when she's less sweet, loving, and fun to be around than your little girl of the past, it often won't be about you. More likely, it means she can use a little extra compassion and patience.

Is Being a Teenage Girl Really That Unpleasant?

A few years ago, I was standing on the floor of a university auditorium, about to pitch my plan for the girls' media platform I was building. I looked up at three balconies packed with hundreds of potential investors, advisers, and business partners, only about thirty of whom were women.

"Who in here has ever known a teenage girl?" I asked in my introduction. People sighed and chuckled, some squirming in their seats, as every hand went up.

"Okay, who in the room has ever been a teenage girl?" The few women in the room raised their hands as the men turned to look at them.

"And who," I continued, "would ever go back and do it again?" People exchanged knowing smiles, and one woman raised her hand—only to lower it immediately after realizing that she was the only one in the room with her hand in the air. Peer pressure, most certainly.

The preteen and teenage years can be exciting, joyful, and positively productive. But it turns out that if you ask women if they would want to go back and be teenage girls again, you'll probably receive a hard "no" in reply. You can't take your daughter's adolescence personally. Girls have a lot on their plates and a lot on their minds, and while you will at times feel frustrated, defensive, and defeated, adolescence is one of the times your daughter most benefits from your presence. It's not all easy-breezy for her, and she needs you—even if she acts like she doesn't even like you.

Your Role and the Recent
Evolution of Fatherhood

Popular conceptions of father-daughter relationships have their roots in age-old gender roles. For millennia, while women acted as caregivers to their children, men were primarily breadwinners and protectors. As a result of these traditional divisions of labor, there continues to be a vast body of knowledge geared toward women that moms can tap into at a moment's notice. There are family stories and old wives' tales, neighborhood networks, mommy blogs, shelves of books and whispered secrets to help mothers do the job of mothering. Mothers and their caregiving powers have always been highlighted in movies, TV shows, and on commercials. Women have a lot of built-in support passed down through generations, and as I've already mentioned, by nature of being female themselves, they have particular insight into the lives of girls. Men have been left entirely out of the brain trust, until recently.

Today, fathers are contributing greatly in the parenting department—but much of society still views women as the most qualified to do the job. Researchers at Pew Research Center have been leaders in exploring the roles and influence of fathers.

"Dads in general are spending about three times as much time caring for children as they did in the midsixties, and today, dads are as likely as moms to say that being a parent is a key aspect of their identity," Dr. Gretchen Livingston told me of their research at the Pew Center.

"But," she went on, "at the same time, we still see that women are more often seen as the default caregiver or as the more natural care-giver."

When Dr. Livingston and her colleagues asked research partici-pants if it's best for children if one parent stays home, if both parents stay home, or if both parents work, survey respondents were more likely to say that it was best if one parent stayed home and that moms, not dads, should be the parents to stay home with children.

The clash of old and new paradigms has led to a palpable tension and friction among parents. Men are more involved parents than ever before, but it's a bit of a double-edged sword. There is both more opportunity for and more expectations placed upon men. Men are expected to engage more with their children, co-parent more actively, and share housework and child-rearing duties with their partners—and they are doing all these things. Findings from Pew Research also show that 60 percent of moms are struggling to find balance between work and family, and 52 percent of dads report feeling the same way. What has been called the "double shift," a concept historically related to women's struggle to balance family and career, is now affecting men at similar rates. Dads are now ex-pected to step up, but they don't have all the information at their fingertips. Moms, springing into action when girls need guidance or are in crisis, often do so without having time to consider that fathers could benefit from some direct coaching on how to handle a given situation. Since dads haven't had the same kind of experience that women have had, they often *feel* clueless and useless, and a destruc-tive cycle can develop that leads to dads feeling like they need to step out of the fray and take a step back from parenting their daughters. If you are feeling like you have expectations to live up to but don't quite know how to do it or feel that you've been largely unsuccessful, this may be why. In my conversations with dads, I hear it all the time:

- Am I ready for her teenage years?
- I'm working long days, and at night, my wife is upset that I'm not home enough with my daughters.
- I don't feel like I know what I'm doing.
- My spouse is constantly correcting my parenting.

But it is crucial to know and remember that the times your daughter, co-parent, or broader cultural forces may make you feel powerless, you are a primary force in fostering your daughter's overall well-being and teaching her the skills she needs to fulfill her potential in every area of her life from here forward.[9]

The Gold Standards of Good Fathering

In a world where girls are seemingly under siege by social drama, social media, and popular ideals of female perfection, knowing where to start being a "good dad" can feel overwhelming. How can your influence possibly hold up against these all-powerful external forces? Three factors make up the foundation of effective parenting when it comes to your daughter:

BEING A POSITIVE PRESENCE

In the field of fatherhood research, there's a focus on a concept called "paternal investment." It's what University of Utah professor Bruce Ellis explained to me as "an umbrella term, capturing factors like father presence versus absence, whether he's living in the home, how often he sees his daughter, and also the quality of father—how warm and supportive he is, how much time he spends with his children, how harsh he is."[10] Positive paternal investment is tied to a broad range of benefits for girls. Contributing to your daughter's health and safety is an important start, since her well-being creates the foundation for her to flourish. Being there for her in all other ways, supporting and guiding her as she navigates the ups and downs of adolescence, can pay dividends when it comes to helping her feel grounded and empowered in the near- and long-term.[11] This is true for biological fathers, stepfathers, and adoptive fathers.[12] And it's true for fathers who don't physically live with their daughters.[13] As I discuss in the next chapter, there are plenty of ways to make your presence known and to connect with your daughter, even from a distance.

TAKING A WARM BUT FIRM APPROACH

Also known as "authoritative parenting," taking a loving approach—even when having hard conversations, setting boundaries, and correcting unfavorable behaviors or disciplining your child—is ideal.[14] (This is as opposed to authoritarian parenting, which is *not* ideal.) It fosters trust and open communication, allowing you to set the guidelines while also making your daughter feel supported and accepted. This parenting style is important for mothers as well as fathers (and for children of all genders, not just daughters), and studies have found that it is universally effective.[15] In one of the most striking studies of father-child dynamics, a team of psychologists from thirteen nations analyzed five hundred scientific studies and found that warmth and love (or lack thereof) shown by fathers can have greater positive (or negative) impacts than mothers' love on girls' development. The reason for this is that men are often seen as authority figures in their homes, and so their love or their judgment can seem to carry more weight for their children.[16]

Regardless of your geographic context, religion, or other cultural characteristics, authoritative parenting is the style most associated with ideal outcomes in the parenting of adolescents, including strong parent-child communication and curtailing risky behaviors among adolescents.[17] As Dr. Steinberg puts it, "It works for everyone."

HAVING CONVERSATIONS

In my early research for this book, I asked other experts across areas of parenting and adolescent development what their main advice was to parents of girls, and the resounding theme was simple: talk with her. Authoritative parenting and being present provide a strong foundation for powerful conversations. But your end goal should be setting the scene to discuss meaningful topics with your daughter, to hear her thoughts and offer her guidance whenever possible.[18] That's what this book is all about.

In the next chapter, you'll read more than two dozen tips that will illuminate what you are already doing well; how you can be a more present, authoritative parent; and how to set the scene for effective conversations. If you do these things, according to the research on father-daughter relationships, these are the positive impacts you have the potential to make on your daughter:

- Boost her grades and inspire her career achievement.[19]

- Help her develop strong self-esteem and a healthy body image.[20]

- Curb risky behaviors including sexual intercourse before she is ready and experimentation with drugs and alcohol.[21]

- Inspire her to develop healthy eating habits, and reduce the risk that she will develop an eating disorder.[22]

- Reduce the risk that she'll become depressed.[23]

- Support strong relational communication skills.[24]

- Help inspire her to have healthy romantic relationships.[25]

The importance of your presence in your daughter's life and the love you show her cannot be overstated.

2

"The Talk" Is Dead

Thirty Ways to Level Up Your Father-Daughter Communication

Now, how do you do it? How do you get through to your daughter in her adolescent years, a time when the multitude of changes she's experiencing can create distance between the two of you? As is the title of this chapter, "the talk" *is* dead. Having the maximum positive influence on your daughter will take countless conversations over time.

While moments of easy, mutually enjoyable, and productive communication do happen between daughters and their parents in the adolescent years, you're not alone if it feels like it's hard to get through to your daughter or if the thought of talking to her about sensitive topics feels scary or even impossible. There are times when everyone feels awkward and when tension is palpable, and you'll feel like you can't say anything right and worry that what you say will be misinterpreted. Adolescent girls are experts at letting parents know that they don't appreciate feedback, guidance, or advice. In conversations with adolescent girls, you might receive one or more of the following verbal or nonverbal responses:

- Preoccupation and disinterest.

- Eye rolls.

- Refusal to make eye contact.

- Hair twirling.

- Fidgeting with her phone.

- Turning on the TV.

- Walking away.

- Slamming doors.

- "Oh, you're coming with us?"

- "Whatever."

- "I know, okay?"

- "Why do you care, anyway?"

- "You don't understand."

- "You have no idea what you are talking about."

- "Ugh, please stop."

- "I have to go."

- "Why can't you be a normal parent like everyone else?!"

What's counterintuitive about talking to your teenage daughter is that this unpleasant list doubles as your rubric for success. As you now know, it's developmentally appropriate, at least at times, for your daughter to find much of what you do and say insufferable, annoying, and/or embarrassing. And so, if you are getting any of this negative feedback, it means you're right on track. Bask in the eye rolls, because it means you are involved in your daughter's life. You are there, making an impact, even if she sometimes (or usually) won't do what you say right away.

When it comes to connecting with your daughter, what you need to remember above all else is this: a lot of what has made you successful in the past—the ways you have approached conflict and communicated to create the outcomes you want—often does not apply when you are trying to get through to your adolescent daughter. You might see yourself as an authority figure, a persuasive communicator, a successful goal-setter, the most polished manager. But when it comes to your daughter, you are going to need to get used to being uncomfortable and having your expertise dismissed. You must come consistently from a place where you expect to be shut down. You cannot always expect rationality. You cannot count on reasonable outcomes in the short term. You're not often going to "win" right now. She's on a whole different frequency.

All of this said, there are plenty of ways to build your bonds and have meaningful, productive talks, all while preventing and de-escalating drama in your father-daughter interactions. Strong communication is about talking and listening. But it's also about your style, the example you set, and the space—literal and figurative—you make for connection and conversation with your daughter. Meaningful interactions with her will grow from the foundation you build day by day.

The following strategies will help you feel more successful as soon as you start using them. You don't have to use all of them, but the more of them you incorporate, the more opportunities you'll create to be there for your daughter to hear you.

Setting the Stage for Conversations

#1: Jump in. You must participate. You must plan to touch on as many topics as possible with your daughter, not only the conversations you find easy and approachable. It's not just about teaching her lessons related to the issue at hand. It's about showing up for her, listening to her, and sharing your viewpoints, so that she feels loved, seen, and supported, and so that she knows you are open to talking whenever she needs you. It's also about preparing her to have uncomfortable conversations. Remember that practicing with you, a man, who differs from her in gender, age, and experience, is great practice for the rest of her life. Talk with your daughter, and she'll be more prepared for and fearless in the face of high-stakes conversations in her personal and business relationships.

#2: Be there. Talk to your daughter when you are in the car together. Sit down next to her and watch what she's watching. You can ask questions and start conversations. Even if you say nothing at times, simply reading a book in a chair near where she's texting on her phone or bringing her a favorite snack when she's studying, you are signaling your presence in her life and making yourself available, if she wants to talk.[1]

#3: Create moments of connection.[2] Consider picking something to watch or read together, planning a father-daughter dinner, or taking a vacation, just the two of you. If you live separately from your daughter or you're traveling for work, text and video-call her.[3] You can also play games together online or watch the same movie or sporting event at the same time. Your daughter isn't usually going to take the initiative to spend time with you, and if you're making the plans, she might not want to go. She might complain and have an attitude when she's there. And you will feel like you are wasting your time and your money. But one-on-one time gives you opportunities to grow your father-daughter relationship and make memories separately from other family influences and dynamics. Some of your best conversations will happen against these backdrops, and when your daughter looks back, she'll appreciate what she learned and the special time you took.

#4: Capitalize on teachable moments. A teachable moment is any instance where you have an opportunity to voice your opinion, make your values known, or ask your daughter for her perspective. Teachable moments are your *in*. They happen all the time, and if you take advantage of them, they will keep you consistent in your communication. If you are watching a TV show together and something comes up that you can comment on, like underage drinking or an unhealthy relationship dynamic, make a comment. Or if your daughter tells you about something happening with her friends at school, ask her how it made her feel and if she thinks everyone handled it the right way. If you are driving your daughter and her friends and you overhear them talking about any questionable behavior, like vaping, take the opportunity to ask some questions about trends your daughter is seeing among her friends and how she feels about it. Explore her feelings on topics together and share your thoughts. This strategy also gives your daughter some insight into how you might handle a conversation about something happening in her life. Talking about friends in the hypothetical allows your daughter to test you, and with hope, come to a conclusion along the lines of "Good. I know my dad is okay. It's not going to be too bad if I talk to him about [fill in the difficult topic]."

"Kids are very sensitive about whether their parents will freak out," Dr. Mitch Prinstein, a developmental psychologist at the University of North Carolina at Chapel Hill, told me. "If they know their parents won't overreact, adolescents will be more likely to talk to them."[4]

#5 Repeat yourself (within reason). You name the topic—intimacy, texting and driving, drinking, drugs, finding a passion, healthy friendships. The list goes on later in this book. But, no matter the theme, no matter the message, saying it once won't do the job. You can't check the box with one conversation. Your chances of getting your message across are far higher if you have a pattern of consistent communication.[5] The more parents repeat their values and make their positions known, the more likely their teens are to adopt those beliefs, even if they seem to reject them in adolescence and incorporate them later in life.[6]

#6: Curb multitasking. Your email can wait. So can your calls. To the best of your ability, step away from your laptop and put your phone away when you are spending time with your daughter. Tune in to her. You can also ask her to put her phone away. (In chapter 3, on page 106, I talk about digital contracts to help lessen the negative effects of technology on family time.) In our distracted world, we all need practice being in the moment together.

#7: Show her that you are paying attention to what matters to her. My dad always orders me water with a straw when we go out to dinner (these days, it's a paper one). He's been doing it for decades because he knows I like it. It wasn't until a little while ago, when I was writing this book, that he let me know that he has no idea why he has to order me a straw. (It's because I have really sensitive teeth, by the way, so I prefer to drink cold water through a straw.) But he always does it with intention and gusto. It's such a small thing, but it's always a reminder that he has me on his mind. What are your daughter's favorite foods? Books? Bands? Take notice and take opportunities to show her that you appreciate and support her individuality.

#8: Don't live for the weekends. We're programmed to work during the week and have fun on the weekends. We brace ourselves to be stressed Monday through Friday, mired in responsibilities, and then we let loose (or collapse) once Friday evening comes around. Teenagers, still driven very much by the examples *and* expectations of parents and teachers, are especially conditioned in this way, trying to stay on top of everything during the week. This pattern isn't great for overall mindset or health, because spending all our Mondays through Fridays amped up and stressed is a lot of time.

My dad has always taken me to Los Angeles Lakers games. When I was in middle and high school, he'd say, "Make sure you get your homework done early in the week or at school, because we're going to the game on Wednesday." On the surface, he was just taking me to a game. But he was also helping me break up my week, actively helping me relax and get my mind off things that were weighing on me. He was also showing me that he prioritized time with me. This practice didn't just benefit our relationship; it boosted my happiness and affected the way I live my life in a positive way.

Sometimes, your daughter just needs a breather, a change of scenery on a weeknight. Go see a movie. Take her to a game. Go to a night exhibit at a museum. Go to a fun dinner. Notice the impact it has on her, and you.

Sending the Right Messages

#9: Keep the lines of communication open. It probably seems obvious, but make sure you're explicit about the fact that you are always there to talk about any topic or to help her if she needs you. It's often at the times she needs you the most that she'll fail to reach out to you. She'll worry that you'll be mad or disappointed, or that she'll be in trouble. Tell your daughter that no matter what is happening in her life, you want to be someone she calls. And, be clear with her that if she is ever in a situation that is unsafe or dangerous—like a party where people are doing drugs, or a date that feels threatening—you will be her getaway. Yes, you can tell her there may be consequences, but make sure those are secondary. And then, when she calls you, keep it together, okay? At least in the heat of the moment. Then, plan to have a conversation with her a little later.

#10: Be a good man. For millennia, fathers of daughters have been taught to be "good men," because "girls marry men like their fathers." It remains true that the example you set contributes to your daughter's understanding of what she can expect from a romantic partner. But, we also know that your daughter's adult life could very well revolve around much more than marriage. The way you talk with your daughter, and the way you interact with, talk about, and treat other women, informs her expectations for how she can expect to be treated in different types of relationships and contexts, both personal and professional.

#11: Mind your hypocrisy. Teenagers are the hypocrisy police, and you are under constant surveillance. If you want your daughter to make good decisions, you have to show her how. If you tell her not to text and drive, put your phone away when you're driving. Send a message that what you are saying is actually important to you, or your daughter won't take your guidance seriously. And, she'll probably call you on being a hypocrite, which I am guessing you want to avoid.

#12: Teach her to listen to her intuition. My friend Coach Angie is the athletic director at a school in Texas. Whenever she sees one of her sixth graders (the youngest students on campus) make a questionable decision, say something unkind, or do something dangerous or unwise, she kneels down, looks at them in the eye, and asks, "Did that feel good in your body?" Then she explains: "There's something in here," making a circular gesture from her heart to her gut, "that lets you know if something is right or wrong, if it feels good to you." I tell this story often in my sex ed classes, and the simple message resonates. We all have an inner sense of knowing, if we can just tune into it. Bring your daughter's awareness to this intuition and remind her to connect to it, because when you're not around, she is going to have to rely on her inner compass.

#13: Don't try to fix everything right away. There will be times when your daughter's tears will flow. You'll want to swoop in, protect, and fix. You'll offer advice, tell her what to do, start asking if she feels better, and then maybe also threaten to confront whoever made her so sad. Resist the urge before you know what she actually wants. Often, she doesn't want or need anything else in the moment except to talk or cry through something and be heard.

#14: Don't always reference gender. Yes, this book is largely about gender, and your daughter will benefit from conversations about strong female role models and what it means to be a strong woman. However, cheering on your daughter with statements like

"You're strong. You can do it" rather than "You're a strong girl. You can do it" can help her focus on her *human* strengths and qualities, intelligence, and skills. This type of message can focus her on her power to achieve her goals, regardless of her gender, which can contribute greatly to her confidence and fearlessness.

#15: Offer up the facts in age-appropriate ways. When teens are informed, they make more educated decisions, resulting in less risk, regret, and lasting consequences. You will see this point referenced in later chapters, but talking to your daughter about her sexual health won't encourage her to have sex. Similarly, you aren't going to cause her harm if you have a thoughtful, age-appropriate conversation about suicidal ideation.[7]

When you are sharing the facts, be mindful of how much information you are offering up and in what terms. Girls can't filter information in the same way adults can, especially in middle school. Certain facts can be traumatizing and scary depending on your daughter's level of maturity and personal experience. If you aren't sure what or how much to share, have a conversation with your spouse, other parents in the community, and even your daughter's school counselor, who, knowing your daughter personally, may be able to help you determine the best approach.

#16: Share your life experience. As you will read later on, there are a lot of specific topics, from relationships to career, for which you can draw from your own life stories and memories to guide your daughter in her own personal growth. You don't need to have a perfect past or have made all the "right decisions" to have something (or a lot) to teach your daughter. Oftentimes, our best learnings come from our biggest mishaps. Let your daughter in on some of your own experiences, using language and a level of detail she can handle. However, tell her too much or share details that could frighten her, and she may worry about your well-being or fear for her own security. But, when the time is right, don't be afraid to use yourself as an example.

#17: Calm down.[8] Girls often get the reputation for being the dramatic ones, but I have to say I hear an awful lot of stories about dads who ratchet up drama in conversations with their daughters. Navigating difficult conversations is an important skill for your daughter to learn, and that starts with you and the tone you set. An aggressive tone, no matter how serious or heated the topic, won't help you get your points across or increase your daughter's respect for you. So, take it easy, or at least pretend that you are. You don't want men in the future yelling at your daughter, right? Don't teach her that it's okay for you to do it now.

#18: Don't judge. Your teenage daughter is going to do and be interested in a lot of topics and activities that you think are dumb and don't understand. News flash: if she is into something, she's not going to feel awesome or think you're awesome if you insult her about it. She'll also assume you're out of touch and not interested in understanding her. If you say things like, "Stop looking at social media, that's such a waste of time," or "How can you listen to this music?" it can contribute to a sense for your daughter that she should be ashamed of or hide parts of herself from you. You don't have to share all her passions, and in many scenarios, such as with social media use, you can of course voice your disapproval. Just take a thoughtful approach.

#19: Don't be controlling.[9] This is not a drill. It turns out that there are actually things you can do to mess up your daughter. Being controlling is one of them (multiple studies have confirmed this across cultures and around the world). Now, I promised you at the beginning of the book that I wouldn't micromanage you, and there are cases where certain girls do need more structure from their parents to stay safe and be productive. But I *will* actively judge you if you are controlling and authoritarian. If your daughter develops an eating disorder, acts out by being sexually promiscuous or doing drugs, sneaks around or lies to you, it could at least partially be her acting out against you. Make her feel trapped or voiceless, and she may do the exact opposite of everything you hope for and worse. What does it mean to be controlling? Here are some examples:

- Micromanaging her schoolwork and encouraging perfectionistic tendencies.

- Criticizing her, even if you think you are being funny or sarcastic—trust me, it's not landing the same way with her, and it's not helping her.

- Making negative, demeaning, or discouraging remarks about her hopes and dreams.

- Being overly strict.

- Being controlling toward your co-parent.

If you are not sure whether you are too controlling, find a trained counselor to help you gauge what kind of parent you are being—and quickly.

#20: Talk to her like she's a peer. There's no faster way to lose ground with your daughter than to talk down to her. In many ways, teenagers are inexperienced and lacking knowledge, but they don't see themselves that way. Teenage girls feel very much like they are adults, like they know themselves and they know about the world. It's tempting to condescend to teenagers, to talk to them like they are children. Especially when conflicts get heated, you may be tempted to pull a "papa bear" and put her in her place with a loud, scary (figurative) growl. But when adults talk down to girls, it doesn't contribute to positive behavior change. It makes girls angry and causes them to shut down on you.

You know she's young and doesn't know everything, but don't let her know that you feel that way. You must signal to her that you respect where she is coming from, even if you don't agree with it or think her logic is faulty. When talking to your teenage daughter, address her in the same tone you would address your closest adult friends or colleagues. You're going to have to leave behind the "Because I said so's." And, don't call her "disrespectful"—you would never say that to another adult. Instead, look her in the eye and talk to her like she's already risen to the occasion. Talk her into the person you envision she will become.

#21: Set rules like a dad.[10] A lot of fathers I talk to are confused by rule #20. "She's the daughter, and I'm the dad. How can I set rules for her if I can't talk to her like she's my child?" That's the trick. You can. Your tone is a different thing from the words coming out of your mouth. Just because you need to talk to her like you respect her and hear her doesn't mean she gets to call the shots. You still need to give her structure, boundaries, and guidance. You still need to parent her.

#22: Focus on safety. Girls can't argue with you on safety, or at least they can't present a strong argument when you are pointing to safety to justify a conversation they think is annoying (like one about the dangers of alcohol, for instance), your rules, or the consequences. When you focus on safety, the conversation becomes less personal. This strategy allows you to present less like you are trying to make her life difficult and more like you have real reasons that you care.

#23: Don't period-shame her. I touch on this topic later in the book, but it's important enough that I am highlighting it here as well. There may be times when you know your daughter is exceptionally irrational, emotional, or irritable because of her monthly cycle, but don't use it against her or make light of it. Menstruation is a natural process that your daughter should not be ashamed of. If menstruation is to blame for her heightened emotional state, she's already uncomfortable enough, so she doesn't need a reminder.

#24: Be clear about whether or not she's in trouble. In adolescence, talking to your daughter about certain topics can make her feel judged or like she's in trouble, even if she's not. To avoid the risk of this type of conversation eroding trust and your daughter's comfort talking with you, be clear about where you stand. You can say things like:

- I know it may feel like you are in trouble. You're not. I just want to make sure you know where I'm coming from.

- I'm not trying to scare you or make you feel like you're being punished.

#25: Apologize. You are going to mess up. You'll say the wrong thing. You'll lose your cool. You'll make her cry. You don't have to be perfect. Just say you're sorry so you can start moving forward. Apologies can sound something like this:

- I apologize. I wasn't at my best.

- I'm sorry, you caught me off guard, and I probably should have responded in a different way.

- I'm sorry, I will try to do better next time.

- I didn't stay as calm as I would have liked to before. I love you, and my primary concern is that you are safe. Sometimes, I can overreact.

Your daughter doesn't need to know that you're perfect as much as she needs to know that you hear and see her. And you'll also be showing her that everyone has their moments of weakness—you, her, her friends, future bosses, and romantic partners—and that there are really simple ways to cope, make things right, and move on.

#26: Let her educate you. We've established that she doesn't know everything. You don't, either. Importantly, you don't have to look like you know everything or actually know everything to parent her. You can be out of touch, vulnerable, awkward, and yet still very effective.

Take social media for instance. As I discuss in chapter 3, in "Technology and Social Media" on page 98, I would argue that there is no way for a parent, other than maybe those working in the app industry or in tech news, to stay on top of social media trends. The trends change frequently as new apps are released and go viral in the teen world. Social media is like a language that is constantly evolving. As with everything else going on in her life, your daughter is the one best positioned to help you understand the facts. Learn from her. And then apply your values and beliefs—something you do know well—to this new territory.

#27: Do not use gifts and cash rewards to motivate her. With all this talk of creating special moments and outings, I don't want anyone to be confused that these things should be positioned as rewards for academic or extracurricular performance. Of course you can celebrate major accomplishments, like finishing finals, wrap night for a play, or reaching another important milestone. But don't tie any kind of cash reward or gift to an academic grade or other success metric in adolescence. You don't want to make these rewards dependent on your daughter achieving a certain grade or score. Financial incentives condition your daughter to focus on extrinsic rewards and pleasing others, rather than helping her connect with internal motivation. Once you start the incentivizing process, the gifts need to get bigger to keep the motivation burning, which is not only unhealthy, but expensive.

#28: Set up times for difficult conversations. This is one of the tips I give my students when I'm teaching them about conflict resolution, and I often hear that young people find it helpful when communicating with their parents. If there is a big, serious conversation you need to have, decide on a time and a time limit. Your daughter will appreciate the respect you show her by giving her a heads-up, and with a time on the day's calendar, you can both prepare mentally. Having a start and stop time can help you consciously contain conflict, compartmentalize the conversation, and move forward with the rest of your day.

#29: Pull in supports. I detail this extensively in chapter 4. Despite your best and most heartfelt efforts, there may still be things your daughter doesn't want to talk to you about, and when it comes to sensitive topics, like menstruation or sexual health, you also may not want to handle conversations alone. Pull in supports to help handle different parts of discussions with you or at different times. It can be a relative or a family friend—someone close who you trust and who your daughter trusts.

I often talk to parents of my students and mentees about the messages they would like to get across to their kids. If those messages align with my recommendations, I'll have a conversation with the teen about them. And because I'm not the parent, kids pay a little more attention. They're a little less resistant—even if it's the same message the parents convey, just coming from me.

In addition to scaffolding your daughter a little more, her having important conversations like this also trains her to reach out for help, to see who is in her environment who cares and has some wisdom. Building her "personal advisory board" will be an important skill for your daughter all her life. Guide her in getting it done.

There may be times when a girl's behavior indicates that there is more going on than what might be classified as "normal." If you've seen a recent behavior or significant mood change with her, if she's withdrawn at all, if she's lying excessively, if her reactions are far beyond what you imagine is reasonable for her, talk to her doctor, school counselor, or a therapist to get a sense of whether what you are seeing is okay or indicative of a greater issue like a mental health challenge, addiction, or health problem.

#30: Get shut down. When it comes to communicating with you daughter, I can't promise that you will ever feel like you've improved or mastered it in the way you might master other skills, but consistency is the key. "Winning" at communicating with your daughter doesn't actually feel like you're winning; it feels like *she's* winning. I would put money on any teenage daughter to prevail in an argument with her father, not because she is right or a better negotiator, but because she has less fear, more stamina, and two secret weapons: irrationality and tears. She's not always going to appreciate your efforts to connect with or help her. There will be times when you will not be able to reason with her. Developmentally, she'll be unable to see your side. She'll shut you down over and over again. But you need to focus on simply being there, and being there consistently, so that she can win and you can feel like you're losing again. Then, you're a real winner.

I've built my career as an expert in girlhood, and I took my dad for granted for nearly three decades before realizing the extent of the positive impact he had on me, that he had done a lot right, and that, in fact, his example could be a beacon for other dads. In the process of writing this book, as I've asked him questions and he's told me stories, and we talked about some of our joint memories from each of our perspectives, everything he did for me and the power of his influence has become ever more apparent. So if you ever feel like you're not getting anywhere, you're not alone. There is a light at the end of the tunnel, even if it is years away. If you don't believe me, come to one of my talks, find my dad (he's often there), and he'll tell you you're going to be fine, too.

3

Maximizing Your Impact

Information and Inspiration
for Key Conversations

Now, let's talk about the information you need in order to have impactful conversations.

In the following pages, you will find briefs on the nineteen fundamental topics relevant to your daughter's life and development. Each section is broken up in the following way:

SOME BACKGROUND—Research, expert perspectives, and anecdotes to strengthen your knowledge base.

YOUR GOAL—The overarching intention you should set for your conversation.

RULE #1—One thing to avoid doing or saying when addressing the topic.

TALKING POINTS—Themes for conversations.

HOW IT'S DONE—Specifics on what to say and what not to say.

BEYOND THE CONVERSATION—Additional ways to reinforce meaningful messages.

The information you will find is drawn from hundreds of health, wellness, and life skills presentations I've given; reflections from fathers and their daughters I've met along the way; insights from leading experts and research labs focused on adolescent well-being; and perspectives and resources from respected, trustworthy nonprofits educating and supporting young people and their families. These briefs are designed to give you meaningful starting points in your own research and to set you in the right direction, if you want to dig even deeper.

Through my years of research, I have found that men's goals for their daughters fall into three clear categories, which I highlight in these pages:

- Boosting Her Well-Being
- Strengthening Her Relationships
- Broadening Her Horizons

Within these three categories are the topics I have learned are of greatest interest to girls and of the most importance in supporting their physical, emotional, and social well-being. These are also essential topics in addressing and inspiring the skills girls need to discover and reach their personal bests in all areas of their lives. Perhaps most importantly, having these key conversations—empowering girls to take care of themselves, pursue healthy relationships, and make decisions to support individual and shared goals—gives rise to the qualities that help them create fulfilling lives for themselves and make a positive impact on the world. Talking with your daughter isn't just about giving her the facts; every conversation can contribute to the growth of her empathy, bravery, grit, and resilience. These are the true building blocks of kindness, confidence, and happiness.

Boost Her Well-Being

Body Positivity

As I mentioned in the first paragraphs of this book, adolescence was a roller coaster for me and my friends. My personal struggle was mental health. Seemingly out of nowhere, I got depressed in high school. I woke up one morning and I felt down and exhausted in a way I couldn't describe, like some inner light had gone out suddenly. In my case, the depression lifted quickly, but it gave way to waves of anxiety that lasted for months while my parents and I figured out what to do. I was scared, and what felt especially worrying was that I knew myself and I didn't feel like myself. I became determined to do whatever it took to feel better and get back to enjoying my life.

This is when I started looking to books and magazines for clues and answers. I talked to mentors. I went to doctors. There was a lot of trial and error and a lot of uncertainty. Ultimately, I learned what it took to thrive, not simply in terms of my mental and physical health, but in the emotional sense, in my relationships, and in all other areas of my life. That's why I do what I do—to help girls learn more quickly the secrets it took me and so many other women years to learn.

SOME BACKGROUND

This whole book is about helping your daughter learn the essentials of health, well-being, and performance in all areas of her life. As promised, I will cover all the big topics like substance use, mental health, sexual health, and managing the stress of the college-admissions process. But I'm starting with the habits of active, daily self-care that support energy, mental clarity, and overall confidence and strength. Girls have a lot of information to gather, figuring out the strategies they like the most and that work best for their bodies—how to eat for health and performance, manage stress, ease their menstrual symptoms, and keep a healthy body image. Your daughter is probably learning a lot from you, her doctor, and health classes at school, but there are some overarching messages and strategies that can make this information even more relevant to her, helping motivate her to take control of her health and supercharge her daily routine.

I call this section "Body Positivity" because the more we can help girls feel better and stronger in their own skin, the better prepared they will be to manage any challenges they face. And, the faster we can help young women figure out the self-care strategies that work for them, the more time they can spend feeling on top of their game.

YOUR GOAL: Teaching your daughter that active, consistent self-care contributes to happiness, confidence, resilience, and performance in all areas of life.

RULE #1: Don't reinforce the idea that her physical appearance determines her self-worth and happiness. Unfortunately, much of the broader cultural messaging girls receive about health is focused on physical appearance.

TALKING POINTS

THE MIND-BODY CONNECTION IS REAL

Focusing on the mind-body connection can be an antidote to the emphasis broader culture places on physical appearance. The idea that "feeling good is looking good" is lost on most young people. Girls are well aware of the value society places on the way they look. (This isn't an issue that only affects girls—young men also struggle with body image, especially with regard to keeping up with masculine ideals around muscularity.)[1] Girls' increased time spent on social media makes them even more susceptible to the negative impact of what are often unattainable cultural ideals.[2] Selfie culture laser-focuses them on their looks.[3] The retouched images they scroll through of celebrities, influencers (social media celebrities), and friends alike can lower their body confidence and boost general insecurities about how their lives measure up to others'.[4] As they take, edit, and perfect photos, then monitor likes and comments from friends and acquaintances, they become ever more focused on covering up their flaws and gaining compliments based on outward appearances instead of inner strengths. Posting selfies can feel to girls like a mindless, entertaining pastime but can lead to drops in self-esteem, heightened anxiety, and eating disorders.[5]

Girls will spend hours doing their hair, applying makeup, or trying on clothes. They'll set weight-loss goals or go on fitness kicks because they believe that they'll be happier if they can just achieve the right look. Emphasize to your daughter that the foods she eats, the exercise she does, and the relaxation strategies she incorporates into her day can help her feel strong, think more clearly, maintain focus, and even put her in a better mood.[6] The added bonus of focusing on feeling good is that when we focus on our internal well-being, outside appearances follow.

MINDFULNESS TAKES MANY FORMS

Many schools are now teaching mindfulness, the Buddhist concept of being fully focused on the current moment, because of the proven benefits it has on concentration, stress relief, and emotional regulation.[7] Teachers often introduce mindfulness in the form of breathing meditations, where students sit quietly with their eyes closed, focusing on their breath. You can practice it with your daughter using apps like Headspace that make it easy to meditate, even if you are a beginner.

But if breathing meditations aren't your or your daughter's favorite activities, you have other options to tune into the present without sitting on the floor, eyes closed, legs crossed. I've found that in addition to breathing exercises, my students also really appreciate more active forms of mindfulness. In a positive psychology class I taught for high school seniors, I would play Jenga with my students whenever I sensed that their stress levels were high due to their work in other classes, exams, or the wait for college decision letters. When we played for the first time, I didn't tell them why. We just played. They didn't have anything to "do" other than watch the blocks, cheer on their friends, plot their next moves, and yell "ooooh" and laugh together when the tower toppled. Afterward, I asked them how they felt, and they answered with "happy," "relaxed," and "energized." We then talked about what mindfulness was and brainstormed other ways to work it into their lives. A couple of my favorite suggestions were baking cupcakes and walking the dog. You can take a similar approach with your daughter and practice mindfulness with her, which will have benefits for you, too.

MINDFUL EATING FOSTERS HEALTHY EATING HABITS

Mindful eating, also based in the principles of Buddhism, is the act of slowing down and paying extra attention to what we eat—our food's appearance, texture, taste, smell, and how it makes us feel.[8] I'm giving mindful eating its own section here because it can transform eating habits for the better. Mindful eating is touted by doctors and nutritionists as a practice that can improve peoples' relationship with food, curb weight gain, and prevent overeating. When people actually pay attention to their food, they are more likely to make healthy decisions, choosing foods that make them feel good and eating just enough to satisfy them and not more.

So what does this all mean for girls and their parents who are in a constant rush, distracted by responsibilities and technology, and often out of reach of "healthy" food choices? Mindful eating isn't necessarily about meditating on your food at each meal or not eating pizza and wings. It's just about thinking a little more about what you are putting in your mouth and why. Are you eating for fuel? Are you eating for enjoyment? Are you eating to cope with stress?

In my health classes, I introduce students to mindful eating with a simple exercise. I bring a variety of sweet and savory snacks, everything from strawberries and chocolate to pretzels and carrots. I give the kids small plates and tell them to pick just a couple of bites of their favorites. Then we spend some silly moments chewing silently together before everyone has to go around, including me, and talk about why they chose the bite they did, how it smells, what the colors and textures are, how it tastes, and finally, how it makes them feel. And then I say what I said before, "The message is simple. Just think a little bit more about how what you are eating makes you feel." If you can talk about mindful eating every once in a while with your daughter and encourage a family eating culture where even a few times a week, you sit around the table and take a few minutes to focus on, talk about, and actively enjoy your food, you will be placing value on an important lifelong practice. In the face of constant media messaging about fad diets, your daughter can benefit from this positive perspective on nutrition.

WATER IS A POWER DRINK

Proper hydration is essential to good health, including for brain functioning, mental focus, and positive mood.[9] Drinking water is also essential for skin health and digestion. Dehydration can have a variety of negative health effects, and girls who forget to drink water or opt for sugary or caffeinated alternatives might experience spikes in irritability and anxiety.

The recommendation for how much water your daughter should have each day will depend on her body weight, how much exercise she is getting, the climate you live in, and the altitude. Talk with your daughter's doctor about how much water she should have each day. To help her keep track, you can get her a water bottle to have during the day and calculate how many times she has to fill it up to get the ounces she needs.

FITNESS PREFERENCES ARE PERSONAL

There is a wide variety of factors that shape young peoples' attitudes toward exercise and fitness habits. Among those are family culture, how active parents are, what types of activity parents do on their own and with their kids, and how parents talk about and reference fitness.[10] It's important for girls to understand fitness as a beneficial and essential part of life and of utmost importance for health, but also as a matter of choice. Your daughter will benefit from being encouraged to find her personal fitness passions.

Organized sports are a great way for girls to experiment with different types of fitness and find the activities they enjoy. In addition to being fun and providing social connection, athletics can provide opportunities for goal-setting and achievement, practicing teamwork, and connecting with others. Your daughter may love team sports, or she may be more of a solo athlete, preferring running, hiking, dancing, or yoga to organized athletics. No matter what she chooses, movement is the key ingredient. And if your daughter doesn't like the team sport that her friends are playing or that you'd love her to play, encourage her to try other activities—she isn't "unathletic" if she doesn't like or isn't good at one sport.

SLEEP IS A GIRL'S BEST FRIEND

Girls need to be taught to think critically of the narrative around sleeplessness. There's a myth that teenagers are tired all the time. Granted, many of them are. They stay up late doing homework, bingeing TV shows, watching what must be the entirety of YouTube, and video-chatting with their friends. Working in schools, I see a lot of exhausted teenagers who love to talk about how little sleep they get and how coffee and energy drinks keep them up cramming for tests.

Fatigue shouldn't be the status quo. In middle and high school, girls are managing a lot. But late hours and sleeplessness ultimately make them less productive, not more. And "sleep debt" (or "a sleep deficit"), defined by SleepFoundation.org as "the difference between the amount of sleep someone needs and the amount they actually get," can have negative effects on well-being, including brain fog, heart disease, and obesity.[11] Healthy decision-making with food can fall by the wayside when people are tired, making it easier to mindlessly reach for high-calorie, unhealthy foods. And, it's important to note, especially for teenagers, that making up for lost sleep on the weekends hasn't been found to protect against these unfavorable outcomes.[12]

Talk to your daughter about the facts of sleep, including how getting a good night's sleep will make her more productive during the days. Encourage her to try, even just once, going to sleep early and waking up early to finish an assignment or exam preparation, and then talk with her about whether it was helpful. Teens mistakenly think they can burn the candle at both ends indefinitely. It's a great time to teach your daughter a different strategy.

Spirituality Can Have Powerful
Health Effects

Among the benefits of spirituality that you can probably list off the top of your head—providing a moral compass, being a grounding force, strengthening family bonds—spirituality has also been tied to positive mental and physical health outcomes for adolescents. Multiple studies have found spirituality and participation in religious practices to be associated with lower rates of recreational substance use among adolescents, lower rates and symptoms of anxiety and depression, and lower rates of sexual activity.[13] Religion and spirituality can increase adolescents' sense of community connectedness, foster friendships, enhance their coping skills in the face of trauma, and even be a protective factor against suicide risk.[14]

During adolescence, spirituality is one more area where girls begin to explore and solidify their beliefs. With the individuation and questioning that comes with adolescence, girls often begin to reconsider and debate the meaning and place of spirituality and religion in their lives—or move away from it altogether. You may notice that they are often no longer content to go to services or listen passively to your religious references the way they were when they were younger. You may also get tough questions and be forced into debate. Like so many ways in which girls are flexing their new reasoning skills and experimenting with their identities, when it comes to religion, she may be trying different beliefs on for size.

Your daughter may begin to question the religious practices and declarations of faith that have been the cornerstone of your family life, and spirituality can become one more area where you feel like you are losing influence and control. It can be an especially painful process, but try to curb your fears that your daughter will "get off track," and give her the space to discover her own grown-up version of spirituality. You can feel free to state your own values and your hopes for your daughter with regard to her spiritual life. The more often you repeat your own values and beliefs (within reason and without proselytizing, which, you remember, can make her tune out), the more likely she is to adopt your beliefs for the long term.[15]

If you aren't part of an organized religion, be sure to let your daughter know about any spiritual practices you incorporate into your life, whether that's going for a run, playing music, or spending time in nature. She won't know that these things have religious or spiritual meaning to you unless you share that with her. Knowing that the adults who love her spend time and energy on spiritual pursuits will give her permission to do the same.

A Healthy Media Diet Is Paramount[16]

As I have already mentioned and will address in more detail in the upcoming "Mental Health" and "Technology and Social Media" sections, media is a major threat to girls' overall well-being, self-esteem, and body image. Encourage your daughter to think about how the media she consumes makes her *feel*. How does it affect her mood and her views of her own life? Does she feel positive or negative after spending time watching a dark show or scrolling through social media? Encourage her to consume media that makes her feel good. Some examples include uplifting TV shows and movies, documentaries (there are so many now on people and topics she might find fascinating, be they social leaders, athletes with inspiring stories, or artists or tastemakers like fashion designers), or social media accounts focused on social action or uplifting or informational content.

Periods Don't Have to Be a Total Pain

As you already know, monthly periods create challenges for girls, and the discomfort and shame they often feel weighs on them. The American College of Obstetricians and Gynecologists lists the following symptoms of premenstrual syndrome (PMS), many of which you've probably heard about, but some of which might come as a surprise:[17]

Emotional symptoms

- Depression
- Angry outbursts
- Irritability
- Crying spells
- Anxiety
- Confusion
- Social withdrawal
- Poor concentration
- Insomnia
- Increased nap taking
- Changes in sexual desire

Physical symptoms

- Thirst and appetite changes (food cravings)
- Breast tenderness
- Bloating and weight gain

- Headache

- Swelling of the hands or feet

- Aches and pains

- Fatigue

- Skin problems

- Gastrointestinal symptoms

- Abdominal pain

Eating lots of lean protein and leafy greens, avoiding sugar, drinking lots of water, getting enough sleep, exercising, and practicing relaxation strategies can alleviate symptoms.[18] For girls who struggle with pain, heating pads and over-the-counter medications can help.[19] If your daughter's premenstrual and menstrual symptoms are exceptionally painful, causing emotional distress, or are otherwise disruptive, she should talk with her doctor about options for relief, such as hormonal birth control options or counseling to help manage emotional lows associated with her cycle.[20] If it seems like your daughter is struggling beyond what you think is normal, it's worth keeping an extra eye out.[21]

When it comes to managing menstrual blood flow, your daughter also has options:

- Mass-market disposable pads and tampons

- Organic disposable pads and tampons

- Machine-washable reusable pads

- Period underwear, which is crafted from proprietary fabrics engineered to capture menstrual blood[22]

- Menstrual cups, which are devices that look like a small
  rubber cup and are inserted into the vaginal canal and
  collect menstrual blood

Even if you aren't the one taking the lead on conversations around menstruation, you can still help by making a run to the pharmacy when needed, offering up a healthy snack, or giving your daughter some extra compassion and patience. In your daughter's world, where she no doubt encounters period-shaming from male peers and mass media, you'll also send a subtle, meaningful signal of acceptance and respect.

SOME BEAUTY PRODUCTS MAY BE SAFER THAN OTHERS

According to research by the Environmental Working Group, more than forty nations around the globe do more to regulate potentially harmful chemicals (like parabens and formaldehyde) in their beauty products than the United States.[23] From Germany to Cambodia, the list includes both developing and industrialized countries. Some of these nations have banned more than fourteen-hundred chemicals for use in beauty products, while in the United States, as of 2019, fewer than ten chemicals were banned in beauty products. Major US companies including Walgreens and CVS have publicly stated that they will enact more restrictions in the coming years, and currently, many US products are labeled "organic," "natural," and "paraben-free" to indicate a potentially higher degree of safety associated with their ingredients (although not all of these terms are federally regulated). This is a trend you and your daughter should track.

HOW IT'S DONE

Do Say

- You are beautiful and even more beautiful inside.

- Pay attention to how food, exercise, and the media you consume make you feel.

- Taking care of yourself in small ways over time builds confidence.

- Nourish yourself from the inside out. Eat well, exercise, do activities that truly make you happy, and it will show on the outside.

- Is there anything I can get you at the pharmacy?

Don't Say

- You don't want to get fat, do you?

- Maybe you should go on a diet.

- Maybe we should go on a diet together?

- You'll be happier if you lose weight.

- Are you on your period or something?

- You're just being emotional because you have PMS.

- Why don't you ever exercise?

BEYOND THE CONVERSATION

LOOP IN A PROFESSIONAL TO ENCOURAGE HEALTHY LIFESTYLE CHANGES

"She's complaining about her weight all the time, but she's always eating unhealthy foods with her friends and snacking late at night. It's frustrating to watch and listen to when she should be taking better care of herself. What do I say?" Don't say what you are thinking, even if you think or know you are right. You may know how your daughter can be healthier, you may see opportunities for improvement in her self-care routine, and of course, you want her to be happy and confident. But don't be the one to deliver the message on this topic or anything related to dieting because chances are it could be taken the wrong way coming from you. The perception will most likely not match your intention. If you think your daughter could benefit from some healthier habits that she isn't already adopting, get your pediatrician involved; have them offer up some recommendations to your daughter, if appropriate; and then do your best to help your daughter follow through with healthy choices and routines.[24]

TAKE CARE OF YOURSELF

When you incorporate healthy habits into your own life, and especially when you invite your daughter to join you, you provide her an important model for what it looks like to balance responsibilities and take care of yourself at the same time. When you make thoughtful decisions about what you eat and how you spend your time, your daughter will learn from your example. But just as important, when you take care of yourself, you reap the benefits to your health, mood, and productivity, and you'll have more energy to be there for your daughter when she needs you.

BOND OVER WELLNESS

One of my favorite ideas for father-daughter time came from a Chicago-area father I interviewed for this book. He and his daughter run together, but what makes this time extra special is that there's a "no headphones" rule. They run and they talk. It's a compound bonding opportunity, incorporating discussion, connecting over shared interests, and setting a positive fatherly example. Think about ways you can join and inspire your daughter in self-care. You don't have to frame it as fitness or stress-relief. Instead, you can just offer up the idea as a way to spend time together.

BE MINDFUL OF HOW YOU TALK ABOUT OTHER WOMEN

This isn't to say that you can't ever comment on the beauty of the female form, but you do want to make sure that your commentary is balanced. If your daughter believes that you place high importance on the way women look, she will internalize that as an important value. Curb your commentary or focus on internal strengths like bravery, kindness, empathy, and intelligence when you are complimenting other women.

Clothing Choices

My friend Jonathan got home one day just as his sixteen-year-old daughter was about to leave the house with her friends. She was wearing a T-shirt and a pair of barely-there shorts. Flustered, Jonathan looked at his wife. "I thought you bought her new shorts because the other ones were too short!" he said in a raised whisper. Unfazed, his wife responded, "Those are the new shorts."

I have to say that the daughter in me is still surprised at how often the topic of dress comes up and how much angst it causes dads. I asked Jonathan what his main concern was in that moment. "My daughter doesn't know teenage boys like I know teenage boys," he said. "She doesn't know how they think and what they are capable of. But I don't feel like I can say anything about what she's wearing because I don't want to shame her."

I remember my own dad freaking out about my clothing choices. I remember rolling my eyes, thinking, "*Reeee-lax*, what's the big deal?" I went to schools that required uniforms, and starting in middle school, the only thing I ever got in trouble for was that my skirt was too short. "My legs are growing too fast. I can't keep up," I would say when I got sent to the office, but the administrators didn't buy it. And, their reaction was warranted. My ever-increasing height was only part of the story. The other reason I didn't wear longer skirts is because I thought they looked ugly and were far less flattering. But either way, I didn't think my wardrobe choices were that big a deal—and your daughter probably doesn't, either.

SOME BACKGROUND

In a conversation several years ago, I asked Dr. Lisa Damour, a clinical psychologist and author of *Untangled: Guiding Teenage Girls Through the Seven Transitions into Adulthood*, what she thought was an area where parents worried too much.[25] You may be happy to know that "girls' clothing" was her answer. She went on to explain that girls aren't always trying to send the highly sexualized messages of parents' nightmares. Girls' clothing choices are often more innocent than you assume.

"It is really common for adolescent girls to experiment with dressing in a way that looks sexy and to imitate what they see on TV, online, or in magazines," Dr. Damour explained. "She is not thinking about the sexual implications or how she might be viewed by others or how it might be viewed by adults. Those things might not be accessible to her. Fifteen-year-old girls might not be able to see themselves through the eyes of a thirty-year-old."

At Northwestern University, Dr. Onnie Rogers studies girls' identity development. In my research for this book, we talked about the importance of physical appearance for girls.[26] While it's difficult to say what specifically motivates each girl's outfit choices every time she gets dressed, what we do know, as Dr. Rogers explained, is that "in adolescence, young people are quite literally trying on different identities and figuring out who they are, and that is partially manifested in their physical appearance. Clothing choices, hair choices, and makeup are all signs of this process."

Dr. Rogers told me she can understand why so many fathers feel terrified and even offended by their daughters' outfit choices. But like Dr. Damour, she draws a distinction between the fear you might feel and your daughter's actual intentions. "Fathers know what they think when they see women dressed in certain ways. They know what message society is bringing to it. And so their anxiety is often more about how girls are being perceived by others, as opposed to whether or not girls, themselves, are trying to communicate a particular message or not."

The worry you feel about how your daughter is dressing is not unfounded, but chances are your perspective is probably totally lost on her. So, what do you do with this information? As a father, you are in a precarious position in talking to your daughter about what she is wearing because of the simple fact that you're not a girl. She may lack awareness of how she's presenting herself, but in her eyes, you aren't the authority on what is "normal" and acceptable in her peer group. And she probably doesn't think you know what is cool, either. Also, by saying anything about her clothing, you run the risk of body-shaming her (more on this in the Talking Points that follow), which can start a fight and have lasting negative consequences. Still, you don't have to stay silent and give your daughter free rein to wear whatever she wants, whenever she wants. There are a few topics you can easily touch on—and some others to definitely avoid.

YOUR GOAL: Support your daughter in developing her personal style as part of healthy self-expression.

RULE #1: Don't freak out about your daughter's clothes all the time. You'll exhaust yourself.

TALKING POINTS

MESSAGING TRAPS TO AVOID

Body-Shaming

It can feel natural to make statements that could feel insulting in order to help your daughter see your side, but this strategy will not help you empower her. Comments like this can drop her self-esteem, make her even more self-conscious, and stick with her, shaping her self-concept for years to come.

Holding Her Responsible for the Clothing Options Promoted to Her

Girls find themselves in a highly sexualized culture, which plays no small part in shaping their views of what are acceptable wardrobe choices. There is no shortage of mass media imagery depicting scantily clad girls and women. Girls see the sexualized images that garner likes on social media. And retailers promote and sell sexy clothing to young women everywhere. As Dr. Rogers told me, "The question is less about what girls choose to wear and more about the options we present as valuable to girls and the sorts of things that they are observing."

Suggesting That She Is Responsible for Preventing Sexual Assault

When it comes to what can be called the "policing" of girls' clothing, there is a tendency to connect what girls are wearing to the risk of sexual assault. A broadly internalized cultural assumption is that girls are somehow responsible for inviting—and therefore preventing—

rape and sexual violence, and that through their clothing choices, they can do this. While situational awareness and the power of perception are important points to speak about with your daughter, there is a gentle balance to strike in helping girls understand messages associated with clothing without buying into a culture of victim-blaming.

DRESS CODES

Every school has a dress code of some kind, even those that don't require uniforms. School dress codes are a great "in" to talk about clothing with your daughter. You can start talking about clothing choices in the context of someone else's rules, not your own, which will buy you some time before becoming the "bad guy," if you do set your own rules. In addition, you have the opportunity to have a meaningful conversation about the messages and impacts of dress codes.

Dress codes are known to disproportionately affect and hold consequences for girls. Schools often include provisions about skirt length, makeup, leggings, sleeveless tops, and heels, which primarily apply to girls. Many teachers and administrators continue to contextualize dress codes as tools to curb distractions to boys, which puts the burden on girls—rather than teaching their peers to be more respectful of others' bodies and space. And there are inconsistencies in on-campus dress standards for girls. For instance, they may have strict skirt lengths to abide by in the halls, but at sporting events, they can wear short, tight volleyball shorts or running shorts.

In addition, dress codes can be especially biased against girls of color, with an analysis by the National Women's Law Center finding that Black female students are especially vulnerable to targeting by school dress codes.[27] Some schools include biased restrictions such as those put on hair wraps, which are commonly worn by Black students, and schools with primarily Black student bodies tend to have more dress code restrictions and punish and suspend Black girls at higher rates than other schools.

Your daughter is probably familiar with the problematic nature of dress codes, not just because of her personal observations but also because girls' dress code issues regularly garner attention and backlash in the media. There are often stories about girls petitioning their schools to update dress code rules to be more fair to young women. Parents have also been known to post about unfair school dress codes on social media, prompting public responses from administrators.

Talk to your daughter about how she views her school's policy. Does she think it's fair? Is there anything about it that bothers her? Where might she agree or disagree?

BEING MINDFUL OF SEXUALIZED PRODUCTS OR PROBLEMATIC MARKETING

If you are shopping with your daughter, either online or in stores, note advertisements and wardrobe items that you think are problematic and those you think are body positive. Your daughter is developing her own taste and style preferences, but, as Dr. Rogers pointed out, the clothing being produced and marketed to your daughter and her peers can have a significant influence. Talk to your daughter about trends she sees in advertisements, on social media, and in popular culture. Ask her why she thinks certain types of clothing are in demand.

Conscious Consumerism: Using Spending Power for Good

Today, there are so many companies that "give back." In an era of transparency, companies are also forthcoming about their production practices, where they are based, and their social and environmental impacts. Your daughter's generation is driving many of these trends as they demand this kind of information and speak their minds directly to brands via social media. Ask your daughter what she knows about her favorite brands and check out their websites. You may learn some things that surprise you. For instance, certain girl-focused brands, such as ModCloth and Aerie, promote body positivity in their marketing campaigns through body-image-boosting messaging and by showing diverse body types in their photos. Encourage your daughter to use her spending power for good and make a positive statement with the brands she wears.

HOW IT'S DONE

Do Say

- How would you describe your personal style?

- What are your main inspirations for the way that you dress?

- Is this [clothing item you want to buy] something popular right now? What do you think is driving this trend?

- What are your favorite clothing brands? Why?

- I trust you, but I don't trust everyone else who will be around, and I'm concerned you may receive unwanted and even

unsafe attention if you wear something like that. What do
you think?

Don't Say

* You look like you're asking for it.

* People will think you're a slut if you wear that.

* I'm not buying you that because I don't like it. (She will think
  you don't understand her and aren't trying to, which will
  likely draw a negative reaction.)

* Why don't you dress more like your friend [insert friend's
  name]?

BEYOND THE CONVERSATION

LEARN HER STYLE

What inspires your daughter's personal style? Is it primarily her
friends? A particular celebrity? A culture like skateboarding? Her
heritage? You can ask your daughter directly, but beyond listening to
her, it would be a good idea to do some of your own research. Pay
attention to the stores and websites she visits to buy her clothes. Sign
up for their newsletters so you can stay on top of the latest trends. If
there is a celebrity or subculture your daughter looks to, follow social
media feeds related to them. Style is an art form and a language, and
the more you understand what your daughter is trying to express in
her clothing choices, the better positioned you will be to have meaningful conversations with her about it.

SEEK A BALANCED PERSPECTIVE

Your daughter's clothing is an area that can get your worst-case scenario brain going, fast. But your level of panic and worry about the risk she's incurring by wearing a certain outfit is likely to be overblown. Have conversations with the women in your life, with a school counselor or school administrator, or with other parents you know to help gauge how worried you should be or if you actually need to have a conversation with your daughter about "appropriate" dress. Brainstorming with other adults will help you decide on the most effective approach given any community, cultural, or religious context affecting your daughter.

Gender and Sexual Identity

My parents have always been the most accepting people ever, and they always made it clear to me that I could love whoever I wanted. But when I was ready to come out to them, I got really, really, really nervous, which was weird and surprising, because I knew they would love me no matter what. People get kicked out of their house and things like that for telling their parents that they are gay or bisexual or transgender. I had heard that happened a lot. I knew my parents wouldn't do that, but I didn't know how they would react. I always had boyfriends in middle school and early high school. I just didn't think my parents would expect it, and saying the words and actually saying them out loud is so hard for some reason. It takes so much courage.

I had just gone out with a girl for the first time the night before, and I wanted to tell my parents. I had already told some of my friends, and they were fine with it. No one said anything mean to me, which was really lucky.

When I told my mom, I had spent the day with her. I would start to tell her and then say "never mind," and my heart would beat so fast. And finally, I said, "You know that girl I was talking about? I kind of like her." And my mom said, "That's awesome! Can you show me a picture?" When I talked to my dad about it, he said, "I don't know why anyone would want to date guys anyway!" I just felt this sense of relief, like I could really be myself. The best part about it was that my parents didn't act like it was a big deal. They just acted like I was normal. It shouldn't be a big deal, even though people make it out to be.

At my school, there is a day when between five and ten seniors talk to the freshman class. It's called the Identity Project, and we make speeches about some aspect of ourselves. I talked about being bisexual and coming out. I felt so good after, being able to tell the story and tell others that it's okay made me feel empowered. And after the panel, multiple faculty advisers came up to me and said that students in their advisories had come out after hearing my speech.

—EDEN, EIGHTEEN

SOME BACKGROUND

As I highlighted in chapter 1, identity development is a natural and key task of adolescence, and gender identity and sexual orientation are central themes of that work. It's common sense that your gender and who you love would be core to your self-concept, right?[28] But while gender and sexuality are topics girls are comfortable with and conversant in, they are also two topics I have found to be among the most daunting and misunderstood by parents I speak with. So, if you're beginning this chapter feeling like an outsider, feeling scared or worried, or wondering why there are so many more news stories and conversations about gender and sex than when you were a kid, you aren't alone. Here are just a few of the questions I encounter regularly:

- Why are kids today thinking about this? We didn't have these challenges when I was growing up. (Short answer: People thought about these things when you were younger, they just didn't or couldn't talk about it. Read on for an explanation.)

- Are transgender people gay? (Short answer: People who identify as transgender may identify as heterosexual, homosexual, or any other sexual orientation.)

- I'm worried that my daughter is going to have a harder life, now that she has come out. What can I do? (Short answer: Being able to present her true self to the world will make her life easier in many ways, and having your support and guidance can help her face the challenges with more knowledge and confidence.)

- How can my child possibly know if they are the "wrong gender"? I don't believe it. (Short answer: Kids know, and they know early.)

- What does "pansexual" mean? (See definition on page 65.)

The language around these topics is a major source of confusion and anxiety. While the language traditionally used to describe gender and sexual identity was limited—male/female, gay/straight—there is now a constantly growing and evolving vocabulary to draw on when describing oneself and expressing support for others. As a gender studies major nearly two decades ago, I became familiar with an early version of this lexicon. But even the language I was exposed to then was far more limited than that in use today. I actively try to keep up, but I still have to ask my students to clarify terms they use and look up definitions as new words emerge.

Adolescents are constantly exposed to this language, and many have an essential level of comfort with it due to the fact that it is so ingrained in their daily lives and cultures. In both rural and urban communities, they encounter people using a variety of pronouns to describe themselves. They are aware of news stories covering gay and transgender rights. They see anti-bullying campaigns highlighting the need to stand up for LGBTQ+ (lesbian, gay, bisexual, transgender, queer/questioning, and all other gender identities and sexual/romantic orientations) peers.[29] They watch YouTubers' accounts of coming out. They participate in pride parades and events and view them unfolding on social media. They watch TV shows and read books featuring gay and gender-neutral characters. Whether they do or do not identify as members of the LGBTQ+ community, adolescents are aware of and are often conversant in the terms and concepts defining it.

The Trevor Project is the world's largest suicide prevention and crisis intervention organization for LGBTQ+ young people. Their trained team is available 24-7 by phone, chat, and text to help LGBTQ+ youth in crisis. They have online communities and comprehensive online training and resources for parents, educators, and other allies. The Trevor Project's social media streams are teeming with up-to-date information, messages from role models, and action steps followers can take to contribute to the movement for LGBTQ+

equality and rights. On their website, The Trevor Project has a glossary of terms used to define gender and sexual identity.[30] The following is a list of commonly used terms reprinted from it. You may just skim it now, but seeing them in this format is a useful primer for understanding LGBTQ+ youth and their experience.

Gender identity and sexual orientation are two very distinct things, but they are often misunderstood, conflated, and confused.

Gender Identity: Our internal understanding and experience of our own gender. Each person's experience with their gender identity is unique and personal.

Sexual Orientation: A person's physical, romantic, emotional, and/or spiritual attraction to another person. Everyone has a sexual orientation.

TERMS DESCRIBING GENDER IDENTITY

Cisgender: Used to describe people whose gender identity aligns with the sex they were assigned at birth.

Gender Expression: The way in which we present ourselves, which can include physical appearance, clothing, hairstyles, and behavior.

Nonbinary: Used to describe people who experience their gender identity and/or gender expression as outside the male-female gender binary. Many other words for identities outside the traditional categories of man and woman may be used, such as genderfluid, genderqueer, polygender, bigender, demigender, or agender. These identities, while similar, are not necessarily interchangeable or synonymous.

Transgender (or trans): An umbrella term used to describe people whose gender identity differs from the sex they were assigned at birth. Many transgender people will transition to align their gender expression with their gender identity; however, you do not have to transition in order to be transgender.

Transitioning: The social, legal, and/or medical process a trans person may go through to make their gender identity fit their gender expression, presentation, or sex. This word means many different things to different people, and a person doesn't have to experience all or any of these common transitioning elements to identify as their true gender.

Two-Spirit: A term created by First Nations/Native American/Indigenous peoples whose sexual orientation and/or gender/sex exists in ways that challenge colonial constructions of a gender binary. This term should not be appropriated to describe people who are not First Nations/Native American/Indigenous members.

TERMS DESCRIBING SEXUAL ORIENTATION

Asexual (or ace): Used to describe people who experience little to no sexual attraction. Many asexual people desire romantic relationships, and romantic orientations are a way for aces to communicate who they prefer to date or form relationships with.

Bisexual: Used to describe people who have the capacity to form attraction and/or relationships to more than one gender.

Gay: In the past, only men who are attracted to men have used the word "gay." Now, it is common for "gay" to be used by anyone who is attracted to their same sex or gender.

Lesbian: A woman who is predominantly attracted to other women. Some women prefer the term "gay"—it's all up to you and what fits your identity best.

Pansexual: Used to describe people who are attracted to people of any gender or to people regardless of their gender. Some people may use the words "bisexual" and "pansexual" interchangeably, and others use only one word exclusively to describe themselves.

OVERARCHING TERMS RELATED TO THE LGBTQ+ EXPERIENCE

Binary System: A binary system is something made up of two opposing parts. Gender (man/woman) and sex (male/female) are examples of binary systems.

Queer: An umbrella term used to refer to an identity that expands outside of heterosexuality. Due to its history as a reclaimed slur and use in political movements, queer still holds political significance.

Questioning: Used to describe a person who may be processing or questioning their sexual orientation and/or gender identity.

PRONOUNS

When I was a teenager and my dad would ask me questions about my social life, he would always ask, "Who's they?" wanting me to be specific, so he could know about the exact friends in a group I was talking about. The answer back then was invariably a list of people. "Vera, Tillie, Angel . . ." Today, if you ask a girl, "Who's they?" she may answer, "They are Kira. Those are their pronouns." In this case, "they" refers to one person who has chosen to go by gender-neutral pronouns.

In 2019, Merriam-Webster's dictionary word of the year was "they." The dictionary cited the fact that "English famously lacks a gender-neutral singular pronoun to correspond neatly with singular pronouns like *everyone* or *someone*, and as a consequence *they* has been used for this purpose for over 600 years."[31] "More recently, though," editors for Merriam-Webster explained, "*they* has also been used to refer to one person whose gender identity is nonbinary, a sense that is increasingly common in published, edited text, as well as social media and in daily personal interactions between English speakers. There's no doubt that its use is established in the English language, which is why it was added to the Merriam-Webster online dictionary this past September." The editors also noted that it had seen a 313 percent increase in lookups for "they" in 2019 over 2018, further highlighting its widespread usage and relevance. "They" is just one example of the gender-neutral pronouns in wide use today. There are others, and we can expect additional options to surface in the coming years. Here are some examples of pronouns that people use (in order of nominative, objective, possessive determiner, possessive pronoun, and reflexive), also from The Trevor Project's website:

- She, her, her, hers, and herself
- He, him, his, his, and himself
- They, them, their, theirs, and themself
- Ze/zie, hir, hir, hirs, and hirself
- Xe, xem, xyr, xyrs, and xemself
- Ve, ver, vis, vis, and verself

GENDER IDENTITY AND SEXUAL ORIENTATION THEN AND NOW

Exploration and questioning of gender identity and sexual orientation aren't newfangled concepts, and as you can see from the definitions of gender identity and sexual orientation, they aren't concepts that apply only to the LGBTQ+ community. Even people who are straight/heterosexual and cisgender engage in a process of solidifying their identities through the clothes they wear, the gender roles they choose to subscribe to, or the romantic attractions they act on. Human sexuality is part of a lifelong unfolding that every person on the planet engages in, whether or not it is a conscious process. There have always been people who did not identify as heterosexual and cisgender. However, in recent decades LGBTQ+ individuals have developed the language to express their individuality and paved the way for younger generations to access such language earlier. LGBTQ+ youth also have role models and community who have helped bring LGBTQ+ identity to the forefront of cultural consciousness and discussion.

In the late 1990s, Elizabeth (now Eli) was a female high school student growing up in Texas who knew that she wasn't comfortable playing into traditional ideals of femininity. From the time she was a small child, she had insisted on a masculine haircut and wearing boys' clothes to school. The only fights Eli got in with her mom were about having to wear dresses to family weddings and funerals. Once, out of frustration, her mom, shouted, "I don't understand. Do you just want to be a boy?!"

"I couldn't even answer her," Eli remembered. "Being able to transition from being female to male wasn't something I could even consider because I didn't know it was possible. The only role models of people I had seen transition from one gender to another were on *Jerry Springer*, and they were all men who had transitioned to being women. I didn't identify with them. That wasn't who I was."

Late in high school, Eli fell in love with a girl and came out to her parents as a lesbian. She thought she had it figured out. Then, she went to college at the University of Texas at Austin. "I joined a group for lesbian, gay, bisexual, and questioning women. I was around a lot of folks like me. A few meetings in, this person gets up and starts telling the story of making the transition from being female to male. And I thought, 'This is my story.' I had never even heard the word 'transsexual' (what is now referred to as 'transgender') before I got to college. But suddenly, I knew where things were headed."

It took Eli years to find a framework for how he felt and who he was. "If I had had role models, I would have been able to verbalize it a lot earlier. It was obvious from the time I was three. If I had the language, I wouldn't have had to come out twice, first as a lesbian and then transgender."

I asked Dr. Tia Dole, The Trevor Project's chief clinical operations officer, why she thought today's young people were talking about gender and sexuality so much more than in past decades. "The Internet has been a game changer for young people in the LGBTQ+ community," she explained. "Being able to find other people like you has been a linchpin for opening up and understanding a spectrum of identities. It's not that there weren't people questioning before, or people who didn't feel like they were in one gender or another, but there was no language for it, there was no connection with other people who were questioning in the same way."

Today, no matter where they are growing up or who they have in-person access to, young people questioning their gender or sexuality can go online, find resources, and find others like them. Years ago, Eli was surprised to find people like him after years of navigating his journey on his own. "Now," Dr. Dole said, "you can google 'maybe I'm not the right gender,' or something like that, and you instantly get a whole list of responses. You're going to find online communities, where you can connect with other young people. We didn't have this access years ago, and now we do."

WHY YOUR SUPPORT IS LIFESAVING

Many young people engage comfortably and effortlessly in exploration and experimentation with gender and sexuality. They adopt new pronouns with ease, try new hairstyles, wear gender-neutral clothing, and date people of different genders, breaking away, even if temporarily, from society's dominant, heteronormative ideals for how they should look and act.

For many other young people, realizing that they do not identify with a given gender identity or assumed sexual orientation can be extremely confusing and distressing.[32] "It doesn't feel right. There's a sense of feeling different and not belonging. You start worrying because you know you aren't following the script," Dr. Dole explains. "If you are trying to put yourself in an identity, for instance, if you were assigned female at birth and have been trying to force yourself into this identity, or if you know you are attracted to the same sex rather than the 'opposite' sex, you can have this feeling of incongruence." Learning how to be oneself, when you feel like you are different from most others, can be a lonesome, scary process.

Another source of stress, as Eden talked about in her account of coming out earlier in this chapter, is connected to family relationships, as LGBTQ+ youth worry about how their coming out will be received by those close to them and their broader community. While young people in the United States (and many, but not all, other countries) live in a more accepting society now than in the past, they are well aware of the discrimination and hostility LGBTQ+ community members continue to face. Not only are they worried about being accepted by the people closest to them, they worry about how coming out might affect others in negative ways. There's what Dr. Dole refers to as a "perceived burdensomeness," a concern many young people have that if they come out, they will humiliate their families. As Dr. Dole explained, "They want to be good children to their parents, but that could seem to come in conflict with being their true selves. If you are one of these children, the connections you value to other people can feel thwarted."

In severe cases, LGBTQ+ youth fear full rejection and being thrown out by their parents, which can threaten their access to basic needs like food and shelter and their ability to go to college. So they feel they have to hide their identities until they are financially independent.

Young people who do clear the hurdles of coming out still face questioning and prejudice from others. Explaining their identity and pronouns to people can be exhausting. Defending their identities to people who try to convince them that they should be heterosexual or cisgender can be jarring. (In a 2019 survey by The Trevor Project of 34,000 LGBTQ+ youth, two out of three respondents reported encountering someone who "tried to convince them to change their sexual orientation or gender identity."[33]) Fielding confused looks or glares when out in public with their romantic partners or when using a public bathroom is uncomfortable. (Fifty-eight percent of transgender and nonbinary youth in the same Trevor Project survey reported "being discouraged from using a bathroom that corresponds to their gender identity."[34]) And the threat of being victims of bullying, physical violence, or assault, or of dying because of their identities, is top of mind. (Seventy-one percent of the youth in the Trevor Project survey reported facing discrimination "due to either their gender identity or sexual orientation."[35])

"The risk that some take to live their best lives is very high," Dr. Dole said. "You have to constantly calculate the risk of being harassed at school or injured on the street and the amount of negative feedback you can handle in a given day."

The stress mounts for LGBTQ+ youth, making them uniquely vulnerable to anxiety, depression, and suicidal ideation and suicide attempts.[36] Thirty-nine percent of respondents to The Trevor Project's

2019 survey admitted they had seriously considered attempting suicide. Those who had been in conversion therapy, a widely discredited practice aimed at changing one's gender identity or sexual orientation, were twice as likely to report a suicide attempt as compared to those youth who had not experienced conversion therapy.[37] In a 2018 study published in the journal *Pediatrics*, researchers looked at suicide rates among members of six gender identity groups and found that female to male transgender youth had the highest rates of previous suicide attempts.[38]

As a parent, you may be scared for your daughter, worried about the difficulties she will face, but you can help protect her as she navigates the challenges that come with living as her authentic self. You may find yourself wishing she identified differently, but you will not be able to change her. Her gender identity or sexual orientation may run counter to your religious values or cultural norms. But you must accept her and support her if you want her to survive and thrive. When parents support their LGBTQ+ children, children are protected against risks both now and in the future.[39] If your daughter is a member of this community, she needs you to be consistently present and supportive.

> **YOUR GOAL:** If your daughter is questioning or a member of the LGBTQ+ community, make sure she knows that she is loved and supported in her individuality.

> **RULE #1:** Let go of any belief that you or anyone else can change your daughter's gender identity or sexual identity. Conversion therapy doesn't work, can be deeply

endangering to your daughter's mental health, and is a contributing factor in suicide attempts.

TALKING POINTS

Your daughter is probably going to drive most conversations about gender and sexual orientation, by bringing the topic up to you or coming out to you. In these cases, having meaningful talks depends less on the information you bring to the table and more on listening and responding in accepting and supportive ways to what your daughter is telling you. If she seems open to it, one area you can bring suggestions is in helping her find other members of the LGBTQ+ community.

WAYS TO CONNECT

Finding like-minded friends and mentors can bring relief, joy, and connection to LGBTQ+ youth who feel like outsiders or like they could use extra support in coming out. Today, your daughter has many pathways to find communities, including through:

- Local LGBTQ+ organizations and community centers.
- School-based LGBTQ+ clubs and alliances.
- Online communities facilitated by trusted organizations.

Even if your daughter does not live in an area or attend a school where there are local opportunities to participate in an LGBTQ+ community, she can still participate in online communities, attend events in other locations, and find and connect with supportive peers and mentors online and by phone, text, and video chat.

HOW IT'S DONE

Do Say

- I love you.
- I'm proud of you.
- I know this probably wasn't an easy thing to tell me about.
- I support you.
- What can I do to best support you?
- Do you feel like you have people to talk to who really understand? I am always available to talk, but I know I may sometimes not understand exactly what you are going through.
- This language is new for me, and I would like to know more. How can I learn?
- Has everyone been respectful and kind to you at school?
- Should we talk to the school counselor together?

Don't Say

- Are you sure?
- This is just a phase, right?
- You are too young to come to these conclusions about yourself.
- Your pronouns will just confuse people.

BEYOND THE CONVERSATION

WATCH YOUR LANGUAGE

Cultivating an accepting environment is in the nuances. Use respectful language when talking about members of the LGBTQ+ community. If you ever use demeaning terms, make insensitive jokes, or even laugh at jokes at the expense of LGBTQ+ individuals, your daughter will get the message that you think less of them. If she is considering coming out to you, this can give her pause, making her fearful that you won't accept her.

FIND AN LGBTQ+-FRIENDLY SCHOOL[40]

School can feel unsafe for LGBTQ+ students who commonly find themselves socially isolated or the victims of teasing and bullying. Going to school in a supportive environment can make all the difference. Talk to an administrator at your child's school or at a school your family is considering and explore the following questions:

- Are faculty and administrators trained in working with LGBTQ+ students?
- What type of support does the school offer LGBTQ+ students?
- Are there any clubs for LGBTQ+ students and allies?
- Are there any all-gender restrooms on campus?

STAY UP-TO-DATE ON NEWS AND EVENTS RELEVANT TO THE LGBTQ+ COMMUNITY

As I mentioned, the language around gender identity and sexual orientation is constantly changing, and society is constantly changing to be more inclusive of members of the LGBTQ+ community. Keep your conversations with your daughter relevant by staying up-to-date on these shifts.

EXPECT YOUR DAUGHTER'S IDENTITY TO TAKE SHAPE OVER TIME

"I talk to a lot of parents who want a decision to be made," Dr. Dole of The Trevor Project said. "They say, 'Okay, you are gender non-binary. Got it. This is the pronoun you want to use? Okay.' Then something changes, which can feel very unsettling. They're not comfortable with an identity being in flux, and they feel so stressed about waiting to see what happens in this process." It's normal for you to want to know how your daughter will ultimately define herself, and it's also normal for her to discover her true self (in many senses, not just with regard to gender and sexuality) over time—so be patient, flexible, and nonjudgmental as she moves through the unfolding process.

Mental Health

Jasmine sailed through elementary school, but when she had to transition to a new campus for middle school, she began crying every morning, telling her parents that she didn't want to go.

When Alexis was a freshman in high school, her parents noticed that she had started to spend a lot of time in her room with her door closed. She was less talkative at the dinner table, unwilling to share the details of her day. She was making fewer and fewer plans with friends and started saying she wanted to quit basketball.

Kai's parents discovered that she was smoking marijuana on an ongoing basis as her grades started tanking junior year.

SOME BACKGROUND

While at first glance these behavior changes might be easily explained as "moodiness," "phases," or "bad days," they illustrate some of the many ways mental health conditions can manifest among adolescent girls.

As you know from chapter 1, girls are under a lot of pressure. While many girls have a high tolerance for stress, others' stress levels will reach beyond what is normal and healthy, can have negative effects on girls' daily functioning, and potentially trigger other mental health conditions. Girls are twice as likely as boys to be diagnosed with a mood disorder, such as anxiety or depression, in adolescence.[41] Eating disorders disproportionately affect girls in their teens and twenties.[42] And multiple recent studies suggest that the rates of suicidal ideation among adolescent girls is increasing at a rate significantly greater than that of their male peers.[43]

The root causes of mental health conditions can be circumstantial (such as a death in the family, questioning one's sexuality, or being bullied), biological, or a combination, and multiple factors make adolescent girls especially susceptible, including their hormonal makeups, greater tendency to ruminate, time spent on social media, and lack of sleep tied to screen time.[44] Unfortunately, the unique physical and social circumstances of girls' adolescence can set the scene for a mental health condition to materialize.[45]

Because mental health conditions can be difficult to identify, untangle, and address, parents are often left feeling directionless when it comes to supporting their daughters in this area. Girls are particularly vulnerable to "internalizing disorders," which can cause extreme suffering, undetectable to others (in contrast to disorders that cause girls to act out).[46] To girls, uncomfortable symptoms can feel scary and difficult to articulate, and mental health remains a taboo topic, preventing important conversations from flowing between parents and their kids. In turn, parents often lack the foundational knowledge and personal experience that would allow them to recognize girls' mental health issues at the outset. For example, researchers at University College London and the University of Liverpool found that adolescent girls in the United Kingdom reported higher rates of mental health problems than their parents reported observing, revealing a tendency among parents to underestimate the prevalence of emotional issues their girls were experiencing.[47]

At the Child Mind Institute in New York City, Dr. Jamie Howard is a psychologist who works with adolescents and their families. As she told me, "We tend to think of adolescents and teenagers as difficult and moody, and so a mental health issue would be easy to miss if that's your working paradigm—thinking, 'She's just being a teenager.'"

It's common that signs of mental illness get dismissed at first by caring adults who think they're just witnessing normal "adolescent strife." Symptoms can creep up, taking months to fully manifest, and it can take years for parents to get their girls the proper treatment.[48] I've had dozens of conversations with parents who, after they realized their daughters had been suffering, felt guilty, like they had missed the signs and were behind the ball trying to get help.

SOME SIGNS TO LOOK OUT FOR

The ways in which mental health conditions manifest can be highly individualized. Symptoms can vary in intensity and may be indicative of one or more diagnoses, some of which can occur simultaneously. Symptoms can also be indicative of a stressor other than a mental health condition, like being bullied or the victim of sexual assault—which is why it is important to take note of the symptoms and seek help from a professional. A good rule of thumb is to look out for any negative changes in your daughter's behavior such as those related to:[49]

- Energy or sleep (including sleeping too much or trouble sleeping).
- Mood (including sad mood, excessive moodiness, or irritability).
- Appetite (including skipping meals or overeating).
- Concentration.
- Social habits (including withdrawing from friends, family, or previously cherished activities).

Additional signs of mental health conditions you might notice include:

- Headaches.

- Upset stomach.

- Self-harming behaviors such as cutting.

- Expressing feelings of hopelessness or suicidal ideation.

- Excessive fear or worrying.

- Avoiding situations that feel scary or make one uneasy.

- Extreme behaviors such as alternating high and low moods, consistent extreme emotionality, or repeated, dangerous risk-taking behavior.

- Using alcohol and drugs, which can be a form of self-medication for uncomfortable symptoms.

TREATMENT OPTIONS

The most effective treatment regimens for mental health conditions are highly individualized and developed with the help of qualified mental health professionals. They may include one or a combination of the following:[50]

- Stress-management techniques like meditation, breathing, or journaling.

- Adopting a healthy lifestyle with plenty of exercise, sleep, and a healthy diet.

- Individual, group, and/or family therapy.

- Medication.

- In-patient treatment or hospitalization.

GETTING THE RIGHT HELP

Conversations around mental health are sensitive and personal, so you want to make sure that if you are taking your daughter for professional treatment, it is to someone who makes her feel seen and heard. In chapter 4, "Building Your Support Team," I list types of mental health professionals, how they can help you and your daughter, and how you can identify the people who are the best fit for your family.

Addressing a mental health concern with your daughter can be tough, and it may feel like there isn't a clear path forward for months or even years. But most girls who are diagnosed and receive treatment can be helped and do recover, and the earlier they get treatment, the better off they are. In the process, girls learn a lot about themselves and learn strategies they can draw on to feel more mentally and emotionally centered throughout their lives.

> **YOUR GOAL:** Make sure your daughter has the support she needs to weather a mental health issue.

> **RULE #1:** Don't tell her to "just calm down," "relax," or "get over it." She may not be able to. Telling people how to feel doesn't work. Helping people work through difficult feelings and sensations works better.

TALKING POINTS

A MENTAL HEALTH CONDITION IS
NOTHING TO BE ASHAMED OF

If your daughter has anxiety, depression, or another mental health condition, it's likely she's experiencing a degree of self-consciousness about it. To help her feel accepted, be clear that mental illnesses are common and nothing to feel shame about. You can also talk to your daughter about how, because mental illnesses can't be seen, they have traditionally been misunderstood. Mental illnesses are just like physical illnesses, such as a broken leg, and no one would be ashamed of that.

SYMPTOMS CAN FEEL PERMANENT,
BUT THEY ARE OFTEN TEMPORARY

Just because your daughter feels hopeless now doesn't mean she will feel that way forever. Most mental health conditions are treatable, and many are curable. Talk to your daughter about how much research has been done on mental health conditions and how even in the last decade, treatments have improved greatly. It may be hard for her to feel optimistic, but it won't hurt for her to understand how much is known about what she is going through and how sophisticated the treatments are, even if it takes a few tries to identify the best one for her.

HOW TO HELP A FRIEND IN NEED

Seventy percent of teens say that anxiety and depression are significant problems for their peers.[51] According to the Pew Research

Center, which conducted this research, "concern about mental health cuts across gender, racial and socio-economic lines, with roughly equal shares of teens across demographic groups saying it is a significant issue in their community." At one time or another, your daughter might be concerned about and wondering how best to help a friend who is struggling. Girls can feel like they have to take on their friends' problems and keep them secret. Emphasize to your daughter, especially if she is concerned that a friend is self-injuring or considering suicide, that she should tell you or another adult. The main priority is keeping her friend safe. Over the years, I have often spoken with girls who are really worried about a friend and believe they need help, but are terrified to tell an adult because they don't want to upset their friend further or betray her secrets.

Importantly, this is one of those scenarios I mentioned in chapter 2, where talking about a friend can give your daughter a sense of how you might handle a conversation or scenario that involved her. Though your daughter may broach the topic out of concern for someone else, you can take the opportunity to restate that you are always there to listen and help if your daughter is ever facing an emotional challenge. One question to ask is "What would you do, if you ever felt hopeless or depressed?" You can emphasize that she should always talk to someone, especially you.[52]

HOW IT'S DONE

It can be disheartening to see your daughter suffering from a mental health issue, but this is one of those times your words really will not be able fix her. To be most supportive, focus on statements that help her feel seen in her struggle and highlight your desire to be there for her.

Do Say

- It's okay not to feel okay all the time.
- We're going to get the help you need.
- What matters most right now is helping you feel better.
- You may not feel like yourself right now or right away, and that's okay.
- We don't have to figure everything out right away.
- You can always talk to me when you need to.
- I love you.

Don't Say

- Get over it.
- Cheer up.
- Calm down.
- Relax.
- Why are you down when you have so many things to be happy about?
- You don't know what it's like to have to really worry about things.
- Focus on your schoolwork, that's what matters right now.

ADDRESSING SUICIDAL IDEATION

If you are worried that your daughter might be considering suicide, you can and should ask her about it directly. And you don't have to worry that you will be putting ideas in her head. "You're not going to induce a desire to die by suicide by asking about it," Dr. Howard at the Child Mind Institute says. "So if you say, 'Are you thinking at all about hurting yourself?' or 'Have you thought about hurting yourself?,' you don't have to worry that you're introducing the topic and now your daughter might do it."

If you bring the topic up with your daughter, Dr. Howard explains that a girl who is not suicidal will probably respond with something along the lines of "No, I'm not. Why do you ask? That's weird." But if your daughter has or is considering suicide, she will likely say something like, "Well, maybe kind of. I don't think I'll do it, but I think about it." If you get this type of response, you know there is some risk, and you'll want to call a mental health professional as soon as possible to help you decide on next steps to keep your daughter safe.

Beyond asking about your daughter's intentions, don't be afraid to be direct with her about your stance. Making clear statements like "I don't want you to hurt yourself," "I don't want you to die," and "You need to be here, and we're going to get you help," can all make a positive difference. In the depths of despair your daughter might feel, wrongly, that she is a burden on you. Make sure you are countering those messages.

If you would prefer for a trained counselor or therapist to broach this topic with your daughter, schedule an appointment as soon as possible. Do not hesitate.

Discussing Your Own
Mental Health Struggles

If you have been diagnosed with a mental health condition, sharing your experiences with your daughter as she navigates her own can be a helpful, connective experience for both of you. It is delicate, though, and I recommend that you seek guidance from people who know your daughter well, and perhaps your daughter's mental health professional (if she has one) on how to broach the conversation and the language to use. Younger adolescents may not be able to handle the information at all. Older girls may benefit from hearing about parts of your mental health experiences but not all of them. If you are going to have this conversation, you want to be mindful that it could cause your daughter additional worry and stress, whether what you tell her scares her or makes her worry about your well-being.

BEYOND THE CONVERSATION

Practice Stress-Management Techniques

Stress-management techniques can help you feel more centered and grounded as you guide your daughter through her adolescent years, and especially through challenges like mental illness. Invite your daughter to join you, especially if she is struggling. One father I interviewed for this book bought journals for himself and his daughter and suggested they journal alongside each other. It turned into a daily ritual.

Avoid Making Any Jokes or Flippant Comments Related to Mental Health

For instance, don't use the words "crazy" or "psycho" to describe people. If your daughter is sensitive to your wording, she may be worrying that you'll judge her if she develops a mental health condition. Or she may hesitate to come to you for help because she doesn't want to disappoint you.

Substance Use

My dad always used to tell me a version of the same story before I went out to parties in high school. "Kimmy, have I ever told you the story about how I used to fake drinking when I was in high school?" Invariably, he would continue on to tell me about the barn parties he went to growing up in a small farm town called Streator, Illinois. "I never wanted to drink. I also didn't want to answer to people about why I wasn't interested or turn down the drinks and make a scene," he'd continue (turns out he just doesn't like alcohol). "So, I would hold the drink and then, over the course of the night, I would slowly pour it out behind the hay bales when no one was looking. If someone hands you a drink, you can just pour it in a plant or something. Sound good?"

"Yes, Dad. You tell me that story all the time, and I got it!" I'd say as I zipped out the door on the way to meet up with my friends.

My dad knew he'd told me the story over and over. He knew I had received extensive substance abuse education in school. He knew he'd get a knowing smile from me. But he also knew he was getting an important set of messages across in a language I could understand.

My dad was well aware that I would have access to drugs and alcohol when I went out in high school. So he took the opportunity, again and again, to reference the realities I would encounter and the pressure I might feel. It was clear that he didn't want me to drink and do drugs—we had talked about it. It was also obvious that I could just say "no" and turn down a drink when it was offered, but my dad knew that it wasn't always that easy. Using himself as an example, he helped me see that I could be creative and make my own healthy decisions while navigating risky social situations.

His strategy worked on me. Before the days of ride-sharing apps, I consistently volunteered to be the designated driver, making it easy for me to turn down drinks. And when I wasn't, I would carry the drinks around sometimes, maybe taking a sip here and there, but more often, slowly trickling them into the houseplants.

SOME BACKGROUND

Many adolescents experiment with drugs and alcohol for a variety of reasons we can all name: curiosity, peer influence, the fun of participating in the party culture of adolescent life so often portrayed in TV shows and movies. In the same ways adults self-medicate, young people may drink and do drugs to numb out difficult emotions stemming from the stresses of their lives or mental health conditions. Additionally, girls might use certain drugs, and smoking or vaping, to control their weight. From just a few of the recent statistics, it's clear that substance use continues to be a relevant issue to address with adolescents:

- Underage drinkers consume 10 percent of all alcohol sold in the United States.[53]

- On average, adolescents have been found to drink more than twice as much as adults will in a single drinking episode.[54]

- More than forty percent of teens report having tried marijuana.[55]

- Nearly two out of ten twelfth graders report using prescription medications without having a prescription.[56]

THE RISE AND DANGERS OF VAPING

At the University of Southern California, Dr. Jon-Patrick Allem and his team analyze social media posts to illuminate trends in health-related attitudes and behaviors. In a study of eighty thousand tweets, he didn't set out specifically to analyze youth "JUULing" habits (at the time of this writing, JUUL is the most popular, name-brand e-cigarette/vaping device).[57] "The research question we wanted to answer was simply, when people are thinking about JUUL, and posting about JUUL on the Twitter platform, what are people saying? It was an open-ended research question."[58] But when Dr. Allem and his team looked at the data, they found kids in elementary, middle, and high school talking about JUULing on school grounds, during school hours. They talked about JUULing at recess and in the bathroom. They mentioned teachers mistaking their JUULs for USB keys. "We were not looking for this theme a priori. The words that were commonly occurring in the data happened to represent underage usage," Dr. Allem told me.

While cigarette usage has declined steadily since 2011, the recent, meteoric rise in youth vaping has been called an epidemic by the US Department of Health and Human Services.[59] In 2011, 1.5 percent of adolescents reported that they were vaping, but by 2019, that figure had risen to 27.5 percent of adolescents.[60] Adolescents are vaping marijuana and flavored oils, often laden with nicotine. Young people are drawn to the fruity, sweet flavors of e-cigarettes, especially mint and mango.[61] They are vaping because they think it is fun, because their friends are doing it, or because they are led to believe by social media that it's an acceptable cultural norm among their peers.[62] They mistakenly believe e-cigarettes to be "safe," safer than cigarettes. And girls are vaping to help manage their weight.[63] They are ignoring the dangers and the warnings, as adolescents often do when it comes to risky behaviors. But e-cigarettes carry huge unknowns and threats to health that researchers are racing to uncover and understand. And, e-cigarettes are an important subject to touch on in conversations about substance use.[64]

Not all girls will experiment with drugs and alcohol, but usage is common enough that you want to be aware of the signs your daughter might be high or under the influence. Partnership to End Addiction lists the following possible signs your child is under the influence:[65]

- Scents of alcohol or smoke on her breath or clothes.

- Red and/or dilated eyes.

- Rosy cheeks.

- Difficulty making eye contact.

- Slurring her speech.

- Mood changes (which can also be indicative of a mental health condition or other worrying situation like being bullied).
- Lying or sneaking around.

Teenagers need information on alcohol, drugs, smoking, and vaping. They need you to be realistic in your expectations and knowledgeable when you talk to them. They need to hear the reasons why substance use in adolescence is especially concerning to you and why it should be for them. And they need to know that you will be there to talk or if anything goes wrong.

> **YOUR GOAL:** Keeping your daughter informed of the latest information and risks associated with different substances, and making *absolutely certain* she knows she can ask you first (even if there are some consequences later) if she ever needs a ride home, needs your help with a substance-related issue, or wants to help a friend.

> **RULE #1:** Don't rely on scare tactics alone. Even if you have a family history of substance abuse and extra reason to be concerned about your daughter ever trying drugs or alcohol, trying to frighten her will likely be insufficient to support her in healthy decision-making. Your daughter needs information and strategies to make educated, healthy choices.

TALKING POINTS

SUBSTANCE USE AND THREATS TO WELL-BEING

Relaying some of these concrete facts about the impact of substance use, beyond what she can probably guess, can help your daughter think about the real impacts her choices will have on her well-being. Drugs, alcohol, and prescription drugs used without prescriptions can:

- Have negative effects on her brain and affect healthy development.[66]

- Impair healthy decision-making, making young people more vulnerable to risky behaviors including driving under the influence, driving with someone who is under the influence, and having unprotected sex.[67]

- Make young people more vulnerable to sexual assault and other forms of dating violence. (The connection between substance use and sexual assault cannot be overstated,[68] which I detail in the "Sexual Health" and "Sexual Misconduct" sections.[69])

- Affect mood in negative ways. While alcohol and drugs are often mythologized by peers and in popular culture and media as being the ultimate mood enhancers, in fact they are depressants. Girls, who are more vulnerable than boys to mental health conditions, need to understand that momentary highs give way to downward spirals.[70] In addition, substances can interact with prescription medications, including those taken for focus issues or a mental health condition.

- Spur substance abuse issues in adulthood. Substance use in adolescence makes teens more likely to develop substance abuse problems in adulthood.[71]

SUBSTANCE USE AND THE LAW

Aside from the threats to your daughter's well-being already mentioned, illegal substance use can come with some pretty serious "adult" consequences. Talk with your daughter about the laws in your state and the policies at her middle school, high school, or college related to being caught using illegal substances.

SUBSTANCES AND BEHAVIORS TO ADDRESS

You don't need to know everything about every potentially harmful substance in order to provide your daughter with essential information. That would be impossible anyway, since new drugs are being developed all the time, and slang names for existing ones are evolving just as quickly. You should focus on educating your daughter about the following broad categories, asking her questions about trends she's noticing among her friends, and jumping on any opportunities to talk about anything she brings up:

- Alcohol.

- Recreational drugs (not including marijuana).

- Marijuana, which is becoming more widely legalized but remains largely unregulated and dangerous. Marijuana is often genetically engineered and modified, laced with chemicals, and portioned at high levels in edibles and in e-cigarette oils.

- Prescription drugs, including friends' ADHD meds, anything she sees you take, or anything that you have in your medicine cabinet.

- Vaping and smoking.

The Business of Alcohol, Vaping, and Smoking

Talking to your daughter about the business of drugs, alcohol, and vaping is one way to broach the topic of substance use without sounding like every school presentation she's already heard. Here are some key points you can get across:

- Producers and advertisers count on the addictive properties of their products—the longer and the more people buy them, the more money the companies make.

- Teenagers have a great deal of buying power and can make things "trendy," so advertisers routinely target them, even when they are not legally supposed to.

- The FDA and the surgeon general have made preventing youth e-cigarette use one of their priorities by prohibiting the sale of certain flavored vape cartridges designed to attract young people.[72]

HOW IT'S DONE

Do Say

- If you are ever in a situation where you need a ride home because you or your driver is drunk or otherwise under the influence, call me. There may be some consequences, but we'll deal with them later. Consequences will be more severe than if you don't tell me what is going on and I find out on my own.

- It doesn't always *feel* okay to say no or set a boundary, but it always is okay.

- Beware of people handing you drinks. You want to see your drink being prepared and trust the person who is making it for you. It's a worst-case scenario, but people can and do put drugs in peoples' drinks.

Don't Say

When it comes to what not to say about substance use, you have a delicate balance to strike. On the one hand, you don't want to encourage habits that could be dangerous or harmful to your daughter. On the other hand, you don't want to drive such a hard line that she doesn't feel like she can come to you with questions or a problem.

- Everyone drinks and tries drugs in high school and college.

- Here, have some of my cocktail.

- If I find out you've been drinking or doing drugs, I will lose respect for you.

Conversation Starters

- What are your friends' views on alcohol/drugs?

- Does it seem like a lot of people are doing alcohol and drugs?

- What is your stance on vaping? You can answer honestly.

- Are you learning about substance use in school? What has stood out to you?

- If there are people doing drugs or drinking at the party you are going to, how would you handle the pressure? What would your plan be?

- What would you do if you thought one of your friends was under the influence of drugs or alcohol and not thinking clearly enough to make safe decisions at a party or in another social situation?

- Do you know how to help someone who you think has a substance-abuse problem?

BEYOND THE CONVERSATION

SET A GOOD EXAMPLE

When it comes to preventing your daughter from developing a substance abuse issue of any kind, setting a good example is paramount. You need to mind your attitude and habits related to alcohol, drugs (recreational and prescription), smoking, and vaping. Now, you are of course entitled to an adult beverage or several. By all means, live it up, but don't forget that what you do and what you believe rubs off. Here are some guidelines:

If You Have a Substance-Abuse Issue of Any Kind, Get Help

Pretending that you don't have a problem isn't an effective way to handle addiction or anger issues and "be strong" for your daughter. Chances are, she can already see right through you and knows you need help. There's no shame in it. Find the right people to support you both for your well-being and longevity and for your daughter's.

Don't Drive Under the Influence

In the era of Uber and Lyft, there is no excuse to get behind the wheel under the influence, even if you think you are totally sober. Cars can almost drive themselves. You can find a ride. You must show your daughter that drinking and driving, or driving with someone who is drunk, is a serious threat and one to be avoided.

Model Healthy Recreational Substance-Use Habits

Do you want your daughter to believe that she can't enter a new social situation without having a drink to loosen up? Do you want her to feel like the best way to have a good time is to get blackout drunk or high to the point that she can't remember much of the night before? Do you want her to feel like recreational drugs are the best way to manage the stress she feels? Think about the habits you want your daughter to form as an adult, and lead by example. For instance, I have talked to parents who will not order drinks in front of their children because alcoholism runs in their families, and they don't want to normalize drinking in any amount.

You'll also want to limit any direct or indirect "I need [fill-in-the-blank substance]" messaging. When parents say things like "I need a drink," or even "I can't function without my coffee," it gives girls very specific ideas about how they should be coping and having a good time. If you are going to have your caffeine fix at the beginning of the day or your cocktail at the end of the night, don't make a big deal about how substances help you make it through life.

Mind Your Medications

Teens and/or their friends might get curious about your medications. To prevent any temptation or unhealthy use, keep them out of sight and out of reach. If you have leftover prescription painkillers from a surgery or for some other reason, talk to your doctor about how to properly dispose of them, rather than leaving them in your medicine cabinet.

Technology and Social Media

One morning, my friend and fellow educator Carolynn Crabtree and I were getting ready to present to a group of high schoolers, loading our slides and testing the projector as the students began to file in and fill the seats in the auditorium. Two of them walked in, sat in the front row, pulled out a set of earbuds to share, and began to stare down at a single iPhone, smiling and laughing at a TV show or movie, something they were clearly streaming. As Carolynn and I got started with our introduction, these students didn't find it necessary to hit pause and listen to our presentation. They just kept watching, visibly reacting to the images on the screen. I was curious for how long they would keep this up, and so I let it happen. They went the entire hour.

What were we teaching that morning? Our media literacy program, Into the Blue Light. Carolynn is a former CIA operative who parlayed insights from her career in intelligence to help students and parents understand what information about them is searchable online, and how they can use the positive power of the Internet to cultivate a sparkling online presence. I draw on my early career experience working in entertainment and in the tech sector. Together, Carolynn and I created Into the Blue Light to show teens how to develop healthy digital habits and take control of their online reputations. We think it's pretty interesting and important stuff, and students and parents always give us rave reviews. But even we, digital literacy gurus with thousands of hours of experience working with teenagers, find ourselves in major competition with teens' ever-present screens.

SOME BACKGROUND

Fifty percent of girls say they are on the Internet "almost constantly" (compared to 39 percent of boys).[73]

Girls are on their screens all the time—at school, during leisure time alone and with friends, and in bed at night. Jameelah, thirteen, told me she routinely wakes up to over 150 messages from her group texts. Her parents store her phone at night, but most of her friends' parents do not. When I asked her what people are texting about in the middle of the night, she told me they say things like "Who's up?" before multiple friends chime in. Brianna, a junior in high school, falls asleep every night with her computer on her stomach, watching TV shows. "I don't have any trouble sleeping," she said, not realizing the negative impact blue light from screens has on the quality of her rest. And when I asked Hazel to put her phone away in one of my classes, she said, "Oh! Sorry, I didn't even realize I had taken it out of my backpack." Screens are ever present in most girls' lives, like extensions of their physical bodies.

Unless you work in the tech sector (and sometimes even then), chances are that your daughter is more technologically savvy than you are. She is part of a generation of digital natives who have grown up in a time of broadband Internet, smartphones, texting, video chat, and social media. And, like all teenage girls since the beginning of time, she's probably more tuned into what is cutting edge than you are, including every new digital product or app.

Feel free to feel overwhelmed and even completely annoyed trying to figure out how to curb your daughter's screen time. It's difficult for anyone to feel like they are doing it well. The latest technological revolution has taken place so quickly that parents, educators, and youth advocates everywhere are constantly looking for the best ways to limit the negative impacts of screen time in young peoples' lives, while helping them reap the benefits of the digital age. Making matters more complicated is the fact that while parents can set technological limits and boundaries for their kids, computers are widely used in schools, and technology and content that is limited or blocked in one family's house may not be banned in another. It's a game of Whack-A-Mole that will test your endurance, and girls are great at finding and exploiting the loopholes.

It's worth noting the benefits of screen time. It helps young people in a variety of ways, from facilitating learning about the world to making complex tasks like writing large papers or applying to college easier to manage. Using digital technology also aids in critical skill-building that will help students in college and in their careers. At young ages, they often have opportunities to learn digital document management (when organizing assignments, for instance) and sophisticated presentation design skills, which they will be able to draw on in their future jobs. During the pandemic, access to technology facilitated social connection and remote learning. The ability to share memes, connect over text and video chat, sign into an app, search a website from the palm of your hand, or reach out to a supportive community is particularly important, and perhaps even lifesaving, for young people who feel bullied or isolated in their home communities.

Even social media, which Lady Gaga has poignantly called "the toilet of the Internet,"[74] has its upsides for teenagers. In a 2018 survey by the Pew Research Center, 31 percent of teens reported feeling like social media had a "mostly positive" effect on their lives for the following reasons:[75]

- Connecting with friends/family (40 percent).

- Easier to find news/info (16 percent).

- Meeting others with same interests (15 percent).

- Keeps you upbeat/entertained (9 percent).

- Self-expression (7 percent).

- Getting support from others (5 percent).

- Learning new things (4 percent).

We know that the power of the Internet and social media to provide sources of education, entertainment, and support cannot be underestimated. We also know that there are some downsides to the digital life. Screen time is tied to poor sleep, a decrease in opportunities to practice and employ face-to-face interpersonal skills, challenges focusing on schoolwork and other sustained tasks, and increased feelings of isolation, depression, and anxiety (even for those who use their screens to feel more connected). Students in the same Pew Research Center study who thought that social media had a "mostly negative effect" on their lives offered the following explanations:[76]

- Bullying/rumor spreading (27 percent).

- Harms relationships/lack of in-person contact (17 percent).

- Unrealistic view of others' lives (15 percent).

- Causes distractions/addiction (14 percent).

- Peer pressure (12 percent).

- Causes mental health issues (4 percent).

- Drama, in general (3 percent).

Girls are especially at risk for falling victim to social media's negative impacts. Girls spend more time on social media than boys, increasing their exposure to harassment and expanding opportunities to compare themselves and their lives to others' based on often manufactured posts.[77] In one study of teenagers in the United Kingdom, researchers at University College London found that girls were twice as likely as boys to experience depressive symptoms tied to their social media use.[78] And as I outlined in the "Body Positivity" and "Mental Health" sections previously, social media can have disastrous effects on girls' self-esteem, body image, and overall mental health.[79] In one study of 110 undergraduate women aged sixteen to twenty-nine, Canadian researchers found that the simple act of taking and posting selfies was linked to decreased feelings of physical attractiveness and confidence, and greater feelings of anxiety.[80] These findings held true even when participants could alter their photos.

In recent years, tech executives themselves have begun to speak out about the addictive and damaging effects of digital devices on young people. Steve Jobs greatly limited his own children's screen use, and Bill Gates has spoken publicly about doing the same.[81] In January 2018, two of Apple's highest profile investors wrote an open letter to the tech industry stressing the importance of being more proactive in controlling for the addictive nature of smartphones for the industry's youngest users.[82]

PROBLEMATIC BEHAVIORS TO LOOK OUT FOR

- *Multitasking during homework time.* Digital devices make it really easy to get distracted and procrastinate.[83] I will often speak to parents who say they cannot believe how much homework their kids have. But when I ask parents if their kids have their phones handy while they work, are FaceTiming with friends (something they do often to help them study, but which can quickly turn unproductive), or are streaming Netflix in the background, the answer is often "yes." The distraction provided by screens affects the time it takes for students to do their work and distracts from independent learning.

- *Excessive evening screen time.* It's hard for everyone to pull themselves away from their favorite shows, text messages, emails, social media, and even work, and it's a particular challenge for girls who are still learning the art of self-regulation. Failing to put screens away at least an hour before bed deprives the brain of much-needed time to unwind before bed, making sleep less restful and renewing.[84]

- *Negative online social behaviors.* As I will explain in more detail in "Drama and Bullying," exclusionary closed-group chats and the posting of real-time photos and videos from exclusive gatherings can have broad-ranging negative impacts.

- *Sending or posting inappropriate content of oneself.* Sexting (texting graphic photos), posting sexually suggestive photos, and posting other photos or videos showing questionable or illegal (including drinking) behavior, creates a multifaceted problem. Anything that is texted or posted can be forwarded and reposted and also "lives forever" on the Internet, extending embarrassment and also potentially jeopardizing college and job applications. To adults, it goes without saying that posting this content is a bad idea. But we know that teenagers' brains aren't the best-equipped to think through future consequences, which is why they will sometimes make posts we wish they wouldn't.

- *Creation of Finstas or "fake Instagram" accounts and other social media streams using aliases.* Girls may create Finstas in order to get around their parents' or school's "no social media" rules. But many girls who have "real" social media accounts will also have a Finsta as a second account, where they post content, of the type listed in the previous bullet point, that they don't want everyone to see, including parents and college admissions officers. Girls believe mistakenly that these accounts are truly private, but Finsta feeds can be traced back to users' true identities.

- *Posting photos of others without permission.* Young people will often post photos of one another without asking. Usually no one means any harm, but it can feel like a breach of privacy to peers who don't know their photos are being posted and who might not like a given picture or might not want their picture posted. As an educator, I have also noticed students taking photos of or recording me and other adults, and I have had to address the issue of privacy and etiquette with them.

- *Posting personal information.* Girls aren't always aware of the implications of posting or entering personal information including phone numbers, credit cards, social security numbers, home addresses, and other sensitive data. They can be unaware of how serious the consequences could be if someone were to access their personal contact details or their physical address.[85] (And I'm not just talking about identify theft, but also about risks like stalking, kidnapping, and sex trafficking, as mentioned in the next bullet point.)

- *Talking to strangers.* As in the real world, there are predators in the digital realm who want to prey on teenagers girls. In the darkest corners of the Internet, there are people who will try to lure girls into dangerous situations, including sharing suggestive photos, entering into abusive relationships, and even becoming a victim of sex-trafficking circles.

- *Extensive unsupervised time with technology.* The more opportunities girls have to use technology without adult supervision, either in the same room or in the digital realm, the less insight parents have into what girls are doing online and on their phones.

Technology is intertwined with every moment of girls' lives and is so naturally a part of their routines that they are often unaware that their behaviors are unhealthy or potentially damaging. It's clear that many of them need coaching on how to use technology mindfully and healthily.

I always say that teaching safe tech is like teaching safe sex. Using technology can be enjoyable and beneficial, but there are risks. Accidents can happen, and missteps can have lasting unfavorable outcomes. Not all girls post negative comments or send mean texts, but a lot do. Not all girls sext, but it happens. And these slipups can have long-term impacts. The challenge is to teach girls to make the right decisions when you're not around, and to give them the tools, strategies, and support they need to address problems when they arise.

YOUR GOAL: Help your daughter develop healthy media habits, while limiting the amount of time you spend feeling frustrated and arguing with her about it.

RULE #1: Don't default to telling her that she's "wasting her time" on her computer or phone when she is using it during her downtime. If you act condescending about one of her favorite pastimes, she'll think you don't understand her.

TALKING POINTS

OUR DIGITAL LIVES HAVE SOME DOWNSIDES

Have conversations with your daughter about the risks and potential negative effects of digital media, even if you feel like you're stating the obvious. Chances are, she'll have heard some of it before from teachers. But I'm also surprised at the feedback I get, like that from Brianna, who falls asleep with her laptop on her stomach—from girls who are truly unaware of some of the drawbacks of screen time that seem so clear.

HOUSEHOLD MEDIA-USE "CONTRACTS" CAN FOSTER HEALTHY HABITS

Talking with your daughter and other members of your household to outline specific rules for social media and technology use can reduce the need for constant discussion and negotiation on the topic. You can find templates online, including at commonsense.org, which can offer useful starting points.[86] You can also use the family media planning tool at healthychildren.org to think through your priorities for yourself and your family, and you can incorporate some of the American Academy of Pediatrics' official recommendations on youth media use.[87] These include:

- "For children ages 6 and older, place consistent limits on the time spent using media, and the types of media, and make sure media does not take the place of adequate sleep, physical activity and other behaviors essential to health."
- "Discourage entertainment media while doing homework."
- "Designate media-free times together, such as dinner or driving, as well as media-free locations at home, such as bedrooms."
- "Have ongoing communication about online citizenship and safety, including treating others with respect online and offline."

PUTTING YOUR BEST DIGITAL FOOD FORWARD

Here are the specific tips Carolynn offers up for students hoping to make a good impression online for colleges and employers. Students love Carolynn because she used to be a spy but also because she knows what she's talking about when it comes to using their social feeds for good and to fuel their future success.

What Works on Social Media

In her time as a consultant, Carolynn has interviewed and surveyed thousands of college-admissions officers, athletic recruiting staff, and HR professionals to stay on top of how they are using online searches to learn about students and how what they find impacts candidates. Here is what this cohort values in online content:

- Genuine positivity about life, friends, teachers, and experiences.

- Well-written content.

- Examples of original creations or projects.

- Signs that students work well in groups, including photos of sports teams, school clubs, and study groups.

- Personal posts related to individual interests.

- Citations of previous academic or personal accomplishments.

What Doesn't Work on Social Media

- Excessive, self-centered, or mindless sharing.

- Publicly venting in a petty or ungrateful manner.

- Small talk.

- Pictures of or references to anything illegal.

Simple Steps to Start Building a Positive Online Presence

- Buy a personal web address (example: www.yourchildsname .com) and build a simple website. This helps people find you easily.

- Once girls meet age requirements (check websites for updated terms of use), start public Facebook and LinkedIn pages showcasing personal interests and accomplishments.

- Link the personal website to Facebook and LinkedIn pages, which helps search engines make the connection and helps schools and employers find your daughter more easily.

* One note. Parents ask me if their child *needs* a "formal" online presence as outlined here. The answer is no. But if there is any content at all about your child online, it is a good idea to take some control over it where possible. Actively populating positive content about your child online on trusted platforms like a personal website or LinkedIn ensures that admissions officers and employers are finding content you want them to see when they search for your child.

HOW IT'S DONE

Do Say

- Technology is powerful, but we all have to be mindful so that it has a positive impact in our lives and not a negative impact.

- The technology available to us has evolved so quickly that there isn't complete research yet on how it affects our brains.

- It's so easy to get sucked into our screens that it's important to really pay attention to how it makes us feel.

- Can you show me how this app works?

Don't Say

- Social media is such a waste of time.

- Why do you care what other people are doing, anyway?

- Your generation doesn't know how to communicate.

- Do you and your friends know how to have a real conversation?

BEYOND THE CONVERSATION

STAY UP-TO-DATE ON DIGITAL TRENDS

The rapidly changing and ever-expanding media landscape makes it difficult to stay on top of exactly what apps girls are using and which content they are streaming. It's perfectly acceptable to let your daughter guide you. But to give yourself a leg up, I recommend subscribing to the *New York Times'* newsletter *Well Family* and Common Sense Media's newsletter. Both of these platforms do an excellent job of communicating the latest digital trends among youth. Common Sense Media also has a robust and constantly updated website, which includes media and app reviews.

GET IN TOUCH WITH YOUR SCHOOL'S RESIDENT TECHNOLOGY EXPERT

Most schools have at least one person on campus who is their go-to technology expert. This might be someone who works in a dedicated technology department, someone who teaches digital literacy or design classes, or a savvy teacher or administrator who knows what students are up to online. Find out who this person is and be in touch with them if you have questions about your daughter and her peers' media habits and current media platforms of choice. Your school's technology expert should also be able to guide you in choosing a digital monitoring app (if you choose to use one) to help you keep track of your daughter's media use time, allow you to view her text messages, and see any sites or apps she is using.

SET STRICTER RULES FOR YOUNGER GIRLS WHO ARE STILL LEARNING SOCIAL MEDIA ETIQUETTE BASICS

- *Put a no-posting rule in place during and after playdates, gatherings, and parties that not everyone was invited to.* Groups of students getting together and live-streaming or posting pictures of their gatherings provides extra opportunities for others to feel left out. (It was also my personal Monday-morning nightmare as a school counselor.) While much of posting is done for entertainment, sometimes students in this age group will post specifically so that others who are not invited will see. The drama plays out for extended periods.

- *Monitor texts closely and deny use of group-chatting apps.* Common behaviors on group chats and texts include excluding people from group chats/texts from the outset, kicking people out of group chats/texts, and leaving group chats/texts when other students are invited or added. Group-chatting is perhaps an even greater threat to girls' well-being than social posting because it is more difficult for parents to monitor. Simple group texts and more sophisticated apps give students opportunities to communicate and interact with one another out of the view of parents, which can result in use of bad language, frequent insults, and exclusionary behaviors that the adults in the room would never accept if we witnessed them. It's as if students have endless opportunities for unsupervised playdates in the digital realm.

The American Academy of Pediatrics encourages parents to go beyond monitoring and interact with kids online, "so you can understand what they are doing and be part of it."[88] What girls are doing online can seem so foreign and even irrelevant to adults. But taking the time to learn what girls are doing online so you can be informed, aware, and engaged with it can be smart. They may not love the idea of your seeing their social media posts, but it shows them you are paying attention and allows you to stay informed.

FACILITATE SHARED SCREEN-FREE EXPERIENCES

It's important to set specific household guidelines for screen-free times, but you can also create tuned-in moments without a big announcement. When you do this, your daughter will be less inspired to shut you down or contradict you, fighting you on why she can't have her phone. Are there things your daughter loves to do, like cooking, shopping, puzzles, games, art, or sports? Are there places you can go where Wi-Fi and service bars are not existent? Is there a hike you can take? A water park to visit? An ocean or lake to swim in? Can you take a trip? Go camping? Girls get tired of listening to adults telling them that technology is bad. Gently creating moments of enjoyment that require a separation from technology can help your daughter understand that screen-free moments can be enjoyable and their digital lives can wait.

PUT YOUR PHONE DOWN AND BE PRESENT

The pull of technology is strong for everyone, not just teenagers. Parents of teens report using screen media for nine hours a day.[89] Martin, who I interviewed for this book, told me that when his daughter was a kindergartner, she asked why adults are on the phone all the time. He and his wife promptly instituted a no-phones rule from the time they get home until they put their children to bed.

From very young ages, kids notice parents' phone use, and adolescent girls are even more aware when parents are checking and distracted by their phones. Family contracts can help everyone in the house stay on the straight and narrow, but no matter what your family rules are, always remember that the small, ungoverned moments, where you can turn your phone off or put it in another room and be a little more present, won't just influence your daughters' own habits and beliefs about technology use, but will increase your opportunities to connect with her.

Grief and Tragedy

I often speak to parents who wonder if their child's reaction to a death, divorce, community tragedy, or other life-altering event is normal.

> *"We found out her grandmother passed away last night, but she wanted to come to school today anyway. Should I be worried?"*

> *"She's still so angry at me about her mother's and my divorce, and I feel like I can't get through to her. Is there anything I can do?"*

> *"We moved here a few months ago, and I'm worried that she is having trouble adjusting to life without her friends from back home. Has it been going on too long?"*

Teenagers face loss just like adults, *and* just like adults, girls' reactions are unique and deeply personal.

SOME BACKGROUND

Think about the things in your life that have been hardest to weather. The trials your daughter faces are just as real to her and can feel just as heartbreaking and difficult, whether they are related to her personal relationships and circumstances or to those of your broader family unit. She may grieve loved ones lost, the death of a pet, or elements of her life she's had to let go. Facing a family member's death or shocking life change like a divorce, geographic move, or sudden loss of a home will be challenging for your daughter, just as it would be for you.[90] And if you are experiencing grief from events affecting your family, your daughter is, too. Her youth doesn't protect her from painful experiences or the unease that can come with major transitions, even if her ways of processing events and managing her feelings differ from your own.[91] For instance, at a time in life when friendships are a primary pursuit, your daughter might be embarrassed, wondering if friends will see her as "broken" or as having a life that's less than perfect.[92] As a parent, you will naturally be more concerned about your daughter's well-being rather than what your friends think of you.

As with so many other experiences in adolescence, what you have to remember is that, while you have experience with life's ups and downs, your daughter is learning a lot for the first time and just starting to develop adult coping skills she'll use in the years to come.

SIGNS YOUR DAUGHTER IS GRIEVING

When, how, and to what degree emotions manifest for your daughter can be unpredictable. If she is wading through deep feelings of despair, sadness, and disappointment, she may not be willing or able to talk about it. She may be consciously or unconsciously overwhelmed. She may feel guilty or somewhat responsible for what happened, and importantly, if she knows you are also having a hard time, she may not want to worry you and risk making your experience more difficult. She may also blame you. You might observe some of the following:[93]

- Worry about the future and what could happen to her.
- Confiding in her friends or sharing on social media (sometimes oversharing).
- Social withdrawal.
- Difficulty concentrating or disinterest in school.
- Expressing anger or notable emotionality, including taking her frustrations out on you.
- Acting out or engaging in risk behaviors like experimenting with drugs or alcohol.
- Self-harm.
- Acting like everything is fine and focusing on her "own life."

The range of her behavior, from acting completely "normal" to utterly enraged—and perhaps both—may be jarring for you.[94]

WHAT YOU CAN DO

If your daughter is under the age of eighteen, I recommend that as soon as a major or tragic event happens, you reach out to a therapist. A therapist you identify can also coach you, even before they meet with your daughter, on how to best help your daughter navigate her healing and when and if it will be a good time for her to start therapy.

Even if your daughter doesn't enter counseling right away, it can become evident suddenly that she needs professional support, and you want to be prepared for that. Counseling helps people of all ages navigate grief and control for possible long-term, negative effects of traumatizing events.[95]

As her dad, it will be enormously tempting to want to shield your daughter from troubling emotions, to "fix" things for her as soon as possible. But if your daughter is going through something terrible, you won't be able to make her pain magically go away. It's going to take work over time. Your daughter will need some time to truly grieve, to be sad, to sit with her feelings. It will be important to validate her, let her know that her feelings are natural and that you understand. Moving through your own grief is essential to your own healing and ability to be there for your daughter. It also sets an example for her, and creates safety for her in knowing she can express and work through her despair in trying times. When you sense the time is right, you can draw on and suggest a variety of coping skills to help support her physical and social health, in addition to her mental and emotional well-being.

YOUR GOAL: Make sure your daughter has the support she needs to grieve, as she learns essential coping skills and processes emotions on her own timeline.

RULE #1: Don't expect her grieving process to fall into a familiar or predictable pattern.

TALKING POINTS

How She Can Expect to Feel About a Loss

Grief can make people feel very alone, especially teenagers who can be self-focused and don't have enough experience or perspective to understand that everyone goes through hard times. Talk to your daughter about the common feelings associated with what she is going through. You can point to your personal experiences, but you don't have to let her in on everything. As I mention in chapter 2, this can make her worry about you more, exacerbating any anxiety or despair she is facing.

Make sure she understands that the following are normal and natural reactions to grief and loss:[96]

- Feeling okay one moment and sad, angry, hopeless, or apathetic the next.

- Feeling "off," but not being able to put her finger on it.

- Wondering if anything will ever feel "normal" again.

- Believing that because one big thing isn't going well, that nothing is.

- Wanting to be alone.

- Not wanting to talk about feelings or a loved one lost.

- Wanting to talk a lot about feelings or a loved one lost.

- Wanting to dive into and distract herself with her responsibilities and life.

- Not wanting to do the things she usually does.

- Blaming herself or wondering if she should have done something differently, even if that's not the case and there is nothing she could or should have done differently.

What She Can Do to Start Feeling Better

Here are some ways your daughter can actively move through her emotions, regain a sense of normalcy, and rebuild confidence and zest for life. You can encourage her to do some of these things on her own, or you can facilitate times to do them together.[97]

- Get moving, even if it's just a walk around the block.

- Take screen time breaks, especially if she's spiraled into the social media vortex.

- Sleep, to give her brain and body time to rest and reset.

- Practice some deep breathing with her (which I explain in the "Mental Health" section).

- Hang out with friends for a healthy distraction, which can provide her mind a break from her worries and sadness.

- Do her schoolwork or practice for one of her extracurricular activities to help regain a sense of routine and forward movement.

- "Fake it until she makes it," deciding to take little steps forward until she feels like she has some momentum.

She may not think anything will help. Without a lot of experience dealing with traumas, letdowns, and heartbreaks, your daughter may not believe you if you insist that taking some kind of action will help her feel better. You can acknowledge that. One thing I always tell teenagers is that a lot of strategies we can use to feel better work in spite of our belief about whether they will work. For instance, girls I talk to aren't always excited to practice deep breathing, but it makes a positive difference anyway.

How to Honor a Loved One Lost

At Harvard Business School, researchers set out to discover the actions that help people process their grief most productively. What they found is that public, social activities like funerals didn't necessarily provide the ideal context for people to cope and grieve. Often, smaller, private, personal rituals can bring peace to the grieving process, helping people regain feelings of control at a time when they otherwise feel as though the circumstances are out of their control.[98] The researchers also found that carrying out rituals after a loss helped lower levels of grief, even for people who didn't believe rituals would have this positive effect. Examples of grief rituals included in the study that might be comforting to your daughter include:

- Lighting a candle.

- Writing a letter.

- Going to a special place that reminds her of the person and spending some time thinking about them or writing about them in a journal.

- Having a regularly scheduled ritual with you where you honor the person, like taking some time to tell stories about them at home, sharing their favorite meal, or visiting one of their favorite places.

Try one of these or ask your daughter if she wants your help designing a different personal tribute.

PROCESSING SCHOOL SHOOTINGS

School shootings are a persistent and widespread problem in the United States. In March 2020, American schools shut down due to the coronavirus pandemic. That was the first March since 2002 in which there was not a school shooting.[99] With the rate at which they occur, these incidents are close to home for students across the country, and even if they aren't in geographic proximity to a tragedy, students are well aware of this type of campus-based violence. In either case, preteens and teens may struggle with grief and stress, questioning their safety and that of their friends and loved ones. They may also feel emotional about gun laws or social factors leading to violence. You can ask her what she has seen or heard about a given incident and check in with her to see if she wants to talk further about it, either with you or with a counselor at her school.[100] Lockdown drills at school are an additional source of anxiety for young people. If your daughter's school lets you know ahead of time that they are planning a lockdown drill, talk through the details with your daughter and how she is feeling about it.

HOW IT'S DONE

"The right things to say" in times of tragedy and transition will depend greatly on your personal circumstances and religious views, especially if you are delivering difficult news. Here are some suggestions you can build on:

Do Say

- I am here for you if you need anything, whenever you need it.

- It's okay to feel exactly the way that you do.

- You might not feel better overnight, but you will begin to, slowly but surely.

- Is there something I could say to you that would make you feel better?

- You may not want to talk about this, but talking about what you are going through can make you feel better.

- You can tell me how you are feeling, even if you are worried about my reaction. I am not worried about that. I want you to talk to me.

- You don't have to talk to me, but there are other people you can and should talk to like a counselor who has been through this with a lot of patients, or any of the other adults in your life who you would feel comfortable with.

Don't Say

- Think about all the things you still have to be happy about.

- It's been long enough, it's time to move on.

- You weren't that close to [grandparent, friend, classmate].

- This doesn't affect you; focus on your life and your work.

Also, don't say nothing, which amounts to ignoring your daughter's experience. Tragedy and grief are some of the most difficult topics to broach. But ignoring the grief won't make it go away, is not recommended by mental health professionals, and will be a missed opportunity to show your daughter your care and concern.

BEYOND THE CONVERSATION

IF YOU DON'T KNOW WHAT TO SAY, LOOP IN ANOTHER ADULT OR GET PROFESSIONAL COACHING

It's not uncommon for people to feel extremely uncomfortable talking about life's most difficult topics. You can pull in another adult in your family or friend circle to speak with your daughter. Mental health professionals can also coach you on what to say to your daughter in specific circumstances.

FEEL YOUR FEELINGS, TOO

You do not need to be stoic if you are also having a rough time. It's healthy for your daughter to see you show some emotion and vulnerability. Again, you don't necessarily want to let her in on everything you are feeling. You want to reveal information that is appropriate for her age and maturity, and you want to give your daughter the sense that you can take care of yourself. Otherwise, as I've mentioned, she may be naturally inclined to start taking care of you.

If your daughter's grief over something in her life triggers your own emotional reaction, get support for yourself. Just as your daughter doesn't have to manage the hardest things in her life alone, you don't, either.

CREATE MOMENTS OF JOY AND GRATITUDE

In times of grief and transition, negative experiences can become all-encompassing. But just as you coach your daughter to take small steps toward healing by giving her body and mind a rest, you should facilitate moments to do so yourself. In the midst of stressful days, take time for some sensory experiences like grabbing an ice cream cone or going on a hike, breathing in some fresh air, and taking in a beautiful view—whether alone or with family, including your daughter. It is natural to feel guilty about taking in some moments of enjoyment, but it is important in the healing process.

Strengthen Her Relationships

Friendship

The only way to have a friend is to be one.
RALPH WALDO EMERSON[101]

SOME BACKGROUND

In adolescence, friends become important sources of support for girls who are exploring their identities and the world around them beyond their family contexts.[102] Girls' friendships provide important opportunities for them to develop and practice their social and communication skills, which they can apply in other contexts including romantic interactions or academic or professional settings.[103] Friends can be positive motivators when it comes to studying or getting involved in activities like volunteering or other fun and enriching pursuits.[104] And, having close friends in early adolescence is tied to higher levels of self-worth and lower levels of depression and anxiety in adulthood.[105] (We also know that peers can have negative impacts on your daughter, which we'll discuss in the next section on peer influence.[106])

In adolescence, your daughter is learning what kind of friend she is, what qualities in others are important to her, and how she wants to be treated by those closest to her. The lessons you want to pass on regarding friendship may come easily to you, and some of this section might seem to be stating the obvious, but what is obvious to adults is not usually obvious to teenagers. Friendship is one more area most people learn to master passively, but some concrete guidance will help your daughter recognize her true friends faster, be a better friend herself, and navigate natural conflicts with more ease and confidence.

> **YOUR GOAL:** Provide your daughter with actionable strategies to help her build and benefit from healthy friendships.

> **RULE #1:** Don't tell your daughter she "needs to be friends with everyone." It isn't realistic. Adults aren't friends with everyone, and kids don't need to be, either. It can actually turn out to be a lot of pressure for girls who can get the idea that they are responsible for everyone liking them.

TALKING POINTS

THE QUALITIES OF TRUE FRIENDS

The drive for popularity and acceptance is a heavy force in determining who girls hang out with and why.[107] But this isn't often the way to build the most authentic friendships. Here are some markers of true friendships to point out to your daughter:

- You feel relaxed and you can be yourself around them.

- You have fun with them.

- They inspire you and open your mind to new ideas and interests.

- They are happy for you when things are going well in your life.

- They don't pressure you to make decisions against your values.

- You don't have to try to keep them happy by going along with whatever they say or want to do.

- They don't find little things to get mad at you for.

- They include you most of the time.

- You know you can trust them.

- They stand up for you.

THE REALITIES OF FRIENDSHIP

Girls can be very literal about what makes or does not make a good friend. Little disputes quickly turn into big blowups, especially in middle school. It's never too early to talk to girls about what they can reasonably expect of friends including:

- Friends aren't perfect people. Their good qualities should outweigh the bad, but it's important to know that they may upset you and let you down from time to time.

- Friends disagree from time to time. This is healthy and good practice for all future relationships.

- You can't expect that people will change their behavior to make you like them better, and so you always have the choice of whether to keep someone close or create distance.

- It's possible to speed up the "getting over it" process. When friends upset each other, they should focus on ways to de-escalate any drama quickly, so they can move on.

- Sometimes, it can take time to get back to "normal" after a fight.

- Even best friends don't invite each other everywhere all the time. Sometimes, you won't get invited somewhere, and while that can be hurtful, it's okay.

- Having best friends doesn't mean those are the only people you should be hanging out with. It's always a good idea to have lots of people to spend time with, even if they aren't your best friends.

- It's important to have friends who aren't exactly like you. Friends can help you discover new interests and views of the world.

How to Apologize

Saying you're sorry can seem like a pretty straightforward skill, but in all my years working with girls, I've seen that it is almost never simple or easy. Here are some things that happen when girls get in fights:

- They call each other names.

- They say and text mean things, including laundry lists of wrongdoings they think their friend is guilty of.

- They take screenshots of texts and send them to other friends, involving a wider circle of people in the fight.

- They lobby their friends to pick sides in the conflict.

- They gossip and stew.

When I'm talking to girls about taking responsibility for their part of a fight, I ask them to think about whether they actually did something wrong. I get two categories of responses:

- "Well, maybe I did something wrong, but she [fill-in-the-blank way she did me wrong]!" This type of response is fueled by anger, defensiveness, denial, and the desire for revenge. In this case, a simple, sincere apology is in order.
  - "I am sorry for my part in this."
  - "Next time, I will try to react differently."

- "It was a misunderstanding, but she got angry, and now I don't know what to say to her." This type of response is extremely common, and I see it a lot with middle school girls. Miscommunications happen naturally as girls are maturing socially and emotionally, often at different speeds. Signals easily cross and intentions are misread on an ongoing basis.

Girls and women can be overly apologetic, even when they have done nothing wrong.[108] In the miscommunications among girls, unnecessary apologies can abound. As guiding adults, it's important that we catch girls if we think they are being unnecessarily apologetic, overly people-pleasing, or sacrificing of their own feelings and needs for others. It's important to highlight times when girls should *not* say they're sorry.

When there is a miscommunication, I coach girls to talk about their intentions and others' perceptions, rather than self-blame. Also, if your daughter talks about her intentions, it helps to de-escalate the emotion, because she is telling the truth without being accusatory toward the other person. It sounds like:

- I understand why that felt hurtful. It wasn't my intention for it to come across that way.

- It's never my intention to make you feel [X]. Can you let me know if something I say or do feels hurtful, so we can talk about it?

In addition to providing your daughter sound bites for apologies and conflict resolution, mention the importance of authenticity in the apology itself. Challenge your daughter to find meaning in her apology or in her efforts to smooth over a conflict: how she can be genuine, even if she is feeling emotional and angry.

HOW TO BE FRIENDLY, EVEN IF YOU AREN'T GREAT FRIENDS

This is such an important lesson for girls. Most of them have a lot to learn when it comes to being diplomatic and polite around people they simply don't like that much. Now, this isn't about letting bullies trample them or putting up with other bad behavior. But girls need to understand that in school, in work, and even in family contexts, they aren't always going to love everyone they are around or find themselves needing to talk with or do projects with. But they need to have patience and be respectful of people. In addition, small acts of friendliness can mean a lot to kids who feel like outsiders or like they don't have a lot of friends. Importantly, girls need to learn that we never know what people are going through, and we can never make assumptions.

I always remind girls that they are powerful, that their words and actions can affect someone's day for better or for worse. Here are some little ways you can encourage your daughter to reach out:

- Saying hi to someone she doesn't know that well.

- Smiling at someone who is having a bad day.

- Inviting someone to join a group study session at school.

- Being patient with someone who doesn't realize they are being kind of annoying.

HOW TO END A FRIENDSHIP

The end of a friendship can feel like a breakup and be just as tricky to bring to a close. Your daughter needs to know that it is okay to distance herself from someone if she feels like the friendship is toxic, if she has felt betrayed by a friend, or if she has simply made other friends who she feels closer to and has more in common with. There's a "nice girl" narrative that can make girls wary of setting boundaries or taking space and time for themselves. Kindness is usually an excellent value to emphasize to your daughter, but she needs to know that if a relationship or dynamic doesn't suit her, it's ok to set a respectful boundary and move on.

Two approaches to focus on are:[109]

- *The slow-fizzle approach*: This method of backing off from a friendship slowly can come in handy when your daughter doesn't want to make a big deal out of dissolving a relationship, perhaps because she doesn't want to cause extra hurt or disrupt other connections she may have in the friend group. Coach her to be cordial, while explaining that it is perfectly acceptable to send fewer texts and not include her former bestie in all her plans.

- *A direct conversation*: Sometimes, especially when ending toxic friendships, girls will need to have direct boundary-setting conversations. In these cases, it's better for your daughter to frame what she says in terms of her needs and her feelings, rather than how the other person has wronged her. She can use phrases like:

> I just need a little bit of space right now.
>
> Sometimes I feel like you are upset with me, even though it has not been my intention to hurt you. So, maybe we should just spend less time together right now.

HOW IT'S DONE

Do Say

- I think you have great friends because . . .

- I really loved seeing you and your friends do . . .

- You don't have to be friends with everyone, but you should aim to be respectful.

Don't Say

- Why can't you hang out with nice girls?

- You need to be friends with everyone.

- Popularity doesn't matter.

- Your friends aren't real friends.

- Why do you like them, anyway?

BEYOND THE CONVERSATION

HELP FACILITATE HER FRIENDSHIPS

For many girls, forming deep friendships can take time. Social dynamics at school can also be especially difficult to manage—for example, if your daughter doesn't feel like she has "her people" there, if she has had a falling out with her core friend group, or if she is facing any bullying (something I will cover at length in the next chapter). If your daughter isn't connecting, consider ways to stealthily broaden her social connections. Encourage her to:

- Get involved in a community service project or organization in line with her passions.
- Explore extracurricular activities that get her thinking outside the box and building confidence in new areas, like a cooking class, dance class, or martial arts.
- Try out for community plays or athletic teams.
- Consider summer camps or summer academic programs where she could connect with new people.

All of these types of activities give your daughter chances to start fresh, meeting new people who share her interests. She may be scared to strike out on her own. Highlight for her how much personal growth and confidence comes from getting outside of our normal circumstances. Sure, she may have some awkward moments and awkward silences, but we all know there is value in these as well.

GET TO KNOW HER FRIENDS' PARENTS, EVEN IF IT'S AWKWARD AND EMBARRASSES YOUR DAUGHTER

It's not uncommon to have less and less contact with the parents of your daughter's friends as she gets older. She's taking more control of her social life. She has a phone of her own that she can use to make plans (unlike when we were kids, and when we called friends' houses to make plans, we often had to talk to their parents first). Many young people meet up with friends using public transportation or using ride-sharing apps (if they meet age requirements).

You probably don't need a scholarly article to lay that this out for you, but there is research showing that when your daughter is spending time with her friends, she is also subject to the influence of their parents.[110] For instance, a friend's parents may be more relaxed and permissive with regard to alcohol use or unsupervised technology use than you are, or have different views on keeping firearms in the household. On the flip side, parents with similar values to your own can directly and indirectly, through the behavior of their children, reinforce the positive values you share.

It takes some effort to get in touch with other parents and to ask questions about their house rules. And your daughter might not appreciate having her parent be the "uncool" one who "oversteps" in her eyes. But communication with other parents is a useful way to ensure your daughter's safety, even when she is out of your view.

CONSIDER SOCIAL SKILLS COACHING

If your daughter has trouble making or keeping friends, she could possibly benefit from some social skills coaching. Of course, you can talk about strategies with her at home, but there are also people you can call in for help. Your daughter's school counselor is a good first person to connect with. See if they have noticed your daughter struggling at all on campus, if they have any insights or suggestions for you. If you decide to have your daughter meet with a professional counselor for social skills coaching, your school counselor might have some recommendations.

Negative Peer Influence

Jojo and her friends organized a limo to take them to their high school winter formal. Against the law, the rules of the driving service, and their school's code of conduct, the students snuck alcohol in the limo and drank on the way to the dance. One of them drank so much he got sick and started throwing up before they arrived. Knowing they faced severe consequences if the school caught them, the students begged the driver to turn around and take them back to the house where they had their preparty. The driver, angry and frustrated that Jojo and her friend had broken the rules and had created a mess in his vehicle, drove them to the dance anyway, where he knew they would have to answer to their school administrators (something he later told their parents). Jojo had one drink, and she told the truth when her principal asked her if she had been drinking. Ultimately, she was suspended from classes for five days and was unable to participate in her winter theater performance.

"We had a talk after that," her dad, Carl, told me. "'Look,' I told her, 'you have two groups of friends. One group of them was on that bus, and they are going in a certain direction. And by nature of you spending time with them, being on that bus with them, you found yourself in a bad situation. You can do a lot right, but it doesn't matter if you are around the wrong people in the wrong set of circumstances. I am not going to tell you that you can't spend time with them, but I want you to think about how much time you should be spending with them.'"

SOME BACKGROUND

Damon, the father of a thirteen-year-old daughter I interviewed for this book, summarized one of the most common fears I hear among fathers when he said, "I think my biggest worry is that I will have put in all of this time, that I will have worked so hard to instill the right values and encourage good decisions, and then she could fall in with the wrong friends and get into trouble." Parents dread the possible negative influence peers can have in adolescence. The fear is not unreasonable or unfounded. But there are steps you can take, and have maybe taken already, to help your daughter recognize and resist negative peer influence.

Decisions you make, including where you send your daughter to school, which friends and family you surround yourselves with, and which religious or community organizations you are part of, will have an impact on who your daughter spends time with.[111] Chances are, you've already done at least a little bit to facilitate some healthy interactions for your daughter. Still, you can feel pretty out of control in the teenager years, as your daughter spends more and more time out of your view, sometimes with friends you don't totally love.

Simply being surrounded by friends, even in the absence of active peer pressure, can increase the chances that your daughter will display some lapses in judgment. This happens across social groups, even among "good" kids. In Dr. Laurence Steinberg's Temple University lab, one of the big questions guiding the lab's research is why it seems that teenagers do more reckless things when they're with their friends than when they're on their own. "We've shown in our research that the mere presence of other kids activates reward centers in the brain, and that leads kids to pay much more attention to the possible rewards of a bad choice, rather than the downside," explained Dr. Steinberg.

For instance, Dr. Steinberg pointed out that when teens are behind the wheel of a car with one other teen passenger, they are twice as likely to exhibit risky behaviors—including speeding, weaving, or showing off—than when they are driving alone.[112] They are three times as likely to be reckless when there is more than one other passenger in the car. Talking and joking in the car can cause distractions, and if a couple of kids in the car seem to be okay with reckless driving, the others are likely to feel like it is acceptable behavior, even if they are a little uncomfortable. You can probably recall at least an instance or two from your teenage years where you made some regrettable decisions that you wouldn't have made if you were on your own. Anything ring a bell?

If you're concerned about your daughter falling in with the wrong crowd, know that it's unlikely that friends would spur behavior that she didn't already have a tendency toward. "Kids are not randomly assigned to the friends that they make," Dr. Steinberg told me. "A lot of research shows that kids tend to select peers that are like them, that have similar interests and attitudes and values. It is typically the case that kids who already have inclinations to do those bad things end up finding friends to join them."

You're allowed to be worried about the fact that having friends around can inspire dangerous behavior and that if your daughter is part of the "wrong crowd," it's possibly because she has the same interests and motivations as they do. If you are truly skeptical of her friends, you can make that known to her and highlight qualities you hope she will seek in close peers. However, girls' abilities to maintain their beliefs and standards and their willingness to stand up for what they believe in can protect against the potential negative impacts of reckless peers. And you can coach your daughter to recognize and resist peer pressure. "The ability to stand up to peer pressure is a capacity that is facilitated by good parenting," Dr. Steinberg said. "You can make sure your child is equipped to not just go along with the crowd."

> **YOUR GOAL:** Teach your daughter to recognize and resist negative peer influence.

> **RULE #1:** Don't explicitly try to control who she is hanging out with unless you absolutely have to. Shutting down a friendship you don't approve of can start a war with your daughter. You have to decide if it's worth it.

TALKING POINTS

THE NATURE OF NEGATIVE PEER INFLUENCE

Help your daughter understand how negative peer influence works by getting some of these messages across:

- Peer influence can affect your behavior, even if you don't realize it.

- By making dangerous or otherwise unfavorable behavior seem "normal," friends' attitudes and outlooks can affect your mindset.

- Peer influence can intensify in certain environments, especially where there is a lack of adult supervision.

HOW TO PREVENT NEGATIVE PEER INFLUENCE AND STAND UP TO PEER PRESSURE

In the upcoming sex ed section, I include a discussion on how you can help your daughter say "no," which can also be helpful in the face of peer pressure and influence in platonic interactions. Here are some other strategies to share with your daughter, some of which may seem obvious to her but are still worth mentioning:

- Choose friends who share your values so that you limit the time you spend feeling pushed outside your comfort zone in unhelpful, unproductive, or dangerous ways.

- Take a moment and a breath before taking any action or doing anything that you think is potentially risky.

- Physically remove yourself from the situation, leaving on your own or calling a parent for help.

HOW IT'S DONE

Do Say

- I really like your friend [name], because of [positive qualities]. They seem like a good person to have in your life.

- Do you feel like your friends bring out the best in you?

- I'm concerned about some of your friends' choices. I always want you to be safe and healthy. Do you feel like these friends are supporting that?

- (In rare circumstances) I would rather you spend less time with [friend], because [explain why the friend's behavior concerns you].[113]

Don't Say

- Why do you hang out with those people anyway? They're a bad influence on you.

- You make dumb decisions when you are around your friends.

- I don't understand the choices you and your friends make.

BEYOND THE CONVERSATION

TAKE STEPS TO CREATE A POSITIVE SOCIAL ENVIRONMENT FOR YOUR DAUGHTER

As you have read, the decisions you make about who you surround your family with have an impact on who your daughter spends her time with. Create additional opportunities for your daughter to interact with people you love and trust.

Drama and Bullying

At the risk of losing your trust, I'll admit I am not a big Star Wars fan. In my wedding vows, I promised my husband that I would watch all the films with him, and over a decade in, I still haven't made good on that commitment. But I will say that when I think about girls navigating their way through the new social scenarios and challenges of adolescence, I picture young Jedis at lunch tables, or at slumber parties, or in group chats. Through adolescence, girls are coming to understand their ability to influence and affect others for better or worse. Like Jedis practicing with lightsabers and the Force, girls are learning to wield the power of their words, actions, and bodies. And it goes without saying that things can get messy.

SOME BACKGROUND

NOT ALL GIRL DRAMA IS BULLYING

"Bullying" is often the default term parents use to describe conflicts between teenagers and their peers. In my years working in schools, talking with the parents of my tutoring clients, and fielding concerns from family and friends, this topic comes up a lot.

- Can you believe that girl didn't invite my daughter to her birthday party? She's such a bully!
- My child is being bullied, and the school does nothing about it!
- Her friends are all such bullies.

The circumstances of these scenarios may reveal that bullying is at play. And then again, they may not. It may be hard to imagine, but the daily drama and ugly interactions that play out routinely among girls actually have an important purpose in their healthy social development. Girls often spar with each other simply because they are new to emotional intimacy, trying to find their balance, and unskilled in relationships. Run-of-the-mill drama often occurs between friends where there is no power differential. It is unintentional—frequently arising due to miscommunication—and it is fleeting, not repeated over time, and without lasting negative physical or emotional effects.

Girls' early relationships give them opportunities to practice their social skills and conflict resolution. Fielding insensitive comments and rudeness, being excluded at times, and feeling betrayed by friends are common social challenges girls may face, not just in adolescence but throughout adulthood. And the more chances they have to learn to navigate conversations with others and manage their own emotions and reactions around given situations, the better prepared and the more centered and grounded they can stay in the face of future conflicts and boundary negotiations. This is not to say that you should delight in or encourage drama. It can be difficult and disappointing to watch, and it can be temporarily hurtful to your daughter. But at the same time, it can also build her resilience.

WHAT IS BULLYING?

So how do you tell the difference between bullying and drama? Bullying is a pattern defined by three specific, co-occurring criteria:[114]

- Bullying is intentional.

- Bullying is carried out by a student or group of students with more actual or perceived power than another.

- Bullying is repeated over time.

Bullying can encompass behaviors that are direct or indirect. It can be verbal, physical, or social.[115] And it can play out in the "real world" and digital realms, commonly referred to as cyberbullying.[116] Certain actions like sending mean texts or giving someone mean looks can be signals of relatively harmless drama, but when repeated and in the context of a power differential, those acts would constitute bullying. Some common forms of bullying include:[117]

- Teasing.

- Threats.

- Spreading rumors.

- Hiding or breaking personal items.

- Interfering with or sabotaging a victim's friendships or romantic relationships (known as relational aggression).

- Shows of force, like pushing in hallways or in PE.

Overall, bullying behavior has been found to be on the decline nationally, which is encouraging. Still, the School Crime Supplement (SCS) to the National Crime Victimization Survey, which collected data from twelve- to eighteen-year-olds on their experiences with bullying, found that 20 percent of students were being bullied at school, with a higher percentage of girls identifying as victims of bullying (24 percent) than boys (17 percent).[118]

The Effects of Bullying

Bullying is serious. Being on the receiving end of any of these behaviors can take its toll and have negative impacts into adulthood. The government's anti-bullying website Stopbullying.gov highlights[119] these negative impacts, including:

- Decreased self-esteem.
- Increased feelings of sadness, depression, anxiety, and isolation.
- Apathy toward or withdrawal from favorite activities.
- Changes in appetite.
- Changes in sleep.
- Lower grades and test scores.
- Poor academic achievement or decreased school attendance.
- Increased likelihood to retaliate with violence.

While the safety and healing of bullying victims should be a primary focus, what surprises many parents is that bullies themselves can experience short- and long-term negative effects stemming from their own aggressive behavior. Bullies are more likely to have substance-abuse conditions in adolescence and adulthood.[120] They may engage in sexual activity sooner than non-bullying peers, and they are more likely to be abusive romantic partners or parents later in life.[121] Bystanders, those who witness bullying, have also been found to suffer the negative impacts of bullying. They have been found to use drugs and alcohol more than peers and have an increased incidence of mental health conditions.[122] So if you have a sense that your daughter is bullying others or even that she has simply witnessed bullying without being directly affected by it, you also have an important job to do in supporting her.

THE LINK BETWEEN BULLYING AND SUICIDE

The news often highlights stories of bullied teenagers who are contemplating or who have died by suicide. While there is a deeply concerning link, bullying is typically understood as the one contributing factor in these scenarios.[123] Factors that can make a child more vulnerable are difficult home circumstances, lack of access to supportive adults, substance use, and learning differences or physical disabilities.[124] If your daughter is struggling in other areas of her life and she is also being bullied at school, your attention is even more important.

WHY BULLYING HAPPENS

Bullies target victims for a variety of reasons. "Even before the onset of adolescence, changes in the brain cause us to crave power, influence, and status over wanting to have positive, fun interactions with one another. That comes from tens of thousands of years of history programmed into us," UNC's Dr. Mitch Prinstein, a developmental psychologist studying popularity, told me. Bullies may be reacting to the stress of family or environmental circumstances, seeking situations they can control, and finding social dynamics with peers to be an area they can influence.[125] Researchers also point to empathy gaps as possible contributors.[126] Bullies will act out against others based on perceived weaknesses or what they see as "undesirable" traits related to body type, facial appearance, race, economic class, religion, gender identity, sexual orientation, learning difference, medical condition, or disability.[127] Bullies may also target others as part of the adolescent process of learning right from wrong. They can act cruelly, just going on impulse, before realizing how hurtful their actions are.

Relational aggression, the disruption or sabotaging of someone's social relationships, is a common type of bullying among teenagers and can happen for many reasons. Dr. Prinstein explained, "Research suggests that females are more socialized than males to feel that their value is measured in social relationships. This need to be liked and feel liked is far more all-encompassing for young women than for young men."

As a result, girls can be driven to do whatever it takes to maintain their social position. At Duke University, Dr. Jennifer Lansford researches the roots of aggressive behaviors among teenagers. "Relational aggression can be a way of establishing social dominance," Dr. Lansford said. "It can also be a way that teenagers cement their relationships with each other. By excluding someone else, you can build a relationship with a different person; or by spreading rumors about someone else, you're, in a sense, making yourself closer to the person that you're telling these rumors to. Rumors can be a way of not just hurting someone else, but trying to build other relationships."[128] At a time when girls can be hyperfocused on fitting in, being accepted, and being "popular," considering "right" and "wrong" can come second to garnering respect from the most desirable crowd.

"Girls, streaming hours of media content each day, may also be influenced by popular depictions of what is acceptable behavior in relationships," Dr. Lansford told me. "Media shows a lot of relationally aggressive episodes, and so teenagers, exposed to relational aggression in TV shows or movies, are more likely to internalize norms about that being an acceptable way that people interact with others—and then they are more likely to engage in that behavior themselves in the future."

In sum, there are, in fact, many reasons why girls bully. Looking at the situation with a more nuanced eye can help you from falling into characterizing anyone as good or bad—including your own daughter, if she is the aggressor. Understanding the behavior is a good start.

WHY BULLYING CAN BE HARD TO IDENTIFY

Every student I've ever talked to about bullying has one worry in common—if they tell someone (like an adult) or do something about it, it will only get worse, either for themselves or a friend they want to advocate for. Research suggests that only 30 percent of bullying victims, at most, say anything to an adult.[129] This is why bullying often continues to occur beyond the view of adults who can step in and help stop it. Your daughter may come to a school teacher, administrator, or you, and tell you about a situation right away, but she is more likely not to. Complicating matters, bullies are commonly bullied, themselves. Few bullying scenarios are straightforward. So it can take time for parents and school administrators to confirm and address bullying dynamics. Additionally, much bullying these days can occur as cyberbullying, meaning the behavior occurs off school grounds and away from adult supervision.

UNDERSTANDING POPULARITY

Though the aggression exhibited by popular girls often stems from insecurity, a heightened sensitivity to rejection, or a type of "loneliness at the top," these girls are often labeled simply as bullies. With the roots of their behavior often misunderstood, they are misparented and misdirected by other adults in their midst, like teachers or coaches, who reprimand them and punish them—rather than coaching them on how to navigate delicate social interactions, learn to handle the pressures of their social lives, and manage their status with grace. Making matters more complicated for "popular" girls, according to Dr. Prinstein, is that there is a lot of evidence that most high-status girls in high school are actively disliked, often by other girls. So girls are socialized to pursue social status and are at the same time penalized for achieving it. (The same is not true for their "popular" male counterparts, who enjoy high levels of likability and respect from peers.) "In order to shift the emphasis from the pursuit of and value placed on popularity, we need to help girls focus on the ways they can make others feel included and valued," Dr. Prinstein said. It's important that all girls understand that likability is more important than status. This isn't to say that girls need to strive to be liked by everyone, but they should aim to be positive, respectful members of their communities. They need to know that how they make others feel, and the positive impact they have on their social environments, is more important than how popular they are.

An example is Lucy, a ninth grader.

I called her into my office and sat across the table from her. "We need to have a little bit of an uncomfortable conversation," I told her. "Several students have come to me saying that they think you don't like them, and they feel like you shut them down when they are talking."

Lucy looked at me, indignant.

"So I have a question for you," I continued. "Do you feel like a lot of people want to be your friend?"

She nodded, refusing to say an actual word to me.

"Okay, do you feel like you want to be everyone's friend?"

She shook her head.

"Okay, and do you feel like some of the people who want to be your friend are really annoying?"

Lucy looked at me. I finally got a word out of her: "Yes."

"Lucy," I said. "This is probably going to be an ongoing problem for you. People will want to be your friend. They will want to be around you because they think you're cool. But where you have an extra responsibility that you may not want is that what you say and do matters to them, even if you don't feel close to them. Does that make sense?"

Lucy didn't have much to say to me that day, but I went on to explain that it was fine if she didn't want to be friends with everyone, but that if she could be more patient with people, letting them voice their ideas or talk to her about stuff she wasn't necessarily interested in, even for a little while, that it would go a long way in how everyone around her felt. I encouraged her to just give people a little time before she set a respectful and gentle boundary, which might sound like this:

- That's a good idea, but for this project I was thinking we could do something a little bit differently.

- We were just talking about something between the two of us, do you mind if we catch you later?

Girls like Lucy aren't necessarily bullies or even villains; they are heroines in training.

When I see girls like Lucy in action, I see a lot of potential that needs to be focused and channeled. A favorite rallying cry in women's empowerment circles is a quote from William Shake-speare's *A Midsummer Night's Dream*: "And though she be but little, she is fierce." With the right guidance, these girls can be some of our strongest leaders.

THE ROLE YOU PLAY

To address your daughter's interpersonal conflicts, you need to be her Yoda, comforting and guiding her with your wisdom, while also challenging her to use her influence for good. Your guidance can help her become a kinder, more empathetic and resilient person. But your mere presence and support in the face of bullying, whether she is a bully, a victim, a "bully victim" (one who is both bullied and bullying), or a bystander, can help keep her safe and healthy. In one study of nearly one thousand fifth, ninth, and eleventh graders in the rural South, researchers set out to discover the influence of parents in protecting their kids against the harmful effects of bullying.[130] The researchers found that when parent support was high, victims, bullies, bully victims, and students not involved in bullying all re-ported lower rates of depression. Being there for your daughter offers her actual protection against the effects of bullying.

In all my years of being a teenage girl and working with teenage girls, I can tell you that at one time or another your daughter will be on both sides of drama, both stoking it or falling victim to it. With hope, your daughter is never the bully and never finds herself the victim of a bully, but these scenarios are also all too common. When it comes to speaking with your daughter about drama and bullying, it's a massive exercise in teaching her to stand up, both for herself and for others.

YOUR GOAL: Building your daughter's self-advocacy skillset and capacity for empathy—while encouraging her to stand up against bullying.

RULE #1: Do *not* let your daughter see you get wrapped up in the drama. Be your best self. Keep your questions positive. Don't ask your daughter every time she gets in the car whether someone wronged her that day. If you see your daughter suffering, it can be very tempting to get petty or vengeful; don't give into that. And if you have a wife, partner, or any other relatives or caregivers talking to your daughter on a regular basis, make sure they do the same. This is not to say that you can't get involved as caring adults. You are allowed to be concerned and to act in ways you think necessary and appropriate. You just don't want to get caught up in gossip or unproductive venting.

TALKING POINTS

HOW SOCIAL INTERACTIONS SHE'S HAVING NOW ARE GREAT PRACTICE

The conflicts your daughter encounters with her peers in the context of drama, while wildly unpleasant at times (both for her and for you), are preparing her to have better and better relationships in the future. When you are helping her find solutions, remind her of this important point. It's an excellent way to offer her some perspective, signal to her that you see her growing into an emotionally competent adult, and potentially help her calm down by de-escalating the drama in her mind.

Sophisticated Conflict Resolution Strategies

Here are some tactics you can talk through with her to help her understand how to decrease the drama in her life. Learning to communicate through difficult periods is a key driver of your daughter's relational health, whether in the context of friendships or romantic relationships.

- *Use technology to facilitate face-to-face conversations.* Tell your daughter that it is okay to send a text that says something like "Hi, I feel like we should talk. Can we meet up for a few minutes?"

- *Talk face-to-face whenever possible.* Most girls I encounter will default to "texting it out" rather than talking it out. Make sure your daughter understands that talking face-to-face can be a much more productive way than texting to smooth things over with a friend. People involved can talk with each other, tune into one another's emotional responses, and be free from other friends' interference and interpretations. In addition, talking face-to-face also limits the risk that your daughter or her friends will say something they regret on text. When girls argue their sides on texts, the messages often get shared with and analyzed by other people "on their side," which can both ratchet up and prolong drama.

- *Remind her that most drama is and should be temporary.* It's entirely possible that your daughter and her friends are engaging in drama for sport. There's something about drama that can just draw a whole bunch of girls into the vortex. Without belittling her emotions, talk your daughter through what is meaningful about her experience. Why is she so caught up? She may not decide to rise above the fray immediately, but it's a good opportunity for you to speak about the true nature and meaning of friendships.

- *Coach her to set a time limit for difficult conversations.* Girls will go and go and go when it comes to talking about what's bothering them. They want to get all their thoughts, zingers, and final words in. Explain to her that having the final word doesn't contribute to healthy resolutions. Her goal should just be to feel like she and her friend have each been *mostly* heard, and then move on.

- *Encourage kindness.* Teenagers today hear a lot about kindness. Still, your daughter cannot be reminded enough to have empathy and be kind to people. Again, it doesn't mean she has to be best friends with everyone, but reminding her often to think about other's feelings, and the possible impact she can have on them, is always good practice.

What Bullying Is and What It Is Not

Understanding the difference between drama and bullying is important for your daughter's well-being and also so she can help be on the lookout for others. Make sure she knows the types of behaviors and understands how power dynamics contribute to unhealthy interactions. She needs to know how serious bullying can be and how it can have extremely negative effects.

STRATEGIES FOR PROTECTING HERSELF
IN THE MOMENT

If your daughter is being bullied, here are some things she can do as it is happening:

- Use a one-line response that she has practiced ahead of time. This can be useful if your daughter is being made fun of for a specific characteristic. The idea with these statements is to help your daughter feel prepared with an answer. She may not be able to stop the aggressive and hurtful behavior coming her way, but she will feel prepared to handle it. Examples include "Ouch!," which is a simple and often unexpected way to draw attention to a hurtful comment, or (perhaps a little sarcastically) "That's original. I haven't heard that before," which can diffuse a little bit of the tension.

- Self-defense. Even if the skills your daughter learns in a self-defense class are more than she needs in the school context or she never needs to use them, confidence can come with feeling like she could take physical charge of a situation.

WHAT IT MEANS TO BE AN UPSTANDER

An upstander is someone who stands up for a peer who is being bullied. While teenagers typically know the right thing to do, they don't always step in to protect another person. Rather than doing something to change the situation, they end up simply standing by. Sometimes they are afraid of the bully. Sometimes they are concerned about compromising their own social status. Explain to your daughter what it feels like to speak up, even if she feels threatened in ways by the situation. Girls need to understand that it is not easy to do the right thing all the time, but that doesn't mean they shouldn't do it anyway.

How to Find Helpful Adults

As I have mentioned, students are often hesitant to let adults into their conflicts because of the worry that adults will make their lives more difficult. Reassure your daughter that adults are there to help and that while she can always seek you out, she should also be talking to teachers and school counselors. You can coach her to voice concerns to them. For instance, you can tell her it's okay to say something like, "I have some information I would like to share. I am concerned that someone is being bullied. But I don't want anyone to find out it was me who said anything." And then she can see how the adult responds. Most likely, school administrators will tell her that they will do everything possible to protect her privacy.

How to Recover from a Distressing Situation

If your daughter has been affected negatively by drama or bullying, explain the various strategies she can use to feel better.

- *Give it time.* Girls can be impatient with and judgmental of their feelings, wanting to feel "happy" and "perfect" again as soon as possible. Emphasize the fact that people don't feel great all the time, and that's okay. Emotional experiences are often temporary.

- *Get distracted.* Encourage your daughter to do anything to "change the channel" in her brain. Listening to music, reading, or going out to do something with you can help her with emotional shifts and relief, even if it's for a short amount of time.

- *Spend time with some new friends.* When girls get into conflict with their friends, it can be a great opportunity for them to branch out. It can feel scary to them because they don't want to distance themselves too much from their core friend group. But encouraging your daughter to have even one conversation a day with someone she's not as close with can help her realize that there are plenty of people to be friends with. It can also simply help her fill the time if she feels awkward at school.

HOW IT'S DONE

On Drama

Do Say

- Pay close attention to the way people around you make you feel.
- Some of the situations that feel really hard right now actually happen a lot, and you will get better at managing them.
- You don't need to like everyone, but let's talk about how we might reach peaceful coexistence.
- It's okay to distance yourself from a friendship that is no longer bringing you happiness.

Don't Say

- Just find new friends.
- It doesn't matter.
- Stop caring so much.

- Your friends sound terrible.

- Why can't you all just be nice to one another?

- Well, maybe you should embarrass *her* next time.

ON BULLYING

Do Say

- If you ever feel unsafe emotionally or physically, tell someone immediately.

- Trust that adults will help you, even if you are worried the bully will be mad or will retaliate.

- Adults at school are there to help you. They can't always tell you what they are doing to correct mean behavior, just like they wouldn't tell people your personal business.

- This is a temporary situation, and we are going to get through this together.

- You can talk to a counselor or therapist, if you would like.

- Sometimes, the right thing to do isn't the most comfortable thing to do.

Don't Say

- Just get over it.

- Stop being so sensitive.

- Punch them in the face next time they pick on you!

- Well, maybe you should turn everyone against them.

Conversation Starters

- Do you ever feel bullied or see people being bullied at school? In which ways?

- Even in my adult life, it can sometimes feel uncomfortable to stand up and do the right thing. Do you find it hard to speak up or does it usually come easily to you? Why?

- When you and your friends get in disagreements, do you feel like you get over them pretty fast? Why or why not?

BEYOND THE CONVERSATION

DON'T MAKE IT WORSE

In my years working with girls, I have seen a lot of parents make some pretty bad decisions that stoke drama. Daughters feel hurt, left out, or threatened, and some adults just can't help but sink to a middle and high school level, actually encouraging or helping their daughters retaliate, rather than taking the high road. Make a pact with your co-parent and your other parent friends that you are not going to give into the temptation.

ACT FAST IF YOU SENSE A PROBLEM

Bullying can threaten girls' mental health. If you notice that your daughter has any sudden behavior changes, like seeming withdrawn, depressed, or angry, ask her if anything has happened or shifted in her social life. It may be that she is involved in or witnessing bullying.

If you find out that your daughter is suffering from the effects of bullying, make sure you engage with adults with influence in the situation, including other parents, teachers, school counselors and administrators, coaches, religious leaders, or camp counselors. You'll also want to pull in any emotional supports for your daughter, including a therapist if possible, to help her process her emotions and create a game plan to move forward. This will help eliminate or curb the intensity of potential negative impacts she experiences.

GIVE YOUR SCHOOL COUNSELORS THE BENEFIT OF THE DOUBT AND WORK WITH THEM

One evening several years ago, I presented my Into the Blue Light digital literacy program to a group of high schoolers' parents at a school. The principal, dean, and counselor were standing to the side as I spoke about some of the unsavory behaviors we've seen rise with the proliferation of cell phones and chat apps. A parent raised his hand, glanced over at the administrators, and then looked at me as if throwing a figurative grenade and said, "What happens if your child is getting bullied all the time and the school does *nothing*?!" It was a little off topic, but he needed an outlet, and I was happy to answer the question. I told him the following:

> *I completely understand why it might feel that way. I often talk to parents who don't think schools do enough to address negative social dynamics and bully-ing. Part of the reason it seems this way is because schools have to protect the confidentiality of all students. They typically can't tell parents and students whether they have talked to another student, what they have said, or what consequences have been enforced. And, even if administrators take steps to make a problem better, that doesn't guarantee that it won't pop up again.*

That's how it works when you are working with adolescents. They don't al-
ways do what you say. [I talk about this in chapter 4, "Building Your Sup-
port Team: Who and How to Call for Help."] But as a parent, you should
rest assured that the grand majority of school teachers and administrators
want to help you and they want your child to feel safe and socially connected
at school. At the baseline, most of them really do care. But in this day and age,
it is also a liability for schools to leave a bullying situation unaddressed. They
want it resolved as quickly as you do. So, call them up if you sense a problem.
Try not to put them on the defensive, and instead, consider them part of a
team of people who can help you understand what might be going on with your
child and what the best solution might be.

This advice holds true for all parents. This isn't to say that schools
will always get it right when you ask them to address instances of
bullying, but just because you don't know everything they are doing
to advocate for students doesn't mean they are getting it all wrong.

Love

Love is my favorite subject to teach. When I teach my Love Class curriculum to middle and high school girls, I never have trouble keeping their attention. My lessons focus on self-love, personal boundaries,
and relational communication. I tell my students that they have the
potential to master relationships, just like they have the potential to
master any other skill or subject area.

And regardless of the age group I am speaking to or the topic at
hand, their eyes are glued on me. Girls want to know what I have to
say. They have questions like:

- When is the right time to get into a relationship?

- How can I get into a relationship?

- How do you know when you're in love?

- My parents are divorced. Will that affect my ability to be in a good relationship?

And they listen closely for the answers. When you talk to your daughter about love, you're likely to encounter a similar response, even if she acts as though she doesn't want to hear it from you.

SOME BACKGROUND

Girls' fascination with love comes naturally. At the most basic level, love is fun and exciting. After all, who doesn't delight in a case of the butterflies? But adolescent girls are also developing physically and emotionally and experiencing more intense attractions.[131] As they mature through middle and high school, so does the nature of their potential romantic relationships, which can last longer and become more intimate emotionally and sexually.[132] Girls are talking about crushes with friends. Many are flirting and communicating with love interests and partners on their phones and on social media.[133] They are becoming more aware of popular culture's glorification of romance through love songs, TV shows, movies, and books. On the verge of adult life, they are beginning to grasp the nature and depth of romantic love. They are curious, and with many good reasons.

Girls' first romantic relationships play an important role in their social development, giving them opportunities to explore their identities and preferences, and practice skills like communication, teamwork, active listening, boundary setting, and intimacy. They learn from and build upon their experiences over time, and the positive habits girls form in their early relationships have been shown to have positive effects on their romantic experiences as adults.[134] As with building any other skill set, practice makes perfect in learning to master relationships. So the earlier in adolescence you start coaching your daughter in age-appropriate ways, the better.

It's worth noting (and may relieve you to know) that according to a 2015 study conducted by the Pew Research Center, only 35 percent of US teens ages thirteen to seventeen report having experience with romantic relationships.[135] The majority of teens will not find themselves in relationships until after high school. Whether your daughter actually enters into a romantic relationship, or whether you have a rule that she's not allowed to date until she is older, doesn't change the fact that she most likely has love on the brain—and that gives you an "in" to educate her, preparing her for dynamics and scenarios she might encounter in the future.

In the 2018 report "The Talk: How Adults Can Promote Young People's Healthy Relationships and Prevent Misogyny and Sexual Harassment," Dr. Richard Weissbourd and his team of researchers from the Harvard Graduate School of Education highlight that 70 percent of participants ages eighteen to twenty-five wished they had more guidance from parents on "emotional aspect[s] of romantic relationships." Additionally, 38 percent wanted to know "how to have a more mature relationship"; 36 percent wondered "how to avoid getting hurt in relationships"; and 27 percent wanted insights on "how to begin a relationship."[136]

Girls often thank me at the end of my classes, telling me that I've helped them. Your daughter will thank you, too, for leveling with her. So don't be afraid to jump in and get real about topics like crushes, love, and boundary setting. And if you've made some mistakes in love, that doesn't disqualify you from being able to advise your daughter. Lessons learned from your past missteps can be invaluable.

> **YOUR GOAL:** Helping your daughter recognize healthy romantic relationships and her power to shape them.

> **RULE #1:** Assume that her feelings, relationships, and heartbreaks are significant to her. Never dismiss her emotions or experiences on the basis that she's "too young to know what love is." Teenagers can experience true love.

TALKING POINTS

Love is one of the highest-impact subjects you can teach. Fortunately, it's also one of the easiest to broach.

THE RISKS OF ROMANTIC RELATIONSHIPS

If you're tempted to open up a discussion of romantic relationships with "no dating until you're thirty!," you wouldn't be alone or entirely misguided. Throughout history, conventional wisdom held that fathers should teach their daughters about the perils of love, stop their potential ravishers at the door, and avenge their heartbreaks. While your role has evolved, and dad jokes about scaring dates away with shotguns are far past their prime, there are some real dangers you want to address.[137] Identifying these risks can help your daughter recognize any potentially harmful patterns in her relationships and help her avoid or address them early on.

- *Loss of personal identity.* Girls can become so wrapped up in their romantic relationships that they get distracted from schoolwork, let their friendships slip, and devote less focus to their own passions.

- *Emotional distress.* Fights, disappointment, and heartbreak can send girls spiraling.

- *Risky sexual behavior.* If girls' relationships become intimate, there is the chance for risky sexual behavior to occur. Girls need to be educated about sexual health, a topic I detail in the next section.

- *Dating violence.* Dating violence, which I cover extensively in the upcoming section on sexual misconduct, is a matter of international concern.

The Building Blocks of Healthy Relationships

Some of these building blocks may seem obvious, but you can't take for granted that your daughter will figure them out easily. Telling her the basics can make a positive difference, saving her time and limiting confusion and heartache. Here are some characteristics of good relationships:[138]

- Partners feel happy and content in the relationship most of the time.

- There are strong feelings of psychological safety and joy, and low levels of drama and jealousy.

- Partners feel accepted. They don't feel pressured to change their appearances, values, hobbies, or other personal characteristics.

- Partners maintain their personal identities and activities and stay focused on their individual goals and responsibilities, enjoying their relationship as just one part of their lives.

- Partners share a strong emotional connection, not just a physical connection.

- Partners communicate openly and directly to voice boundaries, build trust, and solve conflicts quickly.

- Partners speak and act kindly to one another, boosting each other's self-esteem.

- Partners are not physically violent.

- Partners end relationships respectfully.

RED FLAGS IN RELATIONSHIPS

I will highlight unhealthy relationship dynamics in the following sections on sexual health, breakups, and sexual misconduct, but discussion of potential red flags also has an important place in this conversation. Here are some concerning signs your daughter should be aware of:[139]

- Feeling like a romantic partner is excessively jealous.

- When a romantic partner acts controlling or tries to dictate what their significant other is allowed to do, where they can

go, and who they can spend time with outside the
relationship.

- A partner feels guilty, like they can't do anything right,
  or that they are "in trouble" with their romantic partner
  often.

- Any type of physical violence or threat of violence.

- Any type of sexual violence.

GIRLS' COMMON QUESTIONS AND CONCERNS

Why It Seems Like "Everyone Is in a Relationship"

Explain that for a lot of reasons, it might feel to your daughter like
she is the only one not in a relationship. It's easy to focus on what
others have. A lot of movies depicting life in middle and high school
focus on a love story, which makes it seem like having a relationship
in your teens is something that needs to happen or should always
happen. And romantic relationships are glorified and depicted in
the music girls listen to and the Netflix shows they binge. Since our
culture places so much value on relationships, it makes total sense
she may feel like the only single person at one time or another.

Make sure she knows that most people have their first relationships after high school, and that relationships don't always happen
on our timelines. Relationships are about connecting with the right
person at the right time. And make sure she realizes that lots of
people have the moment she is having, where they feel like they are
the only one without a significant other. Her time to be with someone will happen, and it will be worth the wait.

With this approach, you are making her feel heard, honoring her feelings, and reassuring her, while also offering her facts to back up a different point of view. She may not be in the mood to consider her situation from a different perspective, but she may come back to it later.

How to Get into a Relationship

This is another common question for girls. Mention that relationships begin in all different ways. Help her see the benefit in spending time with people who make her happy, and who make her feel relaxed and confident. Sometimes, girls focus on crushes who don't have the same feelings or who are interested in other people. Encourage your daughter to really pay attention in these moments, noticing whether certain crushes and relationships actually make her happy. Explain that you can't always choose the way you feel or who you are attracted to, but you always have the ability to change your focus to the people you feel comfortable around and who value you.

HOW IT'S DONE

Do Say

- I love you.

- Love is an important part of life.

- Healthy relationships can be a fun and meaningful part of life.

- It can feel like everyone else is in a relationship, but that isn't the case.

- Relationships should add to your sense of inner peace and confidence, not cause anxiety.

- You should never feel like you have to change or be uncomfortable to make someone else happy.

- Trust your gut feelings about someone.

- Jealousy, controlling behaviors, and violence are not markers of authentic love.

- Be truthful and kind in relationships.

Don't Say

- You're not dating until you're thirty.

- Relationships don't matter right now, focus on your homework and friendships.

- You're too young to be in love.

- You don't know what love is.

- Relationships never work out.

- All men are dogs.

Questions to Ask

The topic of love and relationships comes up in a song, TV show, or movie. Ask:

- Do you think the way they are talking about love is realistic?

- Do you think the media sets healthy expectations for real-life relationships?

- Do you think the media influences the way your friends view love and relationships? How?

- Who do you think are the most realistic TV or movie couples? Why?

Your daughter and her friends are talking about crushes and/or significant others in your presence. Later on, ask:

- Do you think most people you know in relationships are happy? Or do people get caught up in the drama?
- Do you feel like your friends are always respectful and caring when talking about other peoples' relationships?
- What do you think are the best things about relationships right now?
- What is most exciting to you about relationships?

Your daughter is in a relationship that seems positive. Ask:

- What is your favorite thing about [name]?
- Are there ways you feel like being in this relationship is helping you?
- What do you feel like you've learned so far about relationships?
- What are the ways you communicate best together?

(In the section on sexual misconduct you will find a discussion of how to talk to your daughter about unhealthy relationships.)

BEYOND THE CONVERSATION

MODEL HEALTHY RELATIONAL BEHAVIORS

When it comes to teaching your daughter to recognize healthy relationships and incorporate healthy relationship strategies, the example you set is paramount. You don't have to be perfect, but whenever possible, model the habits you hope your daughter will form, even in trying times. Show her what it means to treat loved ones with respect and resolve conflicts in caring ways. If you have a romantic partner, be mindful of cultivating healthy relationship dynamics together. Your daughter will notice and develop expectations for her relationships based in great part on your actions and behavior.

Sexual Health

"Welcome to sex ed, everyone. Today, we're going to talk about what sexual intercourse is. We're going to talk about the potential outcomes of sexual activity, and we're going to talk about how people can protect themselves, including abstinence and birth control options. I want to warn you that I am going to use words like 'penis' and 'vagina.' Throughout this lesson, you might feel like you want to laugh out loud. You don't have to 'keep it together,' but you should listen, because the truth is, if people can't have some awkward conversations about sexual health, the consequences can be pretty rough."

This is how I open my seventh-grade sex ed lessons. I offer you the same message.

SOME BACKGROUND

I've been teaching sex ed in different formats—in classrooms, through online writing, and to parents of teenagers—for nearly two decades. I have taught in public and private schools, in middle school and high school classrooms, in schools with varying religious affiliations, and on campuses across the country. I can tell you that regardless of their backgrounds or family beliefs, girls are curious about sex.

In my lessons, students have the opportunity to ask anonymous questions, writing them down on pieces of paper that I then collect and read for the class. Here are some that I get frequently:

- When is the right time to have sex?
- Can someone get an STD if they are on birth control?
- Is it illegal to have sex with someone who is older than you?
- Is it a good idea to use two condoms at once?
- What is masturbation?
- Can you get pregnant every time you have sex?
- Is it okay to take a friend's birth control pills?
- If I use a tampon, does that mean I'm not a virgin?

These questions don't necessarily mean that all students are having sex or even want to be in the near future. More than half of girls in the United States ages fifteen to nineteen are not sexually active.[140] However, girls' curiosity signals that they are starting to gather information about sex, and the most trustworthy source of that information is knowledgeable adults. That's your cue.

In adolescence, girls develop an increasing awareness of and interest in sex. As they go through puberty and mature through high school, they experience physical attractions to others that are increasingly intense. And as they gain independence, they find themselves with more freedom from adult supervision and opportunities to be intimate with sexual partners.

Sex also pervades broader culture, and girls pick up on that. They learn about sex and sexual health from online health articles. They see sexualized advertisements. They see sex scenes in the shows and movies they're watching. They hear about it in the music they listen to. Pornography, even though more commonly viewed by boys, still gives rise to unhealthy relationship dynamics and expectations for girls.[141]

It's hard for girls to get properly educated when media presents incomplete, inaccurate, and even detrimental information about sexual relationships and sexual health, older siblings and friends don't have all the facts, and most girls don't have access to doctors or health-care professionals when they have pressing questions. That's why they need you.

It's Safe to Talk About Safe Sex

There's a common misconception that educating teens about sexual health will inspire them to have sex earlier—but the research points to the contrary.[142] The more information young people have about sex, the more likely they are to wait to engage in sexual activity. This may seem counterintuitive at first, but it's not, and it's well established in the academic literature. And, the earlier you start, the better. By educating your daughter *before* she becomes sexually active, you are increasing the chances that she will wait until she is ready and that her sexual experiences are healthy ones when they do happen. The better prepared your daughter is to make informed decisions about her sex life, the fewer regrets she'll have.

The Right Time to Talk to Your Daughter about Sex

Sexual health education should begin early with open, honest conversations about how bodies work, what the parts are named, and the power every child has to say no to unwanted physical contact. When your child's school begins teaching sex ed can inform your timeline, because the conversations are already happening, and you'll want to be part of them. Some other signs you can look for that suggest it's time to jump in yourself include:

- Your daughter is watching movies or television shows, such as those depicting high school life, that have mature sexual content.

- You are watching something with your daughter and a sex scene or advertisement for a sex-related product such as lubricant comes up on the screen.

- Your daughter begins puberty.

- Your daughter has her first relationship or goes on her first dates.

- Your daughter is talking about friends' romantic relationships.

- Your daughter is going to her first dances or parties.

The progressions of your conversations should be informed by your daughter's age, maturity, awareness of the topics, and social context (is she gathering information from her environment that you should address?). In an ideal world, she would hear everything from trusted adults first, at the perfect time, right before or at the moment she encounters information (or misinformation) or imagery from other sources.

YOU WILL SURVIVE THESE CONVERSATIONS

Talking to kids about sex makes a lot of parents anxious. There is no topic with more potential awkwardness than this one. While it may be hard to imagine, not only will you survive these conversations, but you and your father-daughter relationship will be stronger for them. I always say that teaching sex ed to seventh graders at the beginning of my career prepared me better than anything else to have the conversations that matter in all areas of my life. Talking to your daughter about sex will challenge you to tackle complex and uncomfortable topics in age-appropriate and sensitive ways. You are going to have to come up with answers on the spot and keep your cool when she asks you questions that make you want to spontaneously evaporate into thin air. But this is your Super Bowl. If you can have conversations about sex with your daughter, you can talk about absolutely anything else. Even more important, she will know you are up to the task, and she'll know she can ask you and talk to you about whatever is on her mind.

YOU AREN'T ALONE

Keep in mind that you don't have to cover everything at once or all by yourself. If you have a spouse or other adult family member or friend who you and your daughter feel comfortable having involved, they can cover certain topics, and you can cover others. You can also look into what your daughter might be learning in school. She may already be learning about some of the big themes, like human reproduction and STDs, so you won't have to go into depth on the details.

YOUR GOAL: Help your daughter have better experiences and fewer regrets by equipping her with the information she needs to think critically about her decisions related to sexual behavior.

RULE #1: Do not shame her for her sexuality or ever use the word "slut," ever; even if you are thinking it, don't express it. Remember, your words are incredibly powerful. If you respond with anger or degrading comments, you'll not only shut communication down—possibly indefinitely—but you also could damage your daughter's ability to express healthy sexuality with future romantic partners and up the chances she'll find herself in unhealthy relationships.

TALKING POINTS

Get ready. This is a long section because in my conversations with fathers everywhere, sexual health is one of the topics they feel is most important to talk about and also one of the most delicate to approach. It's also one of the topics teenagers are most interested in. I'm giving you a bunch of the high points I use in my Love Class on sexual health, which illustrates the scope of topics your daughter needs to grasp.

WAYS TO GET THE FACTS

I teach sex ed much differently now than I did fifteen years ago. I used to focus simply on the details of human reproduction, healthy relationships, and every sexually transmitted disease and contraceptive method. Now, I assume that kids can and will google much of what I say (if they haven't already), stumbling upon unhelpful or downright disturbing content and imagery, including pornography. So, while I do still teach the details, the broader message of my sex ed classes is teaching young people, who are barraged with sexual imagery and pressure, to use critical thinking in order to make better decisions in their romantic relationships and sexual lives. I stress the importance of thinking through personal values and boundaries and gathering facts from reliable sources. I encourage girls to speak with their parents if they feel safe doing so, and I talk to girls about the importance of knowing how to seek medical advice and attention should they need it. The Internet can be a meaningful first stop for information on sex, but going to the Internet for information on sexuality can bring up more questions than answers, causing unnecessary fear and anxiety. Searching sexual search terms, even for educational purposes, can bring up unexpected pornographic imagery. It's significantly less awkward (for both of you) if your daughter googles answers, but you should also encourage her to talk to a knowing adult, whether that's yourself, someone in your family, a doctor, or a nurse at school.

WHAT IS SEX?

"Sexual activity" refers to a range of intimate behaviors, including intercourse, involving sexual arousal.[143] While sexual activity is potentially pleasurable and connective in healthy relationships, it also carries with it the risks of emotional distress, sexually transmitted diseases, and unwanted pregnancies.

"Sex" refers to different forms of sexual intercourse including:

- Oral sex.
- Vaginal sex.
- Anal sex.

Among the endless misperceptions young people have about sex, some of the most dangerous relate to the belief that only vaginal sex is "sex." Stemming from this belief is the incorrect assumption that vaginal sex is the only type of sexual activity that carries risks. Adolescents may turn to oral and anal sex because they don't realize they can contract STDs from these behaviors. In addition, adolescents who believe that only vaginal sex is "sex" may turn more readily to oral sex or anal sex, believing that they can engage in these types of sexual activity while maintaining their "virginity," which they narrowly define, in certain cases for religious reasons, as vaginal sex.[144]

Anal sex is also an essential topic to cover because surveys of adolescent sexual behavior show a rise in anal sex among young people.[145] I have fielded quite a few phone calls from parents up in arms that their child has come home talking about anal sex after sex ed. I understand why this is alarming, but this topic comes up often in popular culture and all the time in anonymous questions in my classes, and doctors I speak with hear about it from their young patients, illustrating that kids are thinking about it and talking about it. We need to address it for them so that they aren't just learning about anal sex and the potential risks of engaging in it from the Internet and their friends.

An additional point I make to my students is that even if people don't have oral, anal, or vaginal sex, people should be mindful of any behavior including skin-on-skin contact that can result in the transmission of bodily fluids or an STD like herpes or genital warts. It's important to note for young people that activities that are intimate in nature, but don't necessarily involve traditionally understood forms of intercourse, can still carry risks.

THE POTENTIAL OUTCOMES OF SEXUAL ACTIVITY

Getting caught up in the excitement and momentum of romantic relationships can make the risks seem worth it for teenagers. Girls need to understand in no uncertain terms what can happen if they engage in sexual activity and if they don't take proper precautions:

- Intensified emotional connections that can be positive or negative.[146]
- Sexually transmitted diseases (STDs).
    - Viral infections, including herpes and human papilloma virus (HPV), which are not curable but can be treated with medication.
    - Bacterial infections, including chlamydia and syphilis, which are curable with medication.
- Pregnancy.

- Uncomfortable infections like UTIs or yeast infections, which can masquerade as STDs but are easily treatable.

WHY PEOPLE HAVE SEX

Talking to your daughter about why people choose to be sexually intimate with other people can help protect her from making decisions for the wrong reasons, like peer pressure or a belief that it will solidify another person's love for her. When you talk to your daughter about why people have sex, you can set a realistic, balanced tone for your future conversations. You can also provide a foundation for understanding both the potential benefits and risks of being sexually active, and lay out key scenarios that your daughter should be prepared to navigate (even though you hope she can avoid them!).

Reasons why people have sex include:

Positive Motivations

- To express love and caring.
- Partners decide together they want to take their relationship to the next level physically.
- Physical pleasure and fun.
- To have children.

Negative and Risky Motivations

- Peer pressure or feeling like "everyone is doing it."
- Believing that giving in to sex will convince someone to start a relationship or pay attention to you.
- Pressure from a partner.
- The influence of alcohol and drugs.

One of the first questions I ask students is why they think people have sex. They give many answers in quick succession: "because they are in love"; "because they want to have a baby"; "because they are married." But only sometimes does one brave student mention the concept of pleasure. Students are understandably hesitant to offer up "people have sex because it feels good" as an answer to a question asked in a classroom setting. But there is another reason as well, pertaining specifically to girls and women. In popular culture and media, girls receive a lot of messaging about sex being pleasurable to boys and men. Pornography, which has a growing influence on adolescents, is heavily focused on male pleasure. While women's pleasure is more often acknowledged and addressed in broader culture and the media now than previously, it's by no means a primary message that girls are encountering. But girls should understand that sex can and should be pleasurable to them, too, and that that's part of a healthy romantic relationship. This may not be a point that you're comfortable talking about with your daughter, but it's something she should hear, if not from you, then from your spouse, co-parent, or an adult female role model.

When you lead with the positive reasons people engage in sexual activity, even if it is just a couple sentences, you highlight for your daughter that sex can be chosen for positive reasons rather than forced because of peer pressure or unhealthy relationship dynamics and influences. Approaching the conversation from a positive angle will help your daughter understand that sex can and should be a positive aspect of her life, and that she can make strategic decisions to create the best, healthiest outcomes for herself. Talking about the real benefits of sexual relationships also allows you to highlight the risks of sexual activity without being entirely negative—and being negative and scary will make her tune you out.

NOT EVERYONE IS HAVING SEX

Because sex is such a pervasive theme in our culture and because so many teens are naturally preoccupied with it, teens often believe, falsely, that the majority of people are having sex at some point in high school. This misperception can increase the pressure they feel to become sexually active, even if they aren't ready. Emphasize to your daughter the reasons why it *seems* like everyone is having sex—people talk about it, media depicts it as a norm in high school life, music and advertisements emphasize it as key to happiness—and highlight that the majority of teenagers are not having sex in high school.[147] It is also important to note that abstinence is not only entirely normal and acceptable, but it is also the only foolproof way to protect against STDs and unplanned pregnancies.

THE RIGHT TIME TO HAVE SEX

In the majority of sex ed classes I teach, whether single gender or all gender, I get asked when the right time to have sex is. Girls want to get this right. Lucky for you, research suggests that waiting to have sex, and having sex in the context of committed romantic relationships, leads to more positive, healthy sexual experiences.[148] So, you can tell her with confidence that she should wait, and the science will back you up. Beyond that, the way you answer this question may, again, be informed by your religious and cultural context, but some healthy sound bites include:

- When people are of a certain age.

- When people are in a trusting, committed relationship.

- When there are no unhealthy power dynamics from a big age gap or a controlling partner.

- When people have spoken about consent, boundaries, STD testing, and safe sex.

THE HELPFULNESS OF REGULAR STD TESTING

Getting tested for STDs and making sure partners get tested is important because there is often no way to tell by looking at someone whether they are infected. STDs do not discriminate. In addition, many STDs are asymptomatic, especially at the beginning.

Getting tested for STDs can be terrifying. If your daughter makes it part of her ongoing health-care maintenance routine once she becomes sexually active, she will have practice proactively seeking help, guidance, and information from doctors. The earlier doctors can catch a condition, the better chance they have of reducing any discomfort or long-term consequences a patient might face. Importantly, as I noted earlier, there are common conditions, like yeast infections, that girls can mistake for STDs. Worry and fear around symptoms can cause girls to avoid going to the doctor. Your daughter should know that if she ever thinks there is any issue at all, she should make an appointment as soon as possible.

PROTECTION OPTIONS

If you want your daughter to learn about contraceptive methods and STD prevention, you don't need to understand every option or plan to go into detail. Again, you can rely on your daughter's school, if they are covering these topics in class, or you can partner with your daughter's doctor to go over the options with her. When schools ask me to address this topic, I cover the categories of contraception and STD prevention and explain that choosing a method and a brand should be a personal process.

Here is a high-level overview:

- **ABSTINENCE**—the only foolproof way to protect against STDs and pregnancy.

- **BARRIER METHODS**—help prevent STDs and pregnancy.
    - Examples: Condoms (also called external condoms), female condoms (also called internal condoms), and dental dams (latex sheets used between one partner's mouth and another's genitals during oral sex).
    - How they work: Prevent the flow of bodily fluids from one partner to another, and lessen skin-to-skin contact that can lead to transmission of skin-borne infections including herpes and genital warts.

- **HORMONAL METHODS**—prevent pregnancy *only*.
    - Examples: Birth control pills, the patch, and intrauterine devices (IUDs).
    - How they work: Prevent ovulation from happening.

Safe sex methods draw a lot of questions and create a lot of confusion among young people. Here are some points to make sure your daughter understands:

- Contraceptive and STD prevention methods must be used consistently (every time) and correctly in order to be most effective. Even then, such methods can still fail.

- Certain options, such as a barrier method and a hormonal method, may be used together in order to maximize protection.

- Lubrication is important. This is especially important for girls to know about because too little lubrication, either natural or gel, can create pain, lead to genital irritation or vaginal tearing during intercourse, and can create friction that causes condoms to break. Talking about lubrication with girls may seem like an overly sophisticated topic, but it is truly important for your daughter's comfort and safety from the time she becomes sexually active.

- Urinating after sexual activity can help prevent infection because it will clear any bacteria that might have entered the urethra.

- While barrier methods and hormonal methods can be highly effective, they can fail, leading to sexually transmitted infections and unwanted pregnancy.
  - Condoms can break.
  - Barrier methods don't protect entirely against skin-to-skin contact.
  - Hormonal birth control is less than 100 percent effective, including if girls are using it incorrectly or if they are on certain other medications.

- Each person in a sexual relationship is responsible for knowing about and talking about protection.

- Emergency contraception pills, also known as EC or the morning-after pill, are never to be used as contraception. They should be used only in emergency situations.

- There is a vaccine that protects against the human papilloma virus (HPV), one of the most common STDs.

PLANNING AHEAD FOR SEXUAL INTERACTIONS

Teaching sex ed to high school seniors is different from teaching it to seventh graders. At the beginning of my classes, a lot of them have looks on their faces that say, "Tell me something I don't already know." "I assume you know a lot of this," I tell them. My job isn't to tell you about everything you don't know. My job is to help you make the best decisions, in the moment."

There's nothing like getting caught up in the moment that makes people throw caution to the wind in the sexual sense. The safest sexual interactions take place in committed relationships with communicative, respectful partners. Planning ahead with a sexual partner, including talking through consent, boundaries, and protection, boosts comfort and safety. Your daughter needs to know that the more she talks through with her partner before they have sexual interactions, the more prepared she will be and the less likely she will be to compromise her boundaries or put herself at risk.

CONSENT

In the era of #metoo and #timesup, girls' social feeds are often flooded with news stories and first-person accounts from victims of sexual misconduct and those speaking out in support. Sexual misconduct is common, and today's girls are, unfortunately, all too familiar with it. But at the same time, they are receiving plenty of messaging about what is and what is not acceptable behavior. While girls may receive some guidance on it in school, you should address consent directly. Consent is an active agreement to be sexually intimate with another person.[149] Consent should be a topic of ongoing discussion and check-ins between sexual partners because the authentic consent of each person involved in a relationship is a foundational quality of healthy sexual relationships.

How Consent Is Given

When I speak to students about consent, I don't just tell them the ideal way to give and receive consent, I talk to them about the ways people "in real life" give consent and what the benefits and risks are in each type of scenario:[150]

- *Verbally, before each sexual interaction.* This is the safest form of consent, which allows for partners to verbalize what they are and are not comfortable with during each interaction.

- *Verbally, at the beginning of a sexual relationship.* This form of consent is risky because it assumes that if someone is comfortable with a behavior during one sexual interaction, they will be okay with the same or other behaviors in later interactions.

- *Nonverbally.* This is the riskiest form of consent, since facial expressions and physical signs do not allow for an articulation of specific boundaries. Your daughter could think she is consenting to one thing, but her partner could have other ideas.

Barriers to Consent

- *Age.* Check your state laws. Under a certain age, individuals are not legally able to give consent. There are also laws

about age differentials and consent, which vary by
jurisdiction.

- *Coercion and intimidation.* If someone is being intimidated or
  threatened, their consent is null.

- *Influence of drugs and alcohol.* Being under the influence
  negatively impacts individuals' ability to offer consent. If
  someone is passed out, of course they cannot give consent.

One useful tool to fuel a conversation on consent is an advertisement from the Thames Valley Police, in the United Kingdom, which
you can find on YouTube. If you google "tea consent video," you
will find it. (Look for the clean version, particularly if you're going
to watch the video with your daughter. I learned the hard way,
in front of a classroom full of eighth-grade girls, that there are two
versions of this video, and one of them includes some colorful language.)

HOW TO SAY NO

As I've mentioned, I always tell my students that they know what to
do and what boundaries to set, and that somewhere inside them is a
sense of what the right decision is at a given moment. In my Love
Class, I offer my students scenarios and ask what they think they
should do, an exercise you might find helpful in your own conversations. Some examples are:

- At a party, someone wants you to follow them into a secluded
  space. You are kind of excited about it, but you think they
  may expect you to do something outside of your comfort
  zone. What do you say?

- Someone wants you to send suggestive photos of yourself. How do you tell them "no way!"?

- A romantic partner pressures you to "go further" physically, even though you know you aren't ready. What do you do?

Invariably, the girls guess right, that they should simply say "no," and we laugh together because the answers are so obvious when we are talking about them in a classroom setting. The humor is welcome.

And then I say, "Do you think people always say 'no' in the moment?" And they again answer correctly, "No"—and they look at me with renewed interest because I'm no longer stating the obvious. This is always a pivotal moment in sex ed, when students who think they know *everything* realize I can still teach them something: that they can have all the information they need and still make poor decisions in the moment.

"That's right. People say 'yes' when they want to say 'no,' and that's when they make decisions they regret," I tell my students. Then, we brainstorm the reasons why—peer pressure, wanting to impress a crush, feeling too awkward to say "no," feeling like they'll sacrifice the relationship if they say "no," feeling like it won't be that big a deal to say "yes." Then, we talk about how to say "no," even if you feel uncomfortable. You can have this same discussion with your daughter.

THE NEGATIVE INFLUENCE OF
DRUGS AND ALCOHOL

I think high school students get pretty tired of hearing adults tell them not to do drugs or drink alcohol. The message is paramount, but they've heard it before. I repeat it in sex ed. I tell them, "I know I am not the first or the last person to caution you about doing drugs and drinking alcohol. But maybe what you don't know is the extent to which being under the influence of drugs and alcohol can affect your sexual decision-making and safety. I've told you that you can rely on your intuition, that you know what the right decision is in a given moment. When you are under the influence of drugs and alcohol, you know that you might make poor decisions or be more vulnerable to getting taken advantage of. But, perhaps most important, you lose touch with that sense of inner knowing. You cannot access it if you are under the influence." This message resonates. It's true. And it can help your daughter protect against both substance use and risky sexual behavior.

HOW IT'S DONE

As you have read in this section, there is a lot to say about sexual health. Here are some overarching comments to avoid making, and some key messages to send to open up communication on the topic.

It is very possible your daughter will freak out on you for bringing it up. Don't worry. This is definitely one of those times where you can expect her to shut you down, but that doesn't mean you aren't making a positive impact.

If you are unsure whether your daughter is attracted to males, females, or people of other genders—use inclusive, nongendered terms like "sexual partner" and be nonspecific when you are talking about someone your daughter may be attracted to or a future romantic partner. This will signal to your daughter that you are open to talking about sexual orientation and that you will accept her if she comes out to you.

Do Say

- I know I may not seem like the most natural person to go to about topics like this, but I am always here to talk about it.

- If you ever need medical attention, including birth control, I want you to talk to me or [your mother/other adult] about it. It may be uncomfortable for me to know about your private life and I/we may not always agree with your choices, but my/our job is to keep you safe. I/we want to be there for you.

- If you don't feel comfortable talking to me/one of us about it, I want you to talk to [name another trusted adult].

Don't Say

- Nothing.

- You're not allowed to have sex until you are [age here] or married. (You may believe this, but if your daughter doesn't follow your direction, she will not be comfortable talking to you about it. This is especially concerning if she were to engage in a sexual relationship and ended up needing your help with an unwanted consequence, but she didn't want to discuss it with you.)

- You're not ready for this. (Especially if she is asking you about sex, she *is* ready for this conversation, and it's important that you have it now. Telling her she's not ready won't stop her from thinking about or having sexual intercourse. You want to make sure she's prepared with the facts ahead of time.)

- We're not talking about this.

Questions to Ask

- I know you are learning about sexual health in school and probably talking about it some with your friends. Do you have any questions I can answer?

- It seems like you and [romantic partner] are doing really well. As relationships progress, they can become more physical. There are a few things I want you to know. Can we spend a few minutes maybe later this week talking about it?

- *You happen to see a romantic or sexual scene play out in a show or movie you are watching together:*
    - Do you think this is a healthy dynamic?
    - Here's what I think is responsible about this scene . . .
    - Here's what I think is problematic about this scene . . .

- *If you don't know the answer to a question or can't come up with a sensitive response on the spot, you can say:*
    - Let's look it up.
    - Let's make an appointment with the doctor, so you can ask some of these more specific questions.

BEYOND THE CONVERSATION

SET UP A DOCTOR'S APPOINTMENT

If you aren't comfortable or don't feel like you know enough to have conversations with your daughter on certain topics, make an appointment for your daughter with her doctor. Ahead of time, tell the doctor that you think it might be time for your daughter to be learning about sexual health or that it's time to start talking about birth control methods, and enlist the doctor's help. With guidance from your physician, you can address confidentiality with your daughter and what you expect the doctor will or won't tell you, which can help your daughter feel easier about opening up and asking questions or expressing concerns.

Breakups

"Our research suggests that many young people want guidance on how to handle breakups. If we want to teach young people about love, I think it will help a lot to teach them how to break up with each other with decency and care." This is what Dr. Rick Weissbourd, my mentor and a leader in research on young peoples' romantic relationships, said to me when I was first developing my Love Class curriculum for teenagers.

The truth is, most people of all ages are bad at breakups. Whoever learned in any type of reasonable way how to break hearts or be heartbroken? It's not something people usually get guidance on. Adolescents of all genders can get hurt in breakups. Girls can end up heartbroken, but they can also be pretty hard on people they are breaking it off with. Often, girls learn about breakups and getting over them from their friends and media. Productive communication and coping skills aren't usually the norm. Emotion and drama can run high, resulting in a lot of extra heartache for everyone involved.

I can tell you that girls know this is a problem, and when I'm teaching, and I introduce my "bonus section" on breakups, the kids laugh, but they can't hide their interest.

SOME BACKGROUND

In a 2016 study, Australian researchers reviewed records from more than four thousand counseling sessions with ten- to eighteen-year-olds and found that breakups were the leading reason young people sought counseling.[151] The researchers also found that breakups were linked to self-harming behaviors and suicidal ideation. In addition to these outcomes, breakups have been tied to drops in self-esteem, depression, sleeplessness, difficulty concentrating, and distraction from responsibilities and goals.[152]

There are several reasons for the difficulty young people (and yes, adults, too) have with heartbreak:

- Teenage girls are weathering ongoing hormonal shifts, which can contribute to intense feelings.

- When a relationship comes to an end for anyone of any age, it can feel disappointing.

- Romantic love can take on an addictive quality, meaning that breaking up can feel like breaking a habit. In one study at Stony Brook University, researchers used fMRI (brain imaging) to analyze the brain functioning of students who had recently suffered romantic rejections. They found that "intense romantic love" activates the same areas of the brain as addictive substances including cocaine do.[153] Unraveling old patterns and feelings can be a process. Girls' lack of experience (and perhaps interest) in de-escalating drama can exaggerate and prolong heartache.

- Breakups in middle school, high school, and college are relatively public and bring with them the pressure of everyone's curiosity and expectations. Girls will naturally share what is going on with their friends, who may or may not be supportive. Text messages are overanalyzed, screenshot, and shared among friends. Even for more private girls, word can travel fast, especially if their love interest is talking to peers.

- Social media amplifies the drama. Everyone loves a good love saga, and peers watch closely on social media to see if any prior posts are edited or deleted, and to see if former boyfriends and girlfriends are still following each other. Social media provides a platform for each drama to become its own miniseries, and the viewership is hungry.

- Girls' typical proximity (physical and digital) to their romantic partners can make it simply hard to let go and move on. Breakups can happen, but partners stay in touch by text, or continue to hang out as "friends."

- Heartache can recur, because it's common for adolescents to break up and get back together multiple times.[154]

For all these reasons, breaking up is emotionally and physically really hard to do. This is true whether your daughter is breaking up with someone or being broken up with herself.

> **YOUR GOAL:** Teach your daughter practical, caring strategies to minimize the drama and heartache of breakups.

> **RULE #1:** Don't expect her to get over heartbreak in a timely fashion. As with adults, it can take time for girls, especially older adolescents, to recover from rejection.

TALKING POINTS

WHAT REAL BREAKUPS CAN LOOK LIKE

Movies and TV shows get young love and breakups almost all wrong. But the myths of teenage romance perpetuated by media still play a big role in how girls think their love lives should play out. Girls are wrongly conditioned to believe that breakups have to involve unhelpful behaviors like yelling, throwing things, slapping people, and getting revenge. Media also leaves out the depths of emotion that breakups can stir and the length of time it can take to get over someone.

Often, breakups in adolescents are messy and happen over time. If your daughter is in the midst of a breakup, talk to her about how it is playing out. If she talks about any behaviors you identify as being overly dramatic or hurtful, call them out in a way that is gentle and makes it clear you are on her side, but that perhaps there are better ways to come to a resolution.

GIRLS SHOULD FOCUS ON THE FEELINGS OF BREAKUPS AND NOT THE DRAMA

The drama of breakups can distract from the humanity and feelings at stake. If your daughter is breaking up with someone, encourage her to think about the other person's experience. Encourage her to think through her actions and words. Is what she is doing and saying caring? Is it helping get to a peaceful resolution and helping both people move on?

PRODUCTIVE STRATEGIES FOR BREAKING UP

Share these concrete tips with your daughter. As with all things you teach her, she may not listen right away, and instead decide to just milk the drama. But letting her in on these communication secrets can't hurt, and she might draw on them at a time when she needs them most.

- *Know what the goal is and why.* Does your daughter actually want a relationship to end? If she is getting broken up with, what does she want for herself? Even if she is emotional and has trouble letting go of "what could have been," it's good practice to have her try to apply some logic to her circumstances.

- *Have a face-to-face conversation where possible.* Unless your daughter is getting out of a relationship that feels abusive or unsafe to her, or she is geographically unable to get to her significant other, she should have a conversation in person. You can encourage her to use texting to facilitate an offline conversation, but emphasize that important conversations should happen face-to-face.

- *Be straightforward and avoid leading people on.* Emphasize the importance of being as direct as possible. If your daughter is breaking up with her partner, she may be concerned about being too direct because she might not want to hurt another person's feelings. Or she may just feel like it's easier to use language like "maybe we could get back together later" because it seems less final and less mean. But as we adults know, all this approach does is prolong a situation that doesn't help either person involved. Your daughter doesn't have to tell someone all the things she doesn't like about them in order to get her message across. But make sure she knows that it's okay to end things, even if it's painful and even if someone else doesn't like it.

- *Maintain privacy.* As I touched on before, breakups can be very public. It's of course natural and okay for girls to talk to their friends about what is going on for them. But make sure your daughter is aware of the extra damage it can cause if she is screenshotting and forwarding text messages or otherwise sharing private comments made by the person she is breaking up with. The same holds true for making public or disparaging posts on social media about a former romantic partner.

- *Plan the time of day.* "We need to talk" conversations often happen for teens late at night when they are already exhausted. Texting and video-chatting make this even easier to do. Discuss how positive it can be to have conversations at times of day when people are energized and thinking clearly.

- *Be specific about the length of breakup conversations.* Many girls I've known don't know when to stop a difficult conversation. They will just keep talking in circles, trying to say the perfect thing, hear the perfect thing, or get the last word in so they can get "closure." It goes on until they stop making sense and are completely exhausted. I suggest they say things like, "Can we meet up and talk for twenty minutes?" "Things haven't felt great between us. Can we get together and talk for an hour or so later?" It won't feel natural, and I have had students respond to me by saying, "How can I limit the time on what I have to say about something that is such a big deal?" But girls need to know that they don't have to say everything they can think of in order to get a point across.

GETTING OVER BREAKUPS

Charley, a mentee of mine, was a freshman in college, going through her first bad breakup with her high school boyfriend of a couple of years. At the same time, she was navigating the transition to college, making new friends, and living with a new roommate. On top of that, in her first year of school, her parents told her they were getting divorced and she had a death in the family. But what was consuming her most was her breakup.

Heartbreak is real for girls, and most of the time, they don't know how to cycle through the emotional pain they feel and soothe the feelings of loss. They may also be preoccupied wondering what the other person is up to. Here are some things that can help:

- *Resist the urge to get closure.* Talk to your daughter about how it actually feels and what it takes to get over someone. Oftentimes, it's not about hearing the exact apology or explanation you are looking for. It's not about expressing every thought and emotion. Getting over someone takes time.

- *Take space.* It's common for adolescents to stay in contact with their exes, particularly now, with the ease of text messaging, video chat, and social media.[155] They may text on a regular basis or even hang out as "friends." It's also common for them to break up and get back together repeatedly.[156] This behavior can be damaging, and prolong negative emotional experiences. Talk to your daughter about taking time to process her feelings before she jumps back into old patterns with her ex.

- *Curb digital surveillance*: In previous generations, girls simply wondered what their ex was up to. Now, they can watch it in real time. Some unhelpful behaviors include scrolling their ex's social media feeds and comments, and looking at what they are doing, who they are following, and who they are interacting with. If you notice that your daughter is doing this, talk to her about whether it's making her feel better or worse. The answer will inevitably be "worse"—and then encourage her to take a break, maybe from social media altogether.

- *Take time.* The same researchers at Stony Brook who highlighted the addictive quality of romantic love also found that the more time that had passed after students were broken up with, the less reactive their brains were to thoughts of their ex. Remind your daughter that time is a healer.

- *Move through (don't just think through) breakups.* Breakups are a physical as well as an emotional experience. Sleep, healthy foods, and exercise can help girls relieve stress, feel more confident, and bounce back faster.

- *Write the positives down.* Journaling has long been understood as an effective way to process emotions and clear the mind. Research shows that writing down the positive aspects of a breakup can help lessen negative emotions. This exercise can illuminate for your daughter the lessons she has learned and how she has grown as a person from an uncomfortable experience.[157]

- *Get distracted.* It's easy for girls to obsess. Tell her about the positive effects of getting distracted, by giving her brain a break from reliving and/or obsessing about her relationship. Encourage her to make plans with friends and focus on her goals, reassuring her that she won't always feel so bad and that focusing her energy on other things can help pass the time until she feels better.

- *Get support.* Your daughter doesn't have to be in the depths of despair and depression for counseling to help. Therapists can help untangle the complex emotions that come from breakups and help your daughter appreciate any lessons she's learned, despite the heartache. If you think that your daughter's breakup is weighing on her excessively, suggest that she talk to a professional.

HOW IT'S DONE

Do Say (If She's Breaking Up with Someone)

- Your goal should be to end it in a way that is as respectful and low drama as possible, so you can both move on.

- Privacy is really important in relationships. If someone shares something with you because they feel safe, you should think twice before sharing that information.

- You don't need to get the last word in. You could talk for hours and days and still not feel like you've said everything you want to. At a certain point, you just have to believe that you have said enough.

Do Say (If Someone Else Is Breaking Up with Her)

- You aren't going to feel this way forever.

- Do you want to talk about it? I'm here for you when you do.

- Let's go [insert fun, relaxing, distracting activity].

Don't Say (If She's Breaking Up with Someone)

- Tell him all the reasons he sucks.

- Let's start a rumor about him.

- Show him who's boss.

Don't Say (If Someone Else Is Breaking Up with Her)

- Just get over it.
- This wasn't real love.
- One day you'll realize that this relationship doesn't matter. (It matters very much to her right now.)

BEYOND THE CONVERSATION

MAKE PLANS WITH HER

If your daughter is going through a bad breakup, make some special plans with her. Go out in nature together, cook a meal, or pick another one of your favorite shared activities. Not only will you be gently encouraging her to shift her focus, even if temporarily as she processes her emotions, but you'll be making a good memory together in an otherwise dark time for her.

Sexual Misconduct

Taylor was sixteen when she met Raf through mutual friends. They first started talking at a party, exchanged numbers, and kept in close contact for a couple of weeks before Raf suggested they make it official, asking Taylor to be his girlfriend. She was excited to have her first boyfriend, and Raf had been so complimentary of her, sweet and attentive, taking an interest in getting to know her, and knowing just what to do and say to make her feel wanted and seen.

Soon, Raf began pressuring Taylor to have sex, and when she told him repeatedly over the next several weeks that she wasn't ready, he became increasingly aggressive and violent, ultimately raping her. "Saying no was not an option that I had," she recalled. When Taylor said she was going to tell someone what was happening, Raf threatened her with more violence, and Taylor feared for her life.

"I was trapped. I wasn't allowed to leave, and I remember thinking, 'If I was weak enough to get into this relationship, how could I possibly be strong enough to leave it?'" The sexual assaults continued for three months until Raf lost interest and broke up with her, telling her she wasn't "good enough" for him.

It would be two years before Taylor said a word to her parents. "I went through all that without anyone ever knowing," she said.

After she found the courage to tell her parents, Taylor's dad was distraught but found the strength to support her through the healing process. "My dad and I have always been tight. I look like my dad. I act like my dad. It was so painful to see the hurt in his eyes, seeing him realize that so much had happened under his nose. He had a lot of anger, and I had a lot of sadness. But he didn't try to fight his anger. He didn't try to fight my sadness. He didn't tell me to just 'get over it.' We weren't going to skip emotions. He let us be vulnerable and have that moment, together. He helped me find a counselor. He told me that if there was ever a time when I needed him, he was there to talk and listen, and that if anything like this ever happened to me again, that I should tell him immediately. And eventually, he asked me how he could help me move forward."

SOME BACKGROUND

Girls are vulnerable to acts of sexual misconduct, and even the most minor transgressions against young women can spur complex emotions, mark their memories, affect their views of themselves, and, in great part through the responses of those around them, shape their perspectives and expectations for how others will or should see and treat their bodies.

As with all other topics related to girls' sexuality, it can be tempting to take a vigilante tone when talking broadly about sexual misconduct or addressing an assault your daughter has weathered. There is nothing that I've seen bring out the protector in fathers more than this topic. It's understandable, but anger and vitriol can't inform your entire strategy for educating and supporting your daughter. Sexual misconduct is a complex issue, one that can require a delicate approach, and something that needs to be discussed and confronted at all levels—not only the most extreme.

THE LANGUAGE OF SEXUAL MISCONDUCT

Before we jump into statistics and strategies, let's start with some definitions. The language around sexual misconduct is evolving, but these terms will give you a good starting point for understanding this broad, sensitive topic. Later in the chapter, I'll go into additional detail about how you can address these topics with your daughter.

- **Sexual misconduct** is an umbrella term encompassing unwelcome, nonconsensual sexual behavior. Sexual misconduct includes sexual assault and harassment, stalking, rape, and intimate partner violence, among other acts.[158] Victims may be forced, manipulated, or coerced. And victims and perpetrators may be of any gender.

- **Sexual violence** (which includes sexual assault) refers to nonconsensual, unwanted sexual contact including rape, touching, or forced sexual acts.[159]

- **Intimate partner violence** is defined by the Centers for Disease Control and Prevention as "physical violence, sexual violence, stalking, or psychological harm by a current or former partner or spouse."[160] Intimate partner violence is an important category of sexual violence to highlight in conversations about sexual violence because there is a common misperception that sexual violence occurs only between strangers. In fact, as was the case in Taylor's story at the beginning of this section, intimate partner violence occurs at alarming rates with people girls know and may have current or previous relationships with.

- **Sexual consent** is an active agreement to be sexually intimate with another person. A person cannot give consent if they are being coerced or if they are physically unable to give consent, for instance, if they are drunk or unconscious.[161]

- **Victim-blaming** occurs when the responsibility or fault for sexual violence is placed on the victim rather than on the aggressor. The fear of victim-blaming is one of the primary reasons that victims fail to speak up and report what has happened to them.[162] Victim-blaming can sound like:

    "She was asking for it in that outfit."

    "She never should have gone to that party in the first place."

    "What was she doing out at that hour?"

- **Sexual harassment** refers to sexual comments, requests for sexual favors, and unwanted sexual advances taking place in educational or professional environments.[163] Importantly, as noted by the Rape, Abuse & Incest National Network (RAINN), "Sexual harassment does not always have to be specifically about sexual behavior or directed at a specific person."[164] General, negative remarks about a certain gender may fall under the category of sexual harassment.

THE FACTS ABOUT SEXUAL VIOLENCE AND YOUNG WOMEN

Sexual violence is cause of great concern because of the extreme, potentially damaging effects in the short and long-term.

- One in three women and one in four men report being victims of sexual violence in their lifetime.[165]
- One in three females who are victims of rape report that it happened between the ages of eleven and seventeen.[166]
- Sexual violence victims feel fearful, have concerns about safety, and struggle with post-traumatic stress disorder at higher rates than non-victims.[167]
- Sexual violence victims struggle with physical ailments including sleeplessness, irritable bowel syndrome, asthma, and headaches at higher rates than non-victims.[168]
- Sexual violence victims typically know the person subjecting them to sexual violence. Perpetrators might be current or former romantic partners, neighbors, family members, or friends.[169]
- On college campuses, women who identify as lesbian, gay, and bisexual are more likely to experience sexual assault than heterosexual women.[170]

- Individuals who identify as transgender, genderqueer, or gender nonconforming (TGQN) are more likely to experience sexual assault on college campuses than females.[171]

- Female college students have been found to report sexual violence only 20 percent of the time. Reasons young women fail to alert authorities when they are victimized include shame, fear of retaliation, and believing an incident wasn't serious enough to report.[172]

HOW TO KNOW IF SOMETHING HAS HAPPENED TO YOUR DAUGHTER

With hope, your daughter will feel comfortable coming to you and telling you if she has witnessed or been the victim of sexual violence. But it's very possible she could feel too embarrassed, upset, or uncomfortable to tell you. She also might feel ashamed, guilty, or concerned that she has violated cultural or religious norms.[173] She may worry that she'll be in trouble or that you won't believe her, even if you have always taken a warm and loving approach.[174] She might think that you'll be disappointed or overly worried or upset.

The following is a list of signs from RAINN (rainn.org) that your daughter might be struggling.[175] You'll notice that they overlap with symptoms of physical and mental health struggles not associated with sexual misconduct or violence, but it is worth asking some questions to see if the root of such symptoms could be trauma from a sexual encounter.

- Unusual weight gain or weight loss.

- Unhealthy eating patterns, like a loss of appetite or excessive eating.

- Signs of physical abuse, such as bruises.

- Sexually transmitted diseases (STDs) or other genital infections.

- Signs of depression, such as persistent sadness, lack of energy, changes in sleep or appetite, withdrawing from normal activities or friendships, or feeling "down."

- Anxiety or worry.

- Falling grades.

- Changes in self-care, such as paying less attention to hygiene, appearance, or fashion than usual.

- Self-harming behavior.

- Expressing thoughts about suicide or suicidal behavior.

- Drinking or drug use.

WHAT TO DO NEXT

If you find out that your daughter has been the victim of sexual violence, there are a few steps you can take immediately.

- Tell her you love her.

- Tell her you believe her.

- Ask her what she needs from you.

- Ensure she is okay in the moment. If she is calling you and is in danger, it goes without saying to focus on getting her to safety.

- If she has not sought it out herself, get her prompt medical attention, including a sexual assault forensic exam (rape kit), which can preserve important evidence in case of a legal proceeding.

- Contact law enforcement.

- Arrange for mental health counseling, even if she is openly discussing her situation with you. These events can stir unexpected, confusing, or overwhelming emotional reactions in the short- and long-term that can have repercussions into the future. Working with a mental health professional can support and speed healing.[176]

There is information you can pass along to your daughter to help her stay safe and know what to do if she finds herself victimized. These are some of the hardest, and possibly the most emotional conversations you will have. But they are essential in preparing your daughter for the worst while also signaling that you are there to support her, no matter what.

> **YOUR GOAL:** Educate your daughter on the risks and facts of sexual misconduct and what she can do to advocate for herself.

> **RULE #1:** Never victim-blame or slut-shame, whether you are talking in hypotheticals, commenting on someone who is not your daughter, or addressing a specific sexual misconduct incident. If your daughter were ever to find herself a victim of sexual misconduct, you don't want her thinking that you will judge her if she opens up to you about it. Also, we can prevent sexual misconduct by teaching people not to challenge others' personal boundaries and commit acts of sexual violence—not by policing victims more harshly.

TALKING POINTS

THE NATURE AND PREVALENCE OF
SEXUAL MISCONDUCT

Have some realistic conversations with your daughter about what sexual misconduct and violence is and isn't, what her rights are, and how people should treat her. It's also important to talk to her about how she should treat others. Girls are more vulnerable to victimization, but girls can also perpetrate sexual misconduct, and so it is important to instruct her about being mindful of others' boundaries. There's a cultural misconception that *only* females are sexual assault victims, but everyone needs to understand that people of all genders may be perpetrators as well as victims.

ACTION STEPS IF SHE IS SEXUALLY HARASSED

Your daughter needs to know that even though some sexual harassment may seem harmless, it is unacceptable and should serve as a red flag about the environments she finds herself in, at school, work, or in social settings. Being at the receiving end of or witnessing any of the following behaviors should be cause for concern:[177]

- Unwelcome comments about her own or other peoples' bodies.

- Unwelcome flirtation or discussion of sexual topics.

- Unwelcome touching, such as a back rub or even a hug that feels uncomfortable.

- Insinuations that engaging in sexual acts with a teacher, professor, or teaching assistant could help her grades or that

sexual acts with someone in the workplace could advance her
career.

• Comments of a sexual nature that don't relate directly to her
but that give rise to a lack of comfort with colleagues.

If your daughter encounters any of this behavior, she should talk
to someone in administration or human resources, and consider
switching classes or positions if circumstances don't change.

WAYS SHE CAN STAY SAFE WHEN
SEXUAL VIOLENCE IS A POSSIBILITY

While sexual misconduct is never the victim's fault, there are strategies your daughter can use to try to limit her vulnerability.

• *Teach situational awareness.*

- Emphasize to your daughter that she should be
mindful of and paying attention to her surroundings,
especially if she is in an unfamiliar or secluded place.
- Highlight the distractions phones can cause, and
encourage her to put her phone away while walking
from place to place.
- Make sure she knows not to go to secluded spaces
with people she doesn't know well.
- Talk to her about using a buddy system or having
friends look out for each other. For example, she and
her friends might plan to arrive at a house party
together and make sure they all leave together, not
letting any friend disappear to a stranger's
bedroom—especially if that friend has had too much
to drink.

- *Remind her to tune in to her gut feelings.* Girls should trust their intuition about their safety in different contexts. If your daughter has an uncomfortable feeling about her surroundings or the person she is with, tell her to remove herself from the situation as soon as possible.

- *Help her identify resources and come up with backup plans.* Encourage your daughter to always be thinking ahead about how she can remove herself from a bad situation. Who can your daughter call if she feels threatened, such as at a party or on a date? If she is out in public, are there security guards or restaurant managers she could speak to? What excuses can she make to get out fast?

- *Highlight the link between substance use and sexual violence.* As I've already detailed, alcohol and drugs can affect judgment and cut girls off from their gut feelings guiding them safely through situations. Girls should be coached to avoid substance consumption in situations where they feel insecure. They should be protective over their drinks to avoid being drugged, and keep track of how much they have had, if they do decide to consume. Girls should also be mindful of whether others around them are under the influence, as this can lead to uninhibited aggressive behavior.[178]

- *Encourage her to seek help and take action.* For girls wanting to stay safe on college campuses, RAINN highlights the opportunities to utilize campus resources such as security escorts and blue light systems. If necessary, students can also request housing changes, submit a Title IX complaint, or file temporary restraining orders.[179]

Her Role in Consent

If girls have been intimate with the perpetrator in the past or con-
sented to a certain level of intimacy (but not what occurred), girls
may feel at fault for being victimized. Tell her she can always say
"no," that an agreement to sexual intimacy is on her terms, and that
she should not be pushed. If she is, it isn't her fault.

Red Flags in Romantic Relationships

In the section on love on page 158, you'll find outlines for both
healthy relationship characteristics and red flags. Love can be blind-
ing, as we know, and so, in the context of conversations about sexual
violence, it is especially important to reinforce often to your daughter that she is deserving of respectful, loving treatment, and that
anything less is cause for concern. Given that the vast majority of
sexual assaults are carried out by someone known to the victim, your
daughter needs to be able to recognize the signs and take steps to
remove herself from threatening relationships.

What She Can and Should Do If She Has Been Victimized

Make sure your daughter knows the concrete steps she should take
in the event of an act of sexual violence:[180]

- Call 911 if she feels unsafe and needs help getting out of a
  situation.
- Call or text you to help her get the right medical attention,
  provide the emotional support she needs, and coordinate

logistics (for example, whether a friend or family member should go with her to the hospital or campus health services).

- She can also call the National Sexual Assault Hotline at 800-656-HOPE (4673), which will connect her with local resources, or she can text the Crisis Text Line (text 741741) if she doesn't feel comfortable talking or isn't in a location where she can talk.

- Seek immediate medical attention as soon as possible to address medical concerns (including injuries and possible transmission of STDs) and to collect evidence, potentially including the use of a rape kit. RAINN's website offers important recommendations for sexual assault forensic exams, including that victims avoid bathing, showering, or changing clothes, in order to best preserve evidence.[181] RAINN's website also explains the benefits of taking such exams, including that it increases the likelihood of prosecution of a perpetrator and gives the victim time to decide if they want to report the crime.

- Seek emotional support as soon as possible from a qualified mental health professional.

HOW SHE CAN HELP A FRIEND

You can encourage your daughter to use the aforementioned points to help someone she sees in need. In addition, always emphasize that if she knows about something that has happened, she shouldn't hold on to that information—it is imperative that she shares with an adult like yourself, a teacher, an administrator, or law enforcement, who can step in and provide the necessary support or response. Talking to your daughter about how to help a friend in need can be a good conversation starter, and a useful way of discussing the strategies she can use, herself, to stay safe or address a bad situation.

HOW IT'S DONE

Do Say

- You know I always want to help keep you safe. I have been alarmed by what I've read about sexual violence and the risk to young women. Can we talk about it? I'm interested to know what you've heard and learned at school.

- You get to decide who touches you, when, and how. Never be afraid to speak up and set your boundaries in relationships. (She will think this is *very* awkward. That's okay. The message is paramount.)

- Trust your gut feelings about what is safe and what isn't, and who you are safe with and who you aren't safe with.

- Drugs and alcohol will cut you off from your gut feelings. You should never use substances if you feel at all vulnerable in your surroundings.

- Avoid being in secluded circumstances with people you don't know well.

- Always have a backup plan. Circumstances can change quickly. Always know the fastest way to exit a situation, whether by walking away, getting a ride with a friend, or getting an Uber or Lyft.

- If anything ever happens to you, know it is not your fault.

Don't Say

- You're asking for trouble if you wear that.

- People get raped because they make bad decisions.

- If she (another person, not your daughter) was more confident and willing to set boundaries, this wouldn't have happened.

- What were you doing with that guy anyway?

BEYOND THE CONVERSATION

CONSIDER ENROLLING HER IN A SELF-DEFENSE CLASS

As I mentioned in the bullying section, just going through a training session can instill confidence, knowing she has a toolkit to call on if she were ever attacked. Self-defense will also increase your daughter's sense of situational awareness. If you can't get to a class, at least start by pulling up some YouTube videos to watch together.

IF YOU HAVE BEEN A VICTIM OF SEXUAL VIOLENCE, BE SURE YOU ARE RECEIVING THE SUPPORT YOU NEED.

Fathers who have been sexually assaulted, in their youth or otherwise, may worry about their ability to provide guidance to their girls on sexual matters. I have spoken with men who worry about whether they could inadvertently influence their daughters in negative ways because of their own discomfort with or overprotectiveness with sexuality. Being a parent with a history of abuse can make navigating these conversations much more painful. With some professional support, you can raise your comfort level so that you can have these important conversations with your daughter. Don't hesitate to speak to a licensed mental health professional to work through your own concerns and receive important direction on how to approach conversations with your daughter. The effects of sexual violence can be long-term and hard to untangle, but they can be addressed, providing an important sense of healing and relief.

Broaden Her Horizons

Academic Achievement

Education was a huge point of connection for my dad and me, as it can be for many fathers and daughters.

My dad jumped on any opportunity to coach me on mindset. He helped me form goals, stay focused on them, and celebrate when I achieved them. He was always there encouraging me to do my best, being proud of my report cards, reinforcing the value of academic achievement, arranging for extra help if I needed it, and making sure I knew what my options were for which high schools I could attend and colleges I could aim for.

I remember talking to him at the beginning of eighth grade as he methodically went through the reasons I should consider different high schools in the area. In December of my senior year of high school, he went to the post office with me to pick up my early-admission college acceptance letter and then jumped up and down with me, and our mailman, and my best friend, Cydney, when I opened and read it aloud. Years later, when we were at the Phoenix airport baggage claim, grabbing our bags for a father-daughter weekend, and I got the email notification that I got into grad school, he shouted, "Yes, honey! Unbelievable!" And then, unable to contain himself, explained to some onlooking strangers the reason for his excitement and that he was incredibly proud of me.

SOME BACKGROUND

The adolescent years come with increased academic responsibilities and greater expectations from teachers. Educational content is increasingly complex. Students are expected to be more organized, self-sufficient, and proactive when it comes to doing their homework, completing long-term projects, studying for tests, and asking for help and guidance. There are a wide range of responses to this reality: Some girls will dive in and engage out of curiosity and wonder; some will hunker down, as early as middle school, driven by the desire to gain acceptance to their top-choice colleges; some will be more interested in their extracurricular or social commitments; some will flounder; and some will start to question the whole enterprise of education, saying things like, "Why do I need to learn this anyway—it's not like I'll ever use it!" Regardless of what "type" of student your daughter is or what her motivations are, she will learn a lot in the middle and high school years, not just about specific subjects but about the habits that will set her up for personal and career success throughout her life.

Academics can be a great point of connection for dads and their girls.

> **YOUR GOAL:** Help her fulfill her personal academic potential (which may be different from what you think she

is or *should be* capable of), while encouraging the skills that prevent burnout.

RULE #1: Don't fixate on her grades. Instead, focus on her effort.

AND BONUS—RULE #2: Don't even think about tying grades to financial or other material rewards. I mentioned this in chapter 2, and academic achievement is one place I have seen parents try this. But trust me, this never goes well. It's a slippery slope, and it focuses your daughter on extrinsic rather than intrinsic rewards, which will drain her, and you, over time.

TALKING POINTS

When it comes to inspiring your daughter to reach her academic potential, you want to focus on some key building blocks of success.

EFFORT IS PARAMOUNT

Grades are important and play a significant role in determining the course of your daughter's academic future. But singular focus on specific point values or letter grades can:

- Undermine curiosity and prevent true learning, especially if your daughter is studying just to get a good grade and not to learn the material.
- Create an unhealthy preoccupation with rewards.

- Give rise to a fear of failure.

- Foster perfectionism.

- Create unnecessary and unproductive anxiety, especially if your daughter has a learning difference or other challenge that make it difficult for her to get the grades she wants.

Stanford professor Carol Dweck coined the term "growth mindset," which describes the idea that "the brain grows with effort."[182] "The growth mindset," as she describes in her book *Mindset: The New Psychology of Success*, "is based on the belief that your basic qualities are things you can cultivate through your efforts, your strategies, and help from others. Although people may differ in every which way— in their initial talents and aptitudes, interests, or temperaments— everyone can change and grow through application and experience." Dweck and her team found that when students were taught that intelligence could be developed, as opposed to being fixed, their effort, motivation, and achievement increased. This finding has proven to be game changing. Approaching a problem with a growth mindset has huge implications for perseverance and resilience—you can improve in math, you can master a challenging new language with effort over time. Emphasizing to your daughter that she can learn anything by working hard, practicing, and overcoming mistakes and failures can strengthen her growth mindset, setting her up to reach her potential in school and beyond.

DISCOVERING HER PERSONAL LEARNING STYLE

Does your daughter learn best by listening? By reading? By writing? What makes studying fun for her? Does she like to study in a certain place? Study for tests with groups of friends? Have you tested her on important content? Does she listen to music while memorizing? Color-code her flashcards?

Encourage your daughter to think about what works for her and to develop routines that boost her productivity. You can also ask her teachers to observe what works best in the classroom so that you can reinforce the most relevant strategies for your daughter at home. If your daughter has a learning difference, a learning specialist or educational therapist can help identify the tools and approaches that will work best for her. (More on this in chapter 4: "Building Your Support Team: Who and How to Call for Help.")

Importantly, in encouraging your daughter to find her personal learning style, resist the urge to compare her to her friends or siblings. Comparing herself to anyone could get your daughter down, and thinking that you may view her as "less than" in some way can be extremely deflating and demotivating.

Managing Technology Distraction

As I mentioned in the "Technology and Social Media" section (page 98), technology is a big source of distraction for students, even if they need it to do their homework.

Encourage your daughter to think about steps she can take to maximize her concentration, like putting her phone on airplane mode or leaving it in another room, or choosing a place to work, like the kitchen table, where other family members can keep her accountable for staying on task. You can also challenge your daughter to a distraction-free study session where she times how long it takes her to do her work versus how long it takes when she has her phone and checks social media or texts with friends.

Parents ask me if taking away technology would help, but it's simply not realistic, since students typically need computers and the Internet to do their work, or they need video chat for online classes, homework, or group projects. In these cases, your daughter could benefit from having a program on her device that can block certain distracting sites. Many of these programs are easily downloadable for little to no cost. For up-to-date suggestions, ask the technology expert at your daughter's school.

THE POSITIVE IMPACTS OF COMMUNICATING WITH TEACHERS

Academic achievement isn't just about work product, just as accolades and promotions in the workplace aren't just about deliverables. What many students don't realize is that many factors can affect their achievement, including the way they present themselves in the classroom, how neat their work is, the time they take to get to know their teachers, and the way they show they are paying attention in class. Your daughter needs to know that turning work in on time, showing extra effort by setting up periodic meetings with teachers, making eye contact and positive contributions in class (even if your daughter feels shy or uncomfortable), and being a collaborative and contributing group project participant can all help. Teachers appreciate students who are proactive and engaged. It never hurts to be labeled as a conscientious student. If your daughter gets to know her teachers, they can be mentors and advocates for her, including when she applies to college. And all of these proactive habits will also give your daughter additional opportunities to engage with her learning, helping her get the most out of it.

Asking for Extensions

I was working in Houston, Texas, when Hurricane Harvey devastated the city in 2017. I had dozens of conversations with students who were concerned about not having their homework done on time. Some of them had lost their home computers and all their possessions—in some cases, their entire homes. They didn't have Wi-Fi. They didn't have quiet places to do their work because they were staying in hotel rooms with their families or in the homes of family friends and relatives. They were weathering tremendous chaos, grief, and uncertainty, many of them for monthlong periods after the storm. From where I was sitting, their homework was the last thing that mattered, but they were still worried about disappointing their teachers or getting markdowns or zeros. This happens all the time when things go wrong in students' personal lives: when their parents are going through divorces, when siblings have health issues, when there are deaths in the family. Students worry about their grades and their ability to continue meeting expectations at school. What they don't realize is that in these situations, they can and should ask for support and extensions at school.

I always say to students, "I understand why you're nervous about not being able to get your homework done on time, but we adults know that life is in session, that there will be days when things go wrong, when you can't get your homework done, and when you need a breather, or a little extra time. It's okay to be real with your parents and teachers about that." Similarly, your daughter may find it helpful if you talk to her about times in your adult life when your plans were disrupted or you had to ask for an extension.

Self-advocacy is a key skill your daughter needs, and encouraging her to speak up for herself in her toughest moments will give her practice and confidence to ask for what she needs in school and in future professional environments later on.

EXCELLENCE IS MORE IMPORTANT THAN PERFECTION

Perfectionism can lead to extra stress, and paradoxically, a lack of productivity. As perfectionist students strive to turn in flawless assignments or get one hundreds on assessments, they can spend excessive time focused on the details of assignments and become paralyzed in their work, fearing that their best efforts will not be good enough. They may come apart over a few points lost on a quiz or test, even if their performance was excellent.

When I talk to girls with perfectionistic inclinations, I find it helpful to focus on excellence over perfection. If a girl believes that she can perform highly and desires to, I don't fight that narrative. Instead, I show her how strong work doesn't have to be perfect. Here are some of the sound bites I use:

- You can still get an excellent grade, even if you have a few points deducted.

- Excellent grades fall in ranges, which is how colleges view them. Colleges and employers aren't concerned with whether you receive every single point on an assignment, test, or assessment.

- The most successful people in academia and business make mistakes regularly and learn from them.

- Done is better than perfect. Sometimes you just have to be done with an assignment, even if you don't think it's perfect.

A lot of times, you'll be surprised that the feedback you get will be positive.

THE BENEFITS OF HEALTHY TEST PREP

Your daughter will have no shortage of tests. Many students will leave studying until the very last minute, staying up late with pots of coffee, cramming. In a way, it's a rite of passage. But the most stress-free way to get good grades is by:

- Paying attention in class.
- Taking good notes and keeping materials organized at all times.
- Taking advantage of review time with teachers.
- Starting to study days in advance.
- Eating healthy foods for performance (rather than coffee and candy to stay awake).
- Getting good nights of sleep leading up to assessments.

ACADEMIC SUPPORT IS AVAILABLE

In addition to going to teachers for extra help, your daughter should know that there are a lot of different resources to turn to if she wants additional explanation on specific topics or help mastering study strategies and skills like paper writing or public speaking. Encourage your daughter to ask teachers about outside resources, trusted online platforms, or student mentors or tutors who can help her.

If it's a subject you feel comfortable with, offer to help her and then schedule a time to make sure it happens. Be sure you understand what the teacher is trying to teach and how they are teaching.

If you don't know the new math, learn it—but don't teach the old math. You can confuse and frustrate your daughter (and find yourself feeling frustrated) if you leap in with a different method than the one she is learning at school.

ACADEMIC INTEGRITY

Today's adolescents can actually receive too much help. During video-chat homework sessions, students write answers down that one or two people have come up with. Many students are "doing work" but not putting in any thought or effort because friends are doing the thinking for them. Your daughter needs to be mindful of how this affects her learning and how it can put her at a disadvantage when it comes to studying for tests, which she is more likely to feel unprepared for.

Given the ease with which students can pull information off the Internet, it's especially important to talk to your daughter about academic honesty. Most of the time, kids understand that it's a bad idea to buy papers on the Internet or pay people to write original papers for them. Things get fuzzier with regard to citations and paraphrasing, or parents and tutors editing their work. Girls should be well aware of their school's honor code and be on top of the details with regard to listing sources they cited, quoted, or relied on in academic papers.

Resist the urge to overcontribute to your daughter's projects or overedit any of your daughter's work. This goes for English essays, history papers, take-home Spanish quizzes, college-application essays, and any other assignment you can think of for which it might be tempting to take over. Teachers and college-application essay readers know what seventeen-year-old writing sounds like, and they know what adult writing sounds like. You will be doing your daughter a giant disservice if you override her voice. Remember that it's okay for her work to be imperfect and for teachers to correct her. If you play the role of super corrector, you can give rise to self-doubt in your daughter, undermining her confidence, robbing her of the chance to learn, and sending a message that she is not capable—when she is, of course, more than capable.

THE IMPORTANCE OF TAKING BREAKS

Broad cultural messages often wrongly tie busy-ness to productivity. While there are times when all of us have to stay up late and put in extra hours to make a deadline, downtime also plays a huge role in achievement. Talk with your daughter about the importance of breaks to clear and rest her mind. Taking time away can also help with inspiration. If your daughter has been working for a long time and still hasn't finished an assignment or mastered a concept, encourage her to switch her focus to another assignment, sleep on it, and then come back to it.

HOW IT'S DONE

Do Say

- You put in so much work, and it paid off.

- Your work ethic is really impressive.

- What strategies can you use to learn this concept?

- Don't be afraid to challenge yourself. Stretching yourself mentally helps your brain grow.

- Every time you challenge yourself, you prepare yourself better to tackle new concepts in the future.

Don't Say

- You don't try hard enough.

- Don't you care about your schoolwork?

- You'll never succeed in the real world if you don't do well in school.

- Why can't you be more like your [sister/brother]?

- You may not be good at this subject, but you are great at others.

- It's okay, honey, it's just [algebra/trigonometry/calculus], you'll never have to use that.

BEYOND THE CONVERSATION

EXPLORE POTENTIAL LEARNING DIFFERENCES

If your daughter exhibits a combination of the following symptoms, she might have a learning difference:[183]

- Disorganization.

- Doing exceptionally well in one subject but not in others.

- Missing or being late on assignments.

- Difficulty focusing in class.

- Memory challenges.

- Trouble picking out important points from readings, notes, or class lectures.

- Easily distracted or impulsive.

- Studying for tests but still performing poorly.

- Test anxiety.

- Taking too long to finish tests.

- Avoiding school.

- Getting emotional and frustrated about schoolwork.

I go into detail in the coming chapter, "Building Your Support Team: Who and How to Call for Help," about reaching out to your daughter's school counselor or learning specialist to ask them if teachers have noticed anything concerning. It could well be that any of these behaviors add up to little more than the normal challenges of development. But these symptoms can also be indicative of depression, eating disorders, and other challenges teenagers face, so you want to gather information. If you decide to have your daughter tested for learning differences, ask the school for a reference. While academic assessments are not covered by insurance, there are cost-effective options.

College Admissions

"How's it going?" I asked my friend Julie, a college counselor at a high school. It was the fall, the height of admissions season, not just for college-bound seniors but also for juniors feeling the pressure starting to mount.

"Oh, you know, just living my best life," she said on FaceTime, with a chuckle and an overwhelmed half smile. "The kids are on edge. The parents are worse. I just try to calm everyone down all day, every day."

SOME BACKGROUND

The traditional college-admissions process (which is what this section focuses on) is a gateway to an exciting phase of life for college-bound teenagers, but as you know, it can also be stressful and overwhelming for students and their parents alike. Of course, some girls are recruited athletes or have another guarantee for admission (for example, in some states, students in the top 10 percent of their classes are automatically admitted to the flagship state university), which can lessen the intensity of the process and/or shorten it—but most will apply through traditional channels, on the traditional timeline. Years of preparation and anticipation lead up to major application submission deadlines. Prepping for standardized tests, writing essays, asking for reference letters, and filling out financial aid applications is a heavy lift on top of students' existing academic, extracurricular, social, and familial commitments. On high school campuses, kids play off each other's anxiety for months leading up to decision time, which can create awkward competition among classmates and friends. In the age of social media, the process can feel especially public, as acceptance letters start rolling in and students and parents start posting their successes. If your daughter is college-bound, she's feeling some of the intensity.

YOUR GOAL: Take some pressure off a stressful process by helping your daughter understand all her options.

RULE #1: Play it cool, even if you are freaking out about where she'll get in. Your daughter has enough to worry about without also being concerned about how her successes, failures, or decisions might affect you in the admissions process.

TALKING POINTS

The worry about whether they will get into their "top choice" schools is the biggest stressor for most girls I see. The truth is, while select "elite" schools have extraordinarily competitive acceptance rates, the majority of universities accept most applicants.[184] If your daughter wants to go to college, she'll get in (as long as she follows some basic recommendations), and she'll go somewhere great. If she can plan for multiple scenarios for her college experience, she'll be able to relax more while she is waiting to see where she's heading.

FINDING THE RIGHT FIT

Talk with your daughter about what she wants out of college, what her priorities are (academically, athletically, socially, and in terms of culture), and try to understand her motivations for applying to different schools.

There is much more to colleges—and the college-application process—than name brands, prestige, and rankings. These factors don't account for how good a fit a school will be for your daughter. And if your daughter has a specific interest, whether that's volleyball, studio art, business, or robotics, the typical rankings like those of *U.S. News & World Report* may not accurately reflect what schools will be the best for her, given her interests.

When you focus on fit, you are empowering your daughter to think about what she will contribute to a school community and what a school can offer her. For your daughter, this can help her think about her agency to *choose* a place that is right for her, rather than simply wondering if she is "good enough" to be chosen.

HIGHLIGHT ALL THE GREAT OPTIONS

I am going to pull a page out of my own dad's playbook here, because he shined when I was applying to schools. He wasn't perfect. He drove me nuts proofreading my essays—I remember vividly our extreme differences of opinion with regard to comma placement. But my dad was also my main guide during my college visits and applications. Looking back, I remember that time in life as being more illuminating and exciting than stressful and overwhelming, in great part because of him.

My dad never let me get too attached to a single plan or narrative about where I would go to college. He ordered brochures from lots of different schools (this was before all colleges had robust websites). He took me to public and private universities, local schools and campuses on the other side of the country. We explored all the possibilities. My dad was constantly pointing out the unique details of student life at different schools, which really helped me envision my life and potential happiness in several different places—and not get completely focused on going to one school. He turned on a football game on TV for one school so we could watch together, and he insisted I listen to the fight song. When we visited Philadelphia, he walked me through the historic parts of the city and bought me my first cheese-steak. On a road trip through the South, he took me to get authentic barbecue. His constant and specific support for every school we looked at helped me feel relaxed and excited about my choices. My dad was able to travel with me, but these days, it's easier than ever to pull up college websites and take video tours of their campuses. You can do everything my dad did right from your house, and make a similar impact.

THE "WORST-CASE" SCENARIOS

If your daughter has any moments of panic or despair, wondering what will happen if she doesn't get in somewhere she wants to go, take the opportunity once again to talk through the options. Reassure your daughter that people go to colleges all the time that they didn't necessarily think they would like and end up thriving. And talk about what happens if someone doesn't like where they end up, such as the possibilities of transferring or taking some time off to gain work experience.

NAVIGATING TRICKY, COMPETITIVE FRIENDSHIP DYNAMICS

"One of the hardest things I have ever had to witness was when my daughter's friends weren't happy for her when she got accepted to her top-choice college," one father told me in my interviews for this book. What he said exemplifies a common problem: the tension that can arise among friends before and as college letters start coming in. Comparing grades, standardized test scores, and GPAs are all common practice among high schoolers, as much as we wish they would keep it all to themselves. Students find it difficult to focus just on themselves and their own potential because they have to face realities like class rank and the knowledge that "top" schools have limited spots. It's no wonder that girls' friendships get disrupted. Here are some tips you can give your daughter to help her stay out of the fray:

- Focus on your own journey, knowing you will end up at a great school for you.

- Talk about college with people who can be there for you right now.

- Do your best not to share and compare your scores with friends. It only makes people nervous.

- Have compassion and patience for friends who are really stressed and might not be their best selves right now.

- At the same time, if a friend is being exceptionally unkind or unsupportive, you can take some distance from them.

PREPARING FOR COLLEGE LIFE

College life is true practice for independent adult life, especially if your daughter is living away from your house. The transition to college will be one of the biggest she will ever experience, and if you have covered the topics in earlier sections of this book with her, she will be well prepared to meet any challenges that arise. Some issues that you will want to be aware of and make your daughter aware of ahead of time include:

- *Unhealthy lifestyles.* With no parents around, less structured schedules, lots of fun things to do, people to hang out with, and junk food and alcohol at the ready any time of day, college students are known to deprioritize sleep, good nutrition, and fitness. Emphasize the importance that your daughter continue to take care of herself so that she can feel her best and do her best.[185]

- *Roommate conflicts.* Living in close quarters means there will be some boundaries to negotiate, some miscommunication, and most likely, a little bit of cabin fever. Talk to your daughter about how she might handle different scenarios, how she can be a good roommate, and what her plan will be if she and any roommate(s) get into any disagreements.

- *Loneliness and homesickness.* It's normal to feel out of sorts when you have a major shift in your routine and when you are trying to find your true friends. Talk about how your daughter can keep feeling connected as she finds her way at college. She can call you and her high school friends, but she should also identify adults on campus she can go to for support. Research the role of resident advisers, dean's office hours, and her college's mental health services, so if she's having an off day, she'll know where to go. And encourage her to participate in student groups and campus activities—a great way to meet new people and find new friends.

HOW IT'S DONE

Do Say

- You have as good a shot as anyone of getting in.

- We're going to do our best to position you to get into your top-choice school, but there are a lot of places where you can be happy and successful.

Don't Say

- You're going to go to [X college], just like me!

- If you don't study hard now, you'll never get into college.

- Don't apply to [school], that's for people with much [better/worse] grades than you. (It's important to cast a wide net, with both "reaches" and "safety" schools.)

- Don't apply to [school], because it's too expensive and I don't know if we can afford it. (Depending on your financial situation and your daughter's profile, she could receive merit or need-based financial aid at a school that could defray most or all costs of attendance. Many students pay less to attend a top-ranked, out-of-state college than to attend their local state university—for example, Harvard costs less than a public university for more than 90 percent of American families.)[186]

BEYOND THE CONVERSATION

DO YOUR OWN RESEARCH

Make sure that you understand the timeline and how you can help, starting when your daughter is a high school freshman (like keeping a running list of her accomplishments for the résumé portion of her applications). Talk to your daughter's school about any recommendations they have in terms of preparing your daughter. Also ask how they will support her as a college-bound student. Ideally, your daughter will receive personalized attention, help strategizing which schools to apply to (both in-state and out-of-state, and taking into account financial aid options), when to apply to them (in the case of early or rolling applications), and who to ask for reference letters. If you aren't satisfied with the level of support your daughter will be receiving from her school, look into local nonprofits that help college-bound teens or an independent college counselor you can hire to help you and your family navigate the admissions process.

Career

Jaime Casap has two daughters, twenty-two years apart. In her words and his, here's what happened after Elaine, his older daughter, came to him and said she wanted to be a marketing major in college.[187]

ELAINE: *The time came when I was going to apply to school, and I was trying to decide on my college major. I always thought of school and getting my degree in terms of what was practical and safe and what would help me get a job. I thought about science for a while. I came up with the idea of being an immunologist, and my dad said, "Is that really what you want to do? Can you get more specific about why?" I thought it over, and then I went to him in another conversation and said, "I think I am going to be a marketing major. I looked at jobs, and marketing seems to be the closest major that would allow me to find a job in something that I'm good at and passionate about. There aren't a lot of 'help wanted' ads for directors." And he was like, "I'm not paying for college if you do that."*

JAIME: *This is a kid that had been making movies since she was five years old, on whatever device she could get her hands on. She'd made hundreds of movies. In fifth grade, she started the media club at her school and broadcasted the news to students every day. I said, "If you're a film major in the* *arts department, I'll pay for that." I made her be a film major, because I knew that's who she was.*

ELAINE: *When I started film school, teachers constantly talked about how most of us would not even work in film, that work experience is the most important thing you can equip yourself with. That scared me into reaching out and trying to find video work as a student. My first gig was for a national food chain, and they asked me to film something that night. I called my dad panicking, and he gave me his very expensive camera, reassuring me that I could do it.*

I never gave the camera back and used it for the next four years to make all kinds of videos for work and school. I would always send him my finished videos. He was always willing to help my school projects by letting me use his house for a film set, borrow my siblings as extras, and my dad was even one of the main characters in my senior capstone project.

After graduation, I was picking up freelance gigs. I was driving to different states. I kept moving up in the industry. Every time I got a new project that I was scared of, I would call my dad, and he would say, "You can do this. This is why you were hired." I just needed to hear him say, "You got this." He's my rock. He stands for what I believe in.

JAIME: *We have mentor checks. When she's in New York, I call her every once in a while to see how she's doing, but most of the time, she'll text me or call me. She's like, "Are you busy? I need your input," or "I need to vent," or "I need your take on something." And it's just me, providing her thousands of dollars' worth of career advice for free.*

ELAINE: *When I got to New York, I was working freelance, and when you're doing that, all you want is to go full-time. I was making videos for this big tech company, and they were about to hire me full-time. Out of nowhere, I got this phone call from a TV station who wanted me to work two days a week. I called my dad and said, "I have this full-time job offer but then* *network TV just called me for two days a week, meaning I would basically have to go back to freelance. What should I do?" And he said, "Well, why are you in New York?" And I said, to live here and work. And he said, "No, why are you actually in New York?" And I said, "Because I want to work in TV." And he said, "Well, is this tech company TV?" And I said, "No, it's not." That was a pivotal moment for me. I said "no" to the full-time job, and I picked up two days a week editing clips, and then from there, I moved full-time into the branded content studio at the parent company, a major news network.*

JAIME: *When I wanted to launch my YouTube channel, I called her and said, "Hey, where do I start?" She laughed for ten minutes, and then she said, "Just write this down." She said, "Shoot at 1080. You don't need to shoot in 4K. Shoot at 24 frames per second. Double your shutter speed to 50, and keep your ISO at 100. Just keep those settings, and if you want to slow down footage, then you want to increase your frame rate to about 60 or 120, but you're going to need to double your frame rate, which is going to lower the amount of light that you get in. You're going to need a lot light if you do that and if you go outside it actually will blow out your exposure. So you want an ND filter for that." And I said, "Cool. Thank you for all that information. Okay, here's my next question: What do any of those things mean?" I knew zero, but I'm learning.*

ELAINE: *I'm at the point now where I can compete with my dad, since he's starting to vlog [video blog].*

JAIME: *And now, we have this fun banter where I'll say, "I got three hundred thirty views on my YouTube channel for my latest video," and she'll say, "That's great. I got twenty-five million."*

ELAINE: *The best part of that story is that my little sister will be there chanting, "Elaine has more! Elaine has more!"*

SOME BACKGROUND

Women's participation in the labor force has grown significantly since the 1950s. According to the Bureau of Labor Statistics, in 1950, 18.4 million women participated in the labor force, making up about one-third of the total labor force. By 2024, it is projected that 77.2 million women will participate in the labor force, making up a 47.2 percent share of the total.[188] If your daughter decides to work outside the home, she'll have vast opportunities to take advantage of, whether she works for others or starts her own business. However, despite great advancements and opportunities for professional women, men continue to hold the majority of top leadership positions and outearn women as a general rule. In addition, while now under public scrutiny, harassment of and discrimination against women in the workplace remains widespread. Like all young people, your daughter will have a lot to learn about being successful in the professional world. But she will also have to be aware of and learn to circumvent the particular challenges facing women in their careers.

The gender pay gap is an ever-present obstacle to women's professional advancement. In the United States, women make about eighty cents for every dollar men make, and the gap widens greatly for women of color.[189]

Equal Pay Day, launched in 1996, is a public awareness campaign shedding light on this phenomenon. Each year, Equal Pay Day is the date all women working full-time would have to work until in order to make the same amount of money their male counterparts were paid the previous year. In 2021, Equal Pay Day fell on

March 24. Thus, on average, women would have to work nearly a full three months more than men, in the same jobs, in order to make the same amount of money.[190] It's a staggering difference. But when their wages were compared to those of white, non-Hispanic men, Equal Pay Day fell on August 13 for Black women, October 1 for Native American women, and October 29 for Latina women.

In addition to working in lower-paying jobs than men and being paid less for comparable work, women face obstacles to promotions. In a viral 2018 article for the *New York Times* titled "The Top Jobs Where Women Are Outnumbered by Men Named John," reporters Claire Cain Miller, Kevin Quealy, and Margot Sanger-Katz shed light on the absence of women in leadership.[191] They listed key professional positions where the percentage of men with the same name is higher than the percentage of women in the position, including directors of top one hundred grossing films (8 percent named James or Michael versus 7 percent female), Republican senators (14 percent named John versus 12 percent female), and Democratic governors (19 percent named John versus 13 percent female). This was a bit of a tongue-in-cheek approach to exposing a pervasive issue women face, but it's based on a cold, hard truth.

Why do these inequities persist? There are many reasons for the lack of gender parity in the workforce. Conscious and unconscious bias and discrimination continue to adversely affect women, despite extensive evidence that supporting women boosts the bottom line.[192] But there's also research to suggest that women self-promote and self-advocate less often than men do, which can lead to money left on the table and slowdowns in their careers.[193]

Your daughter's success in the workplace depends not just on building professional skills but also on learning to believe in herself, negotiating fearlessly, and addressing gender bias and discrimination head-on. You can coach her while she is still living under your roof.

> **YOUR GOAL:** Help your daughter recognize and develop the concrete skills she needs to capitalize on every future career opportunity.

> **RULE #1:** Support and encourage your daughter in the activities she chooses, but don't emphasize career-building and future accomplishments so much that your daughter begins to define her identity based on them. As you know, directly or indirectly encouraging girls to measure their self-worth and define themselves by the strength of their achievements breeds perfectionism, self-doubt, and confidence gaps.

TALKING POINTS

HER CURRENT SKILLS ARE TRANSFERRABLE

Through her academic classes, activities like sports and arts, and yes, her social life, your daughter is gaining experiences that she will expand and be able to draw upon throughout her life and career. "Real life" can seem like a long way away for adolescent girls, who often wonder if they will use anything they learn in school when they "grow up" or start working.

In addition to being Elaine's dad, Jaime Casap, who I quoted at the beginning of this section, is an educator and leading expert on the future of work. For years, he was Google's chief education evangelist, and he consults with educators, school districts, and educational organizations striving to innovate educational policies and practices. If you listen to his talks, you'll hear him speak on the competencies young people will need to succeed. "Do they know how to learn? That is the question I ask," he says as he goes on to highlight categories of skills that are of utmost importance, including problem-solving, critical thinking, communication, and collaboration.[194]

It's true that your daughter may forget or ultimately find useless some (or most) of the content she is learning now, but whether or not she realizes it, she is honing numerous skills she will be able to use in the future. Transferable skills your daughter is learning in middle and high school include:

- Critical thinking.
- Research and writing.
- Statistical literacy (increasingly important in the era of big data).
- Technology use and management, including familiarity with some of the programs used in a professional setting like Microsoft Word, Excel, and PowerPoint.
- Project management on larger and longer-term assignments.
- Personal focusing strategies.
- Collaboration strategies gained through group projects.
- Negotiating power structures while interacting with teachers and administrators.

- Practicing résumé writing by translating her accomplishments and skills into a college application or for an internship or job.

- Crafting cover letters in the form of personal statements on college applications.

- Networking.

- Connecting with mentors who can guide her and write letters of recommendation.

- Internship and job research.

- Informational interviewing for school projects.

- Writing thank-you notes and correspondence.

SHE DOESN'T HAVE TO BE THE "BEST STUDENT" TO SUCCEED IN BUSINESS

As a father, you may experience worry if you feel like your daughter "underperforms" in academic settings. My own dad can relate.

My parents fought with my sister, Robin, throughout her high school years about all the time she spent talking on the phone. She was chatting with her friends and boyfriend at all hours, tying up the landlines, and not—from my parents' point of view—satisfactorily focusing on her schoolwork. While I was super stressed about getting my work done all the time and my parents struggled to help me relax, my sister was more focused on sports and her social life. But today, one of the running jokes in my family is my dad apologizing to Robin for all the times he got mad at her for being on the phone. She's an executive recruiter with a thriving national business, who spends her days on the phone with candidates and employers. And my dad makes this half-kidding apology to her every time she closes a deal. My sister's social skills, her ability to network, and her true empathy for and interest in people are arguably what have made her so successful in business. Simply by being herself, she was preparing for her career all along.

Traditional schooling encourages and rewards following directions, being respectful in the classroom, handing in assignments on time, and getting the right answers. Students who don't identify as "academic," who have learning differences, who don't get what they perceive to be good grades, or don't find themselves to be teachers' favorites can be left feeling like they don't have a lot to offer academically, and by extension, professionally. Regardless of how your daughter is doing in school, focus on her strengths and help her understand that her natural qualities and the skills she is building upon will benefit her in professional contexts.

ESSENTIAL LESSONS FOR EXCELLENCE IN THE WORKPLACE

Consider what you know about being effective in a job, and let your daughter in on the secrets early. Here are a few lessons to emphasize:

- *Get comfortable with a learning curve.* Emphasize to your daughter that it is okay if she doesn't know everything and needs to ask for help. As you well know, young people think they know a lot, more than most adults around them.

- *Take educated risks.* Spending years in school following directions can kill creativity and confidence. Encourage her to be bold and to take it in stride if her ideas get shot down.

- *Go above and beyond, looking for opportunities to get experience and master new skills.* Work can be fun if people feel like they are growing and learning in a field that they are passionate about. Your daughter should strive for excellence, build her own sense of accomplishment, and show bosses and colleagues that she is a positive, contributing member of the team.

- *Observe leaders around you.* What makes people successful in one field may be different from what makes people successful in another. If your daughter has a certain career goal in mind, encourage her to research and observe standouts in her field.

- *Surround yourself with mentors and advocates.* The power of mentorship cannot be underestimated. Encourage your daughter from an early age to reach out to people other than you and build her personal support network.

NEGOTIATION ISN'T ALWAYS COMFORTABLE, BUT IT'S STILL ESSENTIAL

Explain to your daughter that negotiating job offers and higher salaries and self-advocating for career advances isn't always comfortable, but is essential for professional growth. Money isn't the most relaxing or comfortable topic to discuss, especially if it's with a boss you are afraid of upsetting in any way. For women, this fear isn't entirely farfetched. As Hannah Riley Bowles wrote in the *Harvard Business Review*, "Women get a nervous feeling about negotiating for higher pay because they are intuiting—correctly—that self-advocating for higher pay would present a socially difficult situation for them—more so than for men."[195] Specifically, the "social cost" for women negotiating is higher than it is for men (research study participants indicate that they would be less willing to work with women who negotiate). Most published studies find that there is a significant social cost to women negotiating pay, but not a significant social cost to men.

Still, if your daughter is already at an age where she is negotiating her first paycheck, even if it's for babysitting, tutoring, or a retail job at a local store, help her research pay in her field and strategize how she might maximize her income. If she feels extremely uncomfortable advocating for herself, it is worth considering whether she is working in an equitable workplace, or if she should look for another job.

SPEAK UP AND/OR GET OUT WHEN THERE IS A PROBLEM

The fact is, many people are afraid of their bosses, afraid of looking too high-maintenance, and afraid of losing their jobs or compromising future career opportunities if they bring up a concerning issue. Help your daughter understand that it's her right to speak out against injustices she experiences or sees. She always has the option, if she feels her work environment is toxic, to get out of it.

SUCCESS IS BUILT ON FAILURES

Young people often don't grasp the importance and common nature of making mistakes, of acting on ideas that didn't work well, of giving something your all and still not achieving your goal. Talk to your daughter not just about the importance of learning from mistakes, but also the realities of recovering and growing from them. You can talk with your daughter about failure in the context of academics, sports, or her other activities. You can also take the opportunity to draw from your own experiences. Another great way to broach the topic of failure is by reading or watching shows or movies about your daughter's role models. In recent years, public figures have frequently opened up about their biggest failures and letdowns. Read a book, stream a YouTube video, or watch a movie about someone your daughter looks up to in the public sphere. Talk with her about whether that person's story surprised her and what she thinks the biggest challenges are that the person has overcome in their careers.

SHE SHOULDN'T MAKE UNNECESSARY APOLOGIES

Women apologize more than men.[196] I see it all the time with my students, who apologize for taking my time. "Ms. Wolf, I'm sorry to bother you." "Ms. Wolf, I'm sorry to take your time, I know you are busy." "I know you are probably so busy, I am sorry to ask, but can you write my college recommendation letter?" The apologies go on and on, and rarely are they warranted. Teaching your daughter to apologize only when it's necessary is a way to boost her self-esteem by helping her recognize her self-worth in a very concrete way. She deserves to be in conversation with people, to make her voice heard. If you catch your daughter apologizing unnecessarily, bring it to her attention. If you know that she has a conversation coming up with a teacher, mentor, or boss, be explicit in telling her not to apologize for taking up their time. One approach you can encourage for your daughter is to thank people for their time. Expressing gratitude has a very different feel and effect than apologizing.

YOUR EXPERIENCES CAN INFORM HER

Let her in on what's happening for you at work. Talk about your career path, how you learned what you know, your favorite accomplishments, and your greatest challenges, failures, and triumphs. Talk about how you treat people, your company's policies, and how your company supports women. Your experiences and those of your wife or partner and other adults in your daughter's life can inform her, so don't hesitate to talk about yourself, and how you and others make a living or contribute to the family.

Better yet, talk about how *you* support women at your workplace. When you collaborate with women on projects, or promote women on your teams and in your organization, tell your daughter about it. You'll not only have something inspiring to talk to her about, but you will show her that you're setting an example, engaging in equitable practices, and paving the way for her own future achievement by contributing to a cultural shift that will benefit all women in the long term.[197]

HOW IT'S DONE

Do Say

- In what ways do you want your work to contribute to the world?

- Your work product is a reflection of you.

- The greatest successes you see in business, and the people who have accomplished the things you hope to accomplish, have worked long and hard and overcome challenges to reach their goals.

Don't Say

- You better do well on your test on Friday, or you are never going to get a good job.

- How do you expect to get a good job if all you are doing is socializing all the time? (Remember the story about my sister,

Robin, the successful executive recruiter, who spent so much time socializing, much to our parents' dismay—only for us all to realize that her socializing *was* preparing her to excel in the workplace.)

- If you don't learn how to [fill in the blank], you will never be successful.

BEYOND THE CONVERSATION

Your daughter is doing a lot now that will inform her work life later on. Here are a few things you can do with her now to expand her knowledge of the working world, teach her the language of business, and give her valuable experiences she can draw on later.

- *Bring her to work.* Do you work outside the home? Can you bring her along one day so that she can see what you do, who you interact with, and how you conduct yourself? She'll learn from your example.

- *Write some cover letters with her.* I first encountered this exercise working as a mentor for WriteGirl, a Los Angeles–based nonprofit supporting at-risk girls through creative instruction. I do mock cover letters with students as early as eighth grade because highlighting our best personal qualities doesn't always come naturally, and we can never get too much practice talking up our strengths.

  Working on cover letters is one way not only to help your daughter think about what she's good at but also how she might go about communicating what she has to offer. Encourage her to consider her dream position and write a cover letter that references skills she currently holds that would qualify her to be a productive team member. If she is applying to jobs or internships, offer to help her prepare or edit her materials. Talk her through it, focusing on her strengths and pointing out anything she may not be thinking about.

* *Help her build a positive online presence.* Don't forget the tips I mentioned in the section on social media and technology (page 98). More and more college-admissions officers and employers are researching applicants online. Help your daughter set up personal web pages, including a LinkedIn page (once she meets the age requirements), so people can easily find and learn about her accomplishments, and so she can start building her network of contacts and mentors, even if it's just you and a few adult relatives to start.

Financial Literacy

Gabriela was my college roommate and one of the first people to contribute to my financial education in a meaningful way. Her dad, Mike (whom we all affectionately call Mike G), was a commodities pit trader and brought Gabriela to Take Your Daughter to Work Day when she was eight. "I remember thinking, 'This is a *bit* too aggressive for me,'" she said. "But while I didn't follow in his exact footsteps in finance, he sparked in me early on the notion of hustling and making things happen for myself. He talked a lot about the importance having money to do the things I wanted, without answering to someone."

By eleven, Gabriela was selling her old clothes to classmates, and by fourteen, she had her first real job in an interior design shop. When we graduated from college, she had saved money to put toward a down payment on her first apartment in Manhattan. Mike G said he might be willing to help her bridge the financing gap, but he required a formal presentation on her strategy. So Gabriela made a PowerPoint presentation, pitching her dad on a loan for the rest of the down payment that she would quickly pay back with earnings from her first full-time job. Mike G agreed to the loan but also said he would not participate in cosigning Gabriela's mortgage or even going to see apartments with her.

"If this was my bet, then it was on me to figure out the details and bear the risk if I couldn't complete the payments," Gabriela remembered. "While harsh, it forced me to really assess what I could afford and if I truly felt it was a good financial investment. In essence, I was the only one on the mortgage and therefore the only one on the hook if things went poorly." Gabriela bought her first apartment, and that set her on a path of real estate investing in one of the most competitive housing markets in the world. Today, after a dozen years working in finance (not as a commodities trader), Gabriela is the founder of her own interior design firm and continues to invest in real estate.

SOME BACKGROUND

As I mentioned in the previous section, women are entering the workforce at greater and greater rates.[198] In its 2020 report "Managing the Next Decade of Women's Wealth," Boston Consulting Group reported that women held a third of global wealth.[199] McKinsey & Company's research the same year revealed that women in the United States controlled one-third of household financial assets.[200]

And both of these reports noted that these shares are on the rise. Despite these positive trends, girls and women remain at a disadvantage when it comes to building wealth and maintaining financial independence.

There are, of course, some straight numbers issues—because women working outside the home generally make less than men for comparable work or work in lower paying jobs, they are unable to pay off debt as quickly, save as much, or build the same wealth as men over time.[201] That women's work in the home is unpaid contributes greatly to the difficulty women face in growing their net worth.[202] But arguably, society's disempowering beliefs about "women and money," and the resulting lack of meaningful financial guidance for girls, create greater threats to your daughter's financial future.

As primary and often sole breadwinners until recent decades, men naturally came to be seen as financial authorities, while women, raising children and managing households, traditionally stayed out of budgeting, investing, and planning. These gender roles, though outdated for many young women, continue to influence women's engagement with their finances, society's views of women's financial prowess, and how parents address (or fail to address) the topic with their girls.[203] We know that all kids benefit from early conversations and guidance about money, not just how to save it, but how to grow it and how to manage it on their own, should the need arise (as in the case of a death in the family or other crisis).[204] Schools, for the most part, aren't addressing it in depth. Research has shown that parents hesitate to talk with their kids about money, and when they do broach the subject, they are more likely to talk with boys than girls about investing.[205] After all, it's not always obvious that an adolescent girl, so focused on short-term hurdles associated with schoolwork, weekend plans, and college applications, could benefit from lessons or a brain-storm on finances. The result is that girls grow to be women who feel underprepared, fearful, and apathetic when it comes to financial decision-making.[206]

At UBS, Carey Shuffman is the head of the Women's Strategic Client Segment. With the goal of encouraging women to participate more meaningfully in their financial lives, Carey and the UBS team set out to assess how women around the world were handling financial decisions in their households.[207] Their findings went viral. Millennial women in traditional heterosexual relationships said that they deferred the major long-term financial and investing decisions to their male spouse or partner at a higher rate than any other generation. Similar lack of involvement in financial decisions was true among millennial women who had never been married and had not been in a formal partnership. In UBS's research, single millennial women were the least likely to say that they had a good handle on what was going on in their financial lives and the most likely to acknowledge that they knew they should be doing more when it came to their finances compared to single women of other generations. Single millennial women openly acknowledged that they put many other facets of their lives ahead of their finances. In same-sex female couples, there tended to be one woman taking the lead on financial decisions. What was most surprising to her and her team, Carey told me, was that "rather than breaking the status quo, millennial women are actually perpetuating it."

There is some evidence to suggest an upward trend in financial planning among Generation Z girls and women, the generation following millennials, but your daughter will still need your help to maximize her financial opportunities.[208] Talk to your daughter about money early, and you will give her an edge in grasping important concepts and financial strategies she's not likely to learn anywhere else.

> **YOUR GOAL:** Teach your daughter the essentials of financial management to ensure her long-term financial independence and well-being.

> **RULE #1:** Don't put this conversation off. In the absence of guidance on financial matters, trial and error can set your daughter back.

TALKING POINTS

THE BENEFITS OF FINANCIAL EMPOWERMENT AND INDEPENDENCE

Because the topic of money can feel taboo, a great conversation starter can be discussing everyday ways that money can boost happiness. At the baseline, there is physical and psychological comfort that comes with being able to support oneself and one's family.[209] The importance of building wealth in order to provide basic necessities like food, housing, and medical care cannot be underestimated. In addition, there is much research to suggest that money actually can "buy" happiness in the following ways:

- Spending money on material items has diminishing returns, but spending money on experiences, like travel and socially connective activities, can pay dividends in long-term joy and fulfillment.[210]

- Spending money to buy time, like paying someone to help with household tasks, frees people up to spend more time with loved ones or working on personal passions.[211]

- Money is a top stressor for couples, and participating meaningfully in financial planning can boost relational happiness.[212]

- When women are financially independent, it can free them up to leave unhealthy romantic relationships they would otherwise stay in for financial security.

- There is a large body of research finding that charitable donations increase happiness for the person who donates.[213]

BUILDING WEALTH

Talk to your daughter about the concrete steps she can take toward financial independence. You can teach her by talking her through your saving and wealth-building strategies, and also by using other real-world examples from the news. And of course, you can brainstorm steps you can both take to support her financial future. If you are not confident in your own knowledge, take advantage of online financial education platforms, such as the one offered by the FDIC. Here are some key themes to address:

- *Saving*: Saving is a financial habit everyone can get behind, and one that is pretty straightforward to talk about.[214] To deepen conversations about saving, make them relevant to your daughter by discussing how you save for material possessions or vacations, or how you think her college education (if she's going) will be financed. In addition, make sure she understands compound interest and some of the ways she can benefit from it, like a special savings account or, when she begins working, investing in a 401(k).

- *Wants versus needs*: Encourage your daughter to consider the difference between wants and needs when she is deciding how to spend her money. This is one way to help her think about her daily purchases, conditioning her to be a little bit more thoughtful. Focus not just on how needs often cost less than wants (for instance, she may need shoes for school, but she may want an expensive, brand-name pair),[215] but also how opting to delay gratification now can allow her to grow her money and increase her future spending power. Waiting can facilitate other purchases later on.

- *Assets versus liabilities*: Help your daughter focus on the things she can spend money on that will build value over time. Don't dismiss every meal she eats out with friends or clothing item she wants to buy, but help her think through what the true value is of something she wants to spend her money on.

- *Being smart about debt*: It's really easy to go into debt these days. Credit card companies seek out young people. Almost every website has a payment-plan option so that buyers don't have to wait or think twice about making a purchase, from a sweat suit to a new TV. Make sure your daughter understands interest and the business models of the companies that will attempt to prey on her for monthly payments, and help her understand the negative impacts of paying interest.

- *Investing*: Women are less likely to invest their money than men are, passing up significant opportunities for financial gain. Your daughter needs to know that investing is within her reach and can make a significant difference in her financial life.

HOW IT'S DONE

Do Say

- That's not how I choose to spend money.

- The financial decisions you start making now can have a real positive effect on your future.

- What are your financial goals?

- What is important to you in your life? How will you build a financial foundation to make it all happen?

Don't Say

- That's too expensive! (Focus on where you will and will not spend money based on your family's goals and values. Speak about why or why you won't spend money on something.)

- Why would you waste your money on that? (There's this idea that women are "frivolous spenders." In fact, studies have shown that women are no more likely than men to make impulse purchases. A study by CNBC found that women and men were equally as likely to make impulse purchases, with 23 percent of men and only 16 percent of women saying that they had spent over $100 on a recent impulse buy.[216] Don't reinforce the idea that everything girls want to spend money on is somehow not worth it.)

BEYOND THE CONVERSATION

MEET WITH A FINANCIAL ADVISER

Find a financial adviser in person or online who can speak with your daughter about the steps she can take now to start saving for her future. The conversations you have with her will set the foundation for her financial education, and meeting with a professional and designing a plan will reinforce your message with concrete action steps. If you have a 401(k) or other investment account, or a checking or savings account with a bank or credit union, you may be able to set up a meeting for free with a financial adviser at your financial institution to discuss the basics with you and your daughter. You can also hire an independent financial adviser for an hourly fee.

Global Citizenship

In 2007, Tammy Tibbetts, then the social media editor for *Seventeen*, started her nonprofit She's the First, which is dedicated to helping girls become the first in their families to go to college. As Tammy recalled:

At the time, I was twenty-three years old, and I was working in my dream job at Hearst Magazines with the teen brands. Social media was really taking off. Facebook had come out when I was in college, and I had seen the power of being able to reach all of these friends I knew, just with the click of a button. Crowdsourced fundraising was also on the rise. My cause of choice was girls' education because 130 million girls are out of school around the world. There was all this potential to leverage my network. We started with a Twitter account and a Facebook page, and then we just rallied our friends to get informed about why girls' education was important to us, and we told them about ways to donate.[217]

Capitalizing on the digital power of millennials and Gen Zers, Tammy and her cofounder Christen Brandt have built a thriving global community of adolescent girls advocating for girls' education around the world. As of their ten-year anniversary in 2019, there were nearly 8,000 girls enrolled in She's the First's partner programs in eleven countries; 536 girls had graduated from those programs, and 41,302 of their family members had felt the positive impacts.

SOME BACKGROUND

Oxfam defines "global citizen" as "someone who is aware of and understands the wider world—and their place in it. They take an active role in their community and work with others to make our planet more equal, fair and sustainable."[218] With technology, today's girls have more pathways to drive the changes they want to see locally, nationally, and globally, and they have strong feelings about the areas that need attention. Survey data from the Pew Research Center shows that Gen Zers are more likely than previous generations to believe that Black people are treated "less fairly" than white people in the United States, that humans are driving global warming, and that "society is not accepting enough" of "those who do not identify as a man or a woman."[219] Today's young people are taking

part in protests and online social action campaigns, and some, including Greta Thunberg and Malala Yousafzai, are among the most
outspoken and recognized voices on key issues from global warming
to education.

If you are looking for a way to start meaningful conversations
with your daughter around global citizenship, it's "as simple as opening up a web browser and showing your daughter videos of stories,
so that she understands she's part of this global community," as
Tammy Tibbetts puts it. Never before has it been so easy to show
your daughter the world and her place in it, right from your computer or a phone in the palm of your hand.

There is no shortage of ways your daughter can get involved.
Joining her in thoughtful discussions of the issues that matter most
and helping her find ways to contribute, you can help her discover
her potential to make a difference.

YOUR GOAL: Help your daughter change the world. (No
pressure.)

RULE #1: Don't reinforce the idea that contributing to
her local, national, or international community is a
cumbersome obligation. "Community service" is often
paired with pressure for teenagers—to participate in
ways that don't feel relevant or interesting to them, to
fill school service requirements, or to build their résu-
més for college. This results in many young people simply going through the motions.

TALKING POINTS

UNDERSTANDING SOCIAL JUSTICE

If you want to help your daughter understand her role as a global citizen, I find social justice to be a good starting point. Social justice is a concept promoting equity for all people, throughout society, regardless of race, class, gender, religion, or sexual orientation.[220] Using social justice as a foundation for conversations, you can help your daughter explore her understanding of the world, her biases, unique privileges or disadvantages and those of others, and the power dynamics, economic forces, and environmental factors that contribute to inequality. Talk to your daughter about the social issues she notices in the world and where she thinks they come from. Why do they exist? Talk about what the ideal solutions would be and if there are ways she can influence them. You don't need to have all the answers for your daughter, but you can do the research and discover them with her.

GLOBAL CITIZENSHIP IS ABOUT SHARED ACTION AND SHARED GOALS

"Many parents focus on teaching their sons and daughters to give back to those less fortunate than themselves, and this is a good thing," Tibbetts told me. "In doing so, I think we should avoid language framed around guilt or shame—like 'Eat your vegetables because other kids are hungry!' It's important to remind young people that they aren't doing something *for* those less privileged. Instead, they're working *with* others, people who are closest to the problems, to create change. Everyone has a role to play in creating the world we want to see."

This may seem like a small difference in framing, but it's a huge and empowering mindset shift. Tibbetts continued, "In the She's the First network, all girls are champions of change in their own way. Sometimes, it's just by the sheer force of their example and being a girl in uniform during the day when the other girls in the community are not in school. What she has to go through, just to be that revolutionary example, is a very powerful contribution to the movement for education equality and gender equality."

As I highlighted in Rule #1 for this section, helping your daughter see herself as part of a social ecosystem is a stronger, more authentic starting point to motivate her than an approach marked by pressure, guilt, and shame. With this perspective, your daughter will understand what she has to offer, as well as what others bring to the cause. It can be a humbling experience, which is never a bad thing.

OPPORTUNITIES FOR ACTIVISM

Your daughter has ample chances to explore potential passions and contribute to the world in ways that mean something to her personally. Major categories of social issues she can explore include advocating for people with disabilities, anti-racism, bullying, increasing educational opportunities, elder care, gender equality, homelessness, LGBTQ+ rights, youth health, politics, and the environment. You can help her find opportunities through schools, religious institutions, youth groups, sports teams, online research, and social media. Girls can also easily create their own projects. Here are some types of projects you can suggest:

- Working at organizations and offering direct aid to people the organization serves.

- Administrative work for nonprofits, including help with communications or office work.

- Drives for items such as food, clothes, shoes, eyeglasses, school supplies, electronics, and baby gear.

- Community beautification projects including building houses, planting trees, and tending to gardens.

- Advocating for causes by joining protests, or organizing walks, events, or campaigns to raise awareness and gain support.

- Finding opportunities in everyday life to give back, like using a birthday as a personal fundraiser, encouraging friends and family to donate to a nonprofit rather than giving you a gift.

- Starting a business, like making jewelry or other consumer goods to sell, and giving portions of the proceeds to a cause of choice.

- Letter writing.

HOW IT'S DONE

Do Say

- What do you think are the biggest issues that need to be addressed right now around the world?

- Is there a social justice issue we could support together?

Don't Say

- You and your friends should do something for the world rather than being on your phones all the time.

- Why don't you figure out how to give back rather than being so into your own life all the time?

- Can't you find a better cause to support than [the cause she is supporting]? (If you don't understand the cause she supports, ask her nonjudgmental questions and learn more about it. Maybe you can join her in participating in an event for the cause so that you develop a better appreciation for why the cause is important to her.)

BEYOND THE CONVERSATION

BE A GLOBAL CITIZEN

What you do matters, too. You can have a positive impact on your daughter by involving her in any activism you participate in or decisions about donations you make to the causes that are important to you. As in so many other areas, your daughter is watching and learning from your example.

Building Your Support Team

Who and How to Call for Help

As we've seen, girls can benefit from support in a variety of areas, from academic and social struggles to mental health conditions, eating disorders, addiction, and beyond. Some issues are straightforward, like if your daughter needs extra math help, you call the teacher or get her a tutor. However, figuring out what type of coaching or treatment girls need for more complex problems often takes time and can feel nerve-racking and overwhelming to parents.

Behavior changes can emerge slowly and then seem to suddenly indicate an urgent problem, making parents feel like they were missing something all along. Symptoms like social withdrawal, lack of concentration at school, or mood changes can also have multiple possible causes that may require some untangling before you can identify and pursue the right course of action.

I know a lot of parents who realize there is an issue but try to handle it on their own for far too long. Sometimes it's because their daughters' symptoms don't seem problematic or that out of the ordinary. Some parents feel that getting extra help for a child is to admit that a child has "issues," and that those "issues" may be a result of "subpar parenting" (which is typically not the case). And parents may fear judgment from counselors, doctors, and other specialists. But professionals are not there to judge parents. We work to support children.

At the earliest moment you realize something may be awry, start making phone calls to see if anyone else is seeing what you are. School is a good place to begin—check with your daughter's teachers, counselors, and coaches, as discussed in the upcoming sections. You don't have to ask your daughter about any symptoms right away. Not every symptom is indicative of a major issue. Anything could be temporary, but in case it's not, you want to get help sooner rather than later. Getting to the right professional and the right diagnosis (if there is one) can take months, and so you want to do what you can to shorten any timeline for treatment and recovery, if your daughter does have a treatable issue.

Here are some people you can get in touch with.

School Counselors

School counselors work closely with principals, academic deans, teachers, and coaches to ensure kids are thriving at school.

What they do

- Keep an extra eye out for your child on campus, especially if you call and ask them to.

- Help your child make it through the school day if they are struggling with a mental or physical health issue or a complicated personal circumstance at home.

- Act as a liaison between you, teachers, and coaches, gathering information on your child's behavior or progress.

- Give you additional insight if you think there might be a problem, or sometimes bring it up to you when you don't realize there is one.

- Give you referrals for academic tutors and learning specialists or mental health professionals.

- Give you advice and perspective, so that you realize you aren't the first or last parent to be worried enough about your daughter that you call the school counselor.

When you need the school counselor

- If you are curious about how your child is doing during the school day. In the adolescent years, you will have less visibility into your child's school day; you generally don't see parents roaming middle and high school halls. Counselors can be your eyes and ears.

- If your daughter is struggling socially, emotionally, or academically, and you need help getting to the root of the cause.

- If your daughter has been diagnosed with a mental health condition or is facing a social-emotional challenge, and you want to align your efforts at home with those at school.

- If your daughter has been out of school for an extended period of time due to illness or for another reason, and she needs help catching up on her work.

• If your family circumstances have changed or become stressful, it's a good idea to let counselors know. Sometimes, major life transitions can lead to behavior changes at school, including moodiness, lack of attention, drops in performance, and acting out. It's always good for your child's teachers to know what is going on, even if it's in general terms, so that they can best support your child. If you fail to tell your school what is going on, you will lose a valuable support system. Don't be ashamed about admitting to family troubles. Even though it can feel like your family is the only one in crisis or falling apart at the seams, schools and school counselors interface with hundreds of families, and most of what you tell them wouldn't be surprising in their line of work. Even if you don't want to go into detail, you should strongly consider telling the school that something is going on. If you do provide details to the counselor or administrators, you can ask them to speak in generalities to teachers. You can also request that they don't tell your child you called. Talking to the counselor about new challenges at home can have the added advantage of helping to take the pressure off your daughter. For example, the counselor might talk to teachers about getting your daughter an extension on an upcoming assignment or help preparing for an upcoming test that is stressing her out.

Other reasonable asks for school counselors

• Help addressing on-campus social dynamics.

• Help communicating with or diffusing a difficult situation with a teacher.

• Checking in with your daughter to see how she is doing.

• Providing parenting advice or reassurance. I'm always surprised to hear how relieved parents are when I tell them they aren't the only person who is frustrated or worried that their kid is going to get kicked out of school. If you feel like you aren't on top of your game, or you feel like all the other parents are doing better than you, call the counselor for some perspective.

• Passing along information you heard about another student to that student's parents. As a rule, counselors don't love being a go-between among parents. But if you are really concerned about a student and you don't want to go directly to their parent (which is always encouraged), your school counselor may be willing to help.

What is not reasonable to ask them

• To parent for you.

• To mediate conflicts between you and other parents.

• To manage your daughter's and other people's children's social media lives that do not affect campus life. (If your daughter is being cyberbullied on social media and it's affecting her at school, absolutely contact the counselor.)

• To provide therapy for your daughter on a consistent, ongoing basis. If your daughter needs counseling, you will want to find a therapist.

How to connect with them

• Call the school to set up a time to speak or meet in person.

• Don't be shy! Use them as a resource.

A NOTE ON SCHOOL ADVOCACY

As I touched upon in the section on drama and bullying, remember that while you can report whatever you want to school about your daughter's peers, the school can't disclose all the actions it takes addressing the issue. Just as you appreciate the fact that your daughter's privacy is protected and the school is not talking to other parents about what is happening with your daughter, the school is not at liberty to tell you what is happening with another person's child.

Tutors

Tutors help with homework, study skills, and test preparation. Some tutors handle multiple subjects, while other may specialize in areas such as foreign language or science.

You can try to tutor your own child. I've seen it work sometimes, but I always recommend avoiding it unless it's an undeniably positive and connective experience for both you and your daughter. I say this because tutoring your daughter has the potential to set up a challenging dynamic that can feel frustrating to everyone involved. For example, especially when it comes to math, you may have learned topics differently and therefore teach topics differently from how your daughter is learning in class. There's a lot of room for miscommunication and misunderstanding. Bringing in a tutor is one more opportunity to offer additional wisdom and perspective to your child, and one more supportive relationship you can set up in her life.

What they do

- Help students with study skills and organization.

- Provide homework help.

- Help develop and execute plans for test preparation.
- Boost a child's confidence.

How they can help you and your family dynamic

Tutors reduce everyday stress in the household by being the ones to help manage homework completion and organization, which is something parents and kids often argue about. If you feel like your daughter is struggling not just academically, but socially or emotionally, engaging a tutor can be a good first line support strategy. The right tutor can help her get through a tough time. They do this by offering up undivided attention, a more relevant perspective than your own on school life, and some opportunities to build confidence through skill-building and task-completion. If they form a friendly bond with your daughter, they can also forge a new line of communication, helping you unearth any challenges your daughter is facing that she may not want to talk to you about.

How to find them

- Ask your school counselor.
- Look into volunteer tutoring programs in your school or broader community. For example, in some schools, upperclassmen may offer volunteer tutoring through a student group like the National Honor Society.
- Consider hiring older middle school or high students or college students.
- Research online tutoring services.

Learning Specialists and Educational Therapists

Learning specialists and educational therapists are trained to help students with underlying diagnoses, such as attention deficit/hyperactivity disorder (ADHD) or dyslexia, that cause learning difficulties. Many schools have learning specialists on campus. You can also find learning specialists and educational therapists in private practice. If you need a referral, you can start by asking your school counselor or other administrators.

What they do

- Help discover your daughter's unique learning style and the strategies best suited to help her succeed.

- Provide additional insight into why your daughter may struggle in certain subjects or across classes.

- Refer you to an educational psychologist or educational neuropsychologist who can conduct evaluations measuring your daughter's cognitive strengths and weaknesses and diagnose any learning differences.

- Give you and your daughter strategies and action plans to fuel her success in school. This may involve getting certain accommodations for writing or testing, such as additional time.

When you need them

- When you notice or when your daughter's school calls and tells you that she is distracted, having trouble following directions, or failing to succeed.

- When you notice that your daughter is working hard but bringing home poor grades or failing tests and quizzes.

- If your daughter has been diagnosed with a learning difference and you need to coordinate on-campus support with an on-campus learning specialist.

When you don't need them

- To get your child extended testing time, even though they don't have a learning difference. A major mistake parents make is believing that students who have a learning difference, and receive extra time in school and on admissions tests like the ACT and SAT, have a distinct advantage over students who don't have learning differences. Extended time generally only helps students with learning differences who actually need it. Obtaining extended time for students who don't have learning differences acts to disempower them by:

  - Making them believe that their skills and abilities aren't enough to make them successful. We often see a drop in confidence because kids falsely believe that they need an additional edge.
  - Compromising ethics by making them believe that they need to game the system in order to do well.
  - Putting additional pressure on them to succeed.

Independent Educational Consultants

Independent educational consultants can help you find the school of best fit for your child. These consultants can be especially helpful if your daughter has had trouble fitting in with a peer group or is struggling greatly with behavior or academics in middle or high school and you are thinking about making a change.

What they do

- Help you understand the educational options available to your daughter.
- Help you find the right school fit for your daughter.
- Work with learning specialists, doctors, and therapists to assess the right fit for your daughter.

How they can help

- For nervous parents, they can help you see a path to college early on and help you feel like you have all your bases covered.
- Do the research for you. They often have years of insights to share and connections at numerous schools.

How to find them

- Ask the school counselor.
- Ask an independent learning specialist.
- Online research.

Mental Health Professionals

When talking to parents, I find that "therapy" remains a scary word. It suggests "Your child has problems," or, even worse, "You have problems, and that's why your child has problems." When I've suggested therapy to parents who reached out to me, I've often been met with resistance or fear. But you don't need to be afraid to send your daughter to a therapist. You don't have to frame it as "therapy" or "counseling" or "something we are doing because you [your daughter] have issues." Instead, think about counseling or mental health treatment as going to a private master class on life skills. The class might be in managing family dynamics, understanding social dynamics at school, or determining how best to address a mental health challenge, which can be made easier by practice with a variety of cognitive skills and, if needed, medication. The most successful leaders in the world have therapists and coaches to help them make sense of and master their emotions and life's challenges. There is no harm in getting your daughter started early with an opportunity to feel a little more supported and to build a little more self-awareness. Mental health professionals can have a variety of degrees and certifications and titles, including PhDs, licensed mental health counselor (LMHC), clinical social worker (CSW), licensed professional counselor (LPC), or licensed marriage and family therapist (LMFT). Psychiatrists are medical doctors who treat mental health conditions and are licensed to prescribe medication.

What they do

- Provide valuable life skills, whether or not your daughter struggles with mental health challenges.

- Help your daughter understand her personal thought processes and perspectives.

- Work with you and your family in the midst of a crisis (death, divorce, chronic illness, etc.).

- Help your daughter work through her experience of a difficult situation related to your family or school life.

- Diagnose mental health conditions.

- Help your daughter learn to regulate her emotions and navigate her world in the most effective possible way.

- Prescribe and monitor medication to treat mental, emotional, or behavioral conditions (psychiatrists only).

- Interface with other mental health professionals, other doctors (such as a pediatrician), and school counselors and administrators in order to coordinate care for patients.

How they can help

- Provide extra support for your daughter.

- Help you understand your daughter's struggles in context, so that you feel less alone.

- Coach you on the best ways to support your daughter.

- Help you get to the root cause of an issue.

- Provide guidance and recommendations for additional treatment, such as specific addiction counseling or medical care.

How to find a good one

- Get recommendations from schools, doctors, or other parents.

- Research community organizations that offer free or reduced-fee services for teens.

- Interview several to get a sense of their approach.

- You can also check with your insurance company about what services and providers are covered with minimal or no cost to you.

How to recognize a good counselor

- They have the goal of helping patients get out of therapy. While in many cases therapy can be helpful on an ongoing, long-term basis, therapy doesn't have to be a consistent obligation. Your daughter may need a few sessions here and there, or she may need therapy for several months to get her going, and then continuing every once in a while as needed.

- They take an "integrative" approach. There is extensive research on the benefits of exercise, healthy diet, limiting caffeine and sugar, getting enough rest, and meditation when treating mental health conditions. Working on healthy habits as part of mental health treatment can pay dividends for your daughter in the near- and long-term. And incorporating integrative approaches may also, in some cases, reduce the need for medication. One thing I always encourage parents to consider is engaging an "integrative psychiatrist" who is knowledgeable about and comfortable with incorporating lifestyle changes along with medication when creating a patient's treatment plan.

- They are relatable. As I touched upon in the mental health section, if you want therapy to be helpful, you need to have the right person working with your daughter, someone who she feels comfortable with, wants to open up to, and respects. Personality matches are key when exploring sensitive issues.

- They have an inviting space. Space has an impact on all of us, including teens, who notice everything from the magazines in the waiting room to what is hanging on the walls.

Questions to ask when assessing a therapist or psychiatrist for right fit

- Here is a brief description of the issues we are seeing with my daughter; do you have experience with this?

    Desired answer: Yes.

- Can you tell me about your approach? Do you prefer to see patients on an ongoing basis or can they come to you as needed?

    Desired answer: Every patient is different, but so much of what we see is treatable. Certainly, therapy can be helpful on an ongoing basis if your daughter needs someone to speak with, but my goal is to give them the coping tools to be successful without relying on therapy.

- Will I have insight into what you are speaking about with my daughter when I am not in the room?

    Policies can vary by practitioner, by state, and based on your daughter's age. If your daughter is a danger to herself or anyone else, the therapist is legally required to inform you.

- Would you be willing to interface with our school counselor so that we can make sure our efforts are aligned in each environment?

  > *Desired answer:* Yes, I would be happy to speak with them. I just need to have a release of information form signed by you.

Asking for help is always good practice when it comes to raising your adolescent daughter. It may involve some uncertainty and fear for you to reach out, admitting that you don't have all the answers or that something might be seriously wrong. But that's okay, and you want to be sure you're getting your daughter the support she needs. If you want your daughter to be her healthiest, most grounded self, don't hesitate to get some professionals on your team.

FAQs

Fathers Asking Questions

s I mentioned earlier, personal questions from fathers inspired this book. The previous pages focus on your daughter's well-being, how to tackle the challenges that will ultimately help her become the best version of herself. But your well-being, especially your emotional well-being, is equally important. After all, when you fly, you have to put on your own oxygen mask before you can help your kids. I've touched on some of this already in chapter 3 and in "Beyond the Conversation" under certain topics. But this section starts with you.

Fatherhood is wonderful, but also hard, at least some of the time. And fathers tell me that what can seem most challenging is that it's really not cool to talk about the challenges. Even if you're powerless or disadvantaged in some areas of your life, there are countless arguments for why, as a man, you have throughout history had it better than your nonmale peers. And, because dominant global culture demands that you be strong, capable, and stoic, people don't have a lot of patience for your vulnerability and complaining. For men, it's a "with great power comes great responsibility" type of situation, which also comes with a great deal of pressure. It doesn't feel easy to deliver on the expectations you face as a contributor to the household, a father, a spouse, a professional (if you work outside the home), as a member of your family of origin, or in any other role. That is a resounding theme I hear over and over in the questions I get asked and the conversations I have with men.

The following questions are those I've gotten most often. It's hard to get personal and offer up tailored answers for you. But my hope is that what I say here will offer you some peace, reassurance, and a sense of your path forward.

Beyond the guidance you get here, I encourage you, as I have mentioned previously, to find someone you can talk to.

Common Concerns

I feel overwhelmed by the responsibilities of my career and my home life. Any advice?

If you feel overwhelmed, it's probably because you have a lot going on. It's that simple, and it's understandable. At the baseline, you need to practice active stress-relief strategies, including and especially, eating clean and exercise, which will help clear and refresh your mind. It's easy to let self-care go when you are in survival mode, but exercising and relaxing a little bit will help you feel more energized, think more clearly, and sleep better—all things that will benefit you, especially if you can't change your circumstances or offload any responsibilities right away. When you talk to your co-parent or anyone else contributing to the care of your children about how you are feeling, take a collaborative approach to brainstorming, making it known that you recognize others' needs and also that you need a little bit of extra support.

How can I stay connected to my daughter if I don't live with her?

Family living arrangements take all different forms. So don't be too hard on yourself if you can't be around all the time. (Just because other parents get to live with their children doesn't mean that's the best arrangement—for instance, if there is any physical abuse or substance abuse putting a young person at risk.)

It's true that if you don't live with your daughter, you won't have as many opportunities to passively influence her or interact with her in spontaneous ways as you would if you were home more of the time. But she benefits from knowing that you love her, are interested in her life, are there for her, and make efforts to see her.[1] You can maintain and strengthen your connection in small, simple ways, like sending her regular texts to tell her you love her and ask how she's doing, video-chatting, playing games online together, sending her little care packages, and making exciting plans together for when you get to see one another in person.

I find so much more common ground with my son than my daughter, and I know she knows it. How can I deal with this?

Because you were a teen boy at one time yourself, it makes sense that you might identify more, and more naturally, with a male child. You

don't need to have the same relationships with your son and daughter for those relationships to be meaningful. You won't always share
your daughter's interests. She also may not expect you to understand
or care about her passions and pastimes, which can give you a sense
that it may not be worth trying. But, as I have mentioned, showing
your interest anyway, even if it makes you feel awkward or goofy, will
go a long way. For instance, if you take some time to learn about a
band that she likes, play some of the music in the car or the house, or
take her to a concert, it may be clear to her that you don't love the
music, but she will appreciate (eventually) that you made the effort.
And, take your time, as is one of the foundational messages of this
book; your father-daughter connection will strengthen over time.

I do a lot for our family, but my co-parent feels that they are constantly let down. What can I do?

I get this question all the time. Avoid being accusatory and defensive, even if you feel justified. In your conversations with your co-
parent, try to shift focus to the positives and be matter-of-fact about
how you both can communicate and collaborate better as parents.

One concrete strategy I suggest is to infuse your relationship with
more gratitude. People can feel underappreciated in partnerships
because their spouse simply doesn't offer up enough positive feedback or give credit when credit is due, and it often goes both ways.
Lead by example and start saying "thank you" for little and big
things, like: "Thank you for restocking the toothpaste in the kids'
bathroom," "Thank you for driving carpool. I know it takes some
time, but I really appreciate that you do it," or "Thank you for

handling that meltdown. You were really able to calm [your daughter's name] down in that moment. I may copy your approach next time." You can also have a direct conversation with your co-parent about how it could be good for you both to articulate the things the other is doing to benefit your family and children.

In addition, outlining rules of engagement, so to speak, when it comes to giving feedback about the other's parenting or contributions to the household can be extremely helpful. This can take some of the emotionality out of what is a heated topic. Try using the same tools I recommended that girls use when planning important conversations with romantic partners. For example, try proactively setting a time for such a discussion with your co-parent, rather than letting the conversation occur reactively in the wake of a complaint ("Why am I always the one who has to ground her?").

If you feel that your partner really doesn't appreciate you, you may need to have a more serious conversation so that the situation doesn't worsen unnecessarily or to the point where it is difficult to repair.

I try to be there for my daughter, but my wife (or ex-wife) gives me a lot of negative feedback on my parenting. What should I do?

First and foremost, don't back away from parenting your daughter. Your co-parent may not actively be trying to critique you. She may lack patience or awareness that some of what your daughter is going through is new to you in a way that isn't new to her (the mother). Your co-parent will have insights for you, but these will be easier to hear and put to use if you feel like your co-parent is trying to help you, rather than trying to critique you. You can say the following, which invite discussion and emphasize that you are on the same team:

- I thought my approach on this issue worked well. Why do you think it wasn't effective?

- Here is why I handled [X issue] in this way. Is there anything you would have added?

- From your perspective, is there anything to know about [daughter's reaction/behavior] that I could be missing?

It's also okay to be proactive in communicating with your co-parent about how she is making you feel, and if there are ways she can help guide. If you feel like you may actually be doing something wrong, ask for help directly. And, if you don't trust your co-parent's opinion, check with other people whose opinion you value.

Will I ever have as close of a connection to my daughter as my wife has with her?

It's common for girls to be equally close with male and female parents. There will be times, as you have read, that you may feel distanced from your daughter and when she might naturally turn to her mother or other female adult for advice on certain topics. Just stay consistent with your love, support, and efforts to bond, and that will help ensure you have the strongest relationship with your daughter— even if it doesn't feel like it solidifies for several years.

I'm a single dad. How do I know that my daughter is getting everything she needs emotionally?

Remember that if you are there, telling and showing your daughter that you love her, doing everything you can to guide her, and if you are providing food, shelter, and safety, you are already doing a lot. There are plenty of kids in two-parent households who don't have their needs met. So, even if you feel stretched, give yourself credit. That said, it never hurts to have other people around who can offer your daughter, love, support, and perspective. Try to ensure that your daughter has other supportive family figures she can turn to, whether that's extended family, close family friends, or other role models. And in this era of Zoom and video chatting, it's easier than ever to build and maintain a strong relationship with someone who may not be in the same geographic area as you.

My daughter doesn't have a mother figure in the house. Will I be able to handle all the girl-specific conversations on topics like periods?

I'm a firm believer that you can handle these topics, as long as you're educated on the subject. And remember that broaching conversations lets your daughter know you are open to talking. I do think it's important for your daughter to have a trusted adult female to speak with: a friend or family member, who she might feel more comfortable speaking with at first and who can give her guidance based on firsthand experience. As I've already mentioned, you can also facilitate a conversation with a trusted doctor, so that your daughter can get her sensitive questions answered. In this process, your daughter will not only receive valuable information, but she will get some practice asking knowledgeable adults for help and guidance.

Your Divorce

Is there a right time to get a divorce, if I want to minimize the negative impact it has on my daughter?

There is no cut-and-dried answer here. In deciding whether to leave, you need to weigh the pros and cons. A few things to keep in mind:

If you are in an unhappy or unhealthy relationship, your daughter is likely picking up on the tension, which can be damaging to her mental health and also to her conceptions of what her own romantic relationships should look like.[2] If there are unhealthy, contentious, or violent dynamics playing out in the house, your daughter is learning from that example. If getting a divorce means you are addressing damaging family dynamics, the outcome for your daughter can be very positive, regardless of her age.

It's worth getting professional guidance on timing. Separation and divorce are major disruptions and distractions, and while there is no great time, there may be some times that are better than others. For instance, you might not want to make any big moves during your daughter's junior year of high school, which is very important for her college applications.

My ex is sabotaging my relationship with my daughter. What can I do?

I often hear stories about one parent turning a child against another parent in a separation or a divorce. The advice I can give is in line with that which grounds this book: stay consistent. Be consistent in your messaging, telling your daughter that you love her and care for her. Be consistent in your efforts to connect, even if your daughter doesn't answer you at first or accept your invitations to spend time together. Keep texting. Keep calling. Keep showing up. Keep sending her something on her birthday. When you stay consistent and positive, you create a counternarrative, one that your daughter can look back on and think, "He was there for me all along." It may take some long, frustrating, and heartbreaking months—maybe even years—for your daughter to respond favorably to you, but by being consistent, you are giving yourself the best chance at success.

I just got divorced. Can I start dating again or will that hurt my daughter?

People start dating after their divorces. Be mindful of timing, but you don't need to put your personal life on hold indefinitely. You can expect some reaction from your daughter. She may not be excited for you. She may take it pretty hard, thinking of you with someone else. She may feel hurt and like you are trying to replace her or her mother. The fact that you are beginning to date might add to her stress and worry.

In terms of whether it will cause emotional damage, it certainly can if you bring unhealthy relationship dynamics or an abusive person into your family system. But with a new love interest, you can also introduce someone to your family system with whom you can model caring, positive relationship dynamics. And having someone additional around who loves and supports your daughter, and who she connects with, can bring added benefits. So often, divorce brings with it a sense of brokenness and incompleteness, but one message I always share with young people weathering their parents' divorces is that it doesn't have to be about the family "breaking." Rather, now there are opportunities for the family, and the love among family members, to expand.

What do I need to know about introducing my daughter to my new partner?

Prepare your daughter ahead of time to meet your new partner. If you're lucky, your daughter will be accepting of them right away, but I don't usually hear from fathers that this is easy. You can expect that the first interactions will be awkward and uncomfortable. Your daughter may even act in ways you see as disrespectful. Remember that she is young and might find it difficult to process and express difficult emotions. She may do and say things that are hurtful because she feels hurt and scared. You can parent her, perhaps having a talk with her after the fact. But more importantly, you are going to have to keep calm and help your daughter understand that she is still a priority for you, even though you have someone new in your life. And it may take time to settle into a new dynamic.

You also want to plan for the worst with your new partner. Talk through how you will both handle it if your daughter is rude or distant. You want to avoid your daughter creating a wedge between you. Your partner will need to know they have your support. If the first meetings are rocky, be sure to make special plans with your partner, something that will demonstrate your continued commitment to them and help you recalibrate after what is likely to be an unsettling event.

Your "Flaws"

I'm afraid my daughter will be disappointed in me when she learns about my past. Is there anything I can do?

First, if you are going to share details of your personal past with your daughter, choose your words carefully, so that you deliver the information in an age-appropriate way. As I mentioned in chapter 2, you want to share with your daughter in a way that she can digest, without her worrying too much about you or feeling that she needs to take care of you. (She may anyway, but you want to try to prevent it.)

Second, you don't have to be perfect. You don't need to have a perfect past for your daughter to love and accept you. What you do need is to make sure you've grown from your past mistakes, and that you are aware of and working through patterns in your thinking and behavior that are unhealthy and could have negative impacts on your daughter. This will allow you to maximize the amount of wisdom you pass along to your daughter, while reducing the transfer of bad habits. It can be scary to think of your daughter finding out about the parts of you that you are most ashamed of. It's possible she could be disappointed and need some space from you. But I've heard a lot of stories of young women who are accepting and very caring in the moments their dads reveal personal details, including when they learn about their father coming out or that their father has had past brushes with the law (both of which are scenarios that have come up to me repeatedly as causing worry for fathers about to tell their kids). Revealing this information can help you build a stronger relationship with your daughter. And, if you think she is going to learn this information at some point, it is likely better coming from you than from someone else.

You've Got This

You and Your Daughter in the Long Game

Remember when I told you that experts are at odds when it comes to defining an endpoint for adolescence? The truth is that social-emotional development is a lifelong process.[1] It never actually ends. The physiological transitions of puberty will be a thing of the past, but your daughter's personal growth and development will continue throughout her life.[2] As she gets older, she'll get the hang of a lot of things herself, but she's not going to wake up one day and magically not need you anymore. For as long as you're around, you can be someone she turns to.[3] All you have to do is put the foundation in place early on.[4]

I launched my first girls' media platform when I was twenty-six. It had been a dream of mine since graduating from high school. I just knew that if I could harness the positive power of media, I could change a lot of girls' lives for the better. I'd worked in several start-ups, earned two degrees qualifying me to be an expert in my field, and had a plan. I gathered the courage to get started, got the support of my husband and my family, built the website, and ordered the business cards. Then, I bought a ticket to the National Coalition of Girls' Schools conference in Dallas, Texas. The theme of the conference was the influence of media in girls' lives. Many of the experts and scholars I admired would be there, as well as representatives from girls' schools and girl-focused nonprofits from around the world. I was excited to meet them, hoping to form new relationships, so that more girls could discover our resources.

I was ready to go, and then three days before I was supposed to fly from Boston to Dallas for this "debut" event, I freaked out. Suddenly, I didn't know if I could make it happen. I didn't know what to expect, and if I had what it took to "make it." Could I trust myself to achieve my dreams?

I called my dad, as I do whenever I feel like I've lost my compass, especially in my work life. He's one of the people I can be the most vulnerable with, and one of the people I've always felt understood me the best. Plus, he built his own insurance business from the ground up, as a newlywed hustling around Los Angeles, so he knows a few things about starting and thriving in business.

"Dad?" I said. "Can I pull this off? Will people take me seriously? I'm so much younger, and I just started my company and—"

"Kimberly," he cut me off. "Stop, you're so awesome. Stop that . . . Wait. Do you want me to come there? Do you want me to come to Dallas? I can fly there, and I can be with you. If you start spiraling, you can come talk to me when you need to, and I'll also be there so we can have dinner together, and you won't be alone."

It only took me a moment to agree to the plan. Since I had moved away from home for college, my dad had always been up for travel— any excuse for time away with me. This was the kind of thing my dad lived for. He's never been able to contain his excitement about being involved in my life.

"Yes, Dad," I said. "That would actually be great."

The plan came with one caveat: "You just need to promise me one thing, Dad: You can't stand in the lobby of the hotel and tell anyone with a conference name tag that you are my dad and that you are proud of me," I said with a laugh. "I'm trying to be cool, here."

Sound familiar? Here I was, in my twenties, telling my dad not to embarrass me.

Dad bought a ticket and flew to Dallas two days later. Since the conference hotel was booked, he shared my room, something we hadn't done since I had mono in college and he came to take care of me.

On our first night in Dallas, I woke up in the darkness of the middle of the night to hear my dad shouting in his sleep: "You're awesome! What do you mean, 'How do I know?'" he exclaimed, with his eyes closed, head on his pillow. "I know because that's my gift in life and you can't fake what's in your heart!"

In the morning, I woke him and asked if he remembered talking in his sleep, and he said he didn't. And when I told him what he was saying, he replied, "At least I'm consistent." Then, he rolled over and fell back to sleep as I left for the second day of the conference.

My dad came to the conference not because he thought I was going to self-destruct—I think he knew I would have a great time and that my work would be well received. He just wanted to give me the extra support, let me know he was there, and take my mind off my worries so I could be more focused and in the moment. He was there when I called him on his cell phone so we could eat lunch together. He talked about my outfits with me when I was wondering if I looked professional enough. He joined me and some new friends for dinner at a barbecue joint on the outskirts of town. He contained himself when I introduced him to some conference participants in the elevator, even though I *knew* he wanted to tell everyone how excited he was for me to start this new phase of my career. I will never forget that trip for as long as I live. I needed my dad and he was there.

The conversations my dad and I had when I was in high school provided a foundation for the relationship we still have today. I still call him for advice or a pep talk. We still sit on the beach in Los Angeles together. We still go on trips together. We spoke together on a panel at the Dad 2.0 conference a few years ago.

Being there for your daughter in her preteen and teen years positions you to be a force in her life into adulthood. You don't have to talk in your sleep like my dad does—he's an extreme communicator—but you do need to talk with your daughter over and over again, create moments of connection wherever you can, and plan for the long game. Consistency is your key. In the moments when you feel shut down by her, like you can't say anything right, or like nothing you say even matters, hold the line. Remember that she may not be listening to you, but she can hear you, and that is what matters most. Communication works, even if you can't feel it in the moment. You are ultimately more powerful than the social and cultural influences at play. So be fearless in your approach. Be loving, awkward, and emotional. Be vulnerable and wrong sometimes. Be there when she is insufferable. Be there for her until she starts coming to you. Talk with her until she starts talking to you.

ACKNOWLEDGMENTS

This is a book about dads, but, Mom, I never would have been able to write this book without learning everything you have always taught me about focus, perseverance, grit, resilience, unshakeable self-belief, positive mindset, optimism, prioritizing family time and self-care, keeping my sense of humor, not sweating the small stuff (admittedly something I haven't yet mastered), and how to cook my favorite comfort foods. At the same time I was finishing my manuscript, I became a mom myself, and amid my search for all the experts on fatherhood, you were my most trusted source on motherhood. I love you.

To Jennie Nash, my literary secret weapon. You helped me find my voice, and you helped me write my proposal and manuscript through two and a half years of fertility treatments, while I was working full-time and then pregnant with my first baby. You helped me plan so I could finish my manuscript on deadline at the height of the pandemic, right after the birth of my son. I'm pretty sure that together, we can do absolutely anything. What's next?

To my agent, Laurie Abkemeier, I knew you were the one to guide this book. You are an unmatched creative, guide, and advocate. A not insignificant portion of my motivation to write more books is so I can schedule more calls with you. To James Jayo, who saw a way for this book and my editor, Elda Rotor, at Penguin and the whole Penguin team, thank you for creating the path for *Talk with Her*.

To the experts willing to lend their perspective and voices to this project: Jon-Patrick Allem, Jonathan Baxter, Jaime Casap, Lisa Damour, Tia Dole at The Trevor Project, Bruce Ellis, Bill Hoppock, Jamie Howard at the Child Mind Institute, Jaehee Jung, Abdul Khaleque, Jennifer Lansford, Gretchen Livingston, Susan McHale, Darlene Mininni, Onnie Rogers, Carey Shuffman, Laurence Steinberg, Tammy Tibbetts.

To the hundreds of people across the world who helped me connect with the fathers and daughters who interviewed for this project. To the fathers and daughters who lent your time and wisdom, I hope this book makes you proud and helps countless people following in your footsteps.

Woven through the pages of this book about the power of men to influence the lives of girls and women is inspiration I've drawn from the men who have been the most important in my youth and career, whose presence, wisdom, and positive role modeling has had a lasting impact on my life. My dad; my brothers, Todd and Steve; my uncle Jack and cousin Paul have been constant sources of love, advice, and guidance my entire life. Growing up, I was fortunate to be surrounded by family friends and the fathers of my childhood friends (many of whom I remain in touch with), fathers who were present, involved, and engaged in their kids' lives. I am certain that the difference they made wasn't just for their children, but for all of us little girls in their presence, making us all feel safe and protected, encouraged to explore the world around us, reach our potential, and be good to one another: Chevy Chase, Bob Lang, Bob Hutcherson, Steve Durbin, Ralph Buoncristiani, Bob Madden, David Schiff, John Quinn, Jurg Lang,

Mike Colvard, Len Brisco, Bob Klein, David Wood, Bud Jacobs, Roger Wolk, Rick Katzenbach, Brian Peterson, and the late great Lou Meyers, Hugh Wilson, Nick Diaco, and Jim Shellenberg. To educators like Les Frost and Bruce Harlan at St. Matthew's Parish School in Pacific Palisades, who suspended my friend and classmate for snapping my bra in the hallway, sending the message to him and to all of us that women's bodies and space are to be respected. I thought the response was pretty over-the-top back then, but I understand now why you did what you did and how being in the presence of men like yourselves helped cement my self-confidence and willingness to set boundaries for myself later in life. To the men I have worked for and among, who have mentored me and opened doors in my career, including the good men of Hollywood and Silicon Valley who I have been so fortunate to know, who look out for girls and women in their presence, lifting them up and creating safe, collaborative work spaces where everyone thrives—Patrick Roscoe, Justin Herber, Gino Sullivan, Ray Leonard, Norbert Chung, Jesse Dylan, Patrick McGovern, Jon Funk, Greg Sinaiko, Alan Greene, and John Pacini. To my longtime mentor, Dr. Rick Weissbourd, you have answered every email and every call for years. You have helped me see insights, patterns, and opportunities in my work and exposed me to the vast potential human development research and education has to create positive shifts for humanity. To Bernadette Leonard and Kristin Martin for believing in a world where girls have everything they need to thrive and encouraging me to help build it. To Veronica Cortez and Amy Herold for being the best possible friends and team in our early days of creating inspiring resources for girls. To Jayni Chase for steadfastly believing in me since I was two weeks old and always being there to help bring my creative visions into reality.

To Tracy Scott for being our pandemic family, for caring for and helping us raise Max, night and day, for the long stretches of 2020. And to Beau for helping keep us all safe. To Darcie Durham for the friendship, understanding, and idyllic (and quiet) guest house where I worked on my manuscript. To Adri, Blake, Cydney, Gabri, Janna, Rebecca, Serena, Stefan, and Travis for the pep talks, insight and quick reads. To Bonnie, Gary, and Theo for the love, excitement, encouragement, and moral support from start to finish of this project and for the time you spent entertaining Max by FaceTime so that I could review my pages.

Ethan, Abe, Jamie, and Noa, you are my favorite teenagers, and you inspire me every day. Daleet, thank you for being a steadfast source of advice and insight on my creative journey for the last two decades. Robin, thank you for encouraging me in every aspect of my life in the writing of this book and beyond. One of the greatest silver linings of the pandemic was that you were home all the time and available to FaceTime with me and Max for as long as I wanted. Thank goodness for that timing. It was such an incredible bonus.

And to Alex, my great love, the best dad, and a better line editor than I could search the four corners of the earth to hire, I knew that there was something different about you when you didn't flinch at hearing I was a gender studies major in college. You have always believed in me and this project. You always knew exactly what to say to me in the face of my creative blocks and my writerly spirals of self-doubt. It would have been physically impossible to finish this book without the care you took of me and the baby in the home stretch. You make the best cheese plates and homemade ice cream and take-out orders from Sweetgreen. Thank you for helping me make all my little and big dreams come true. I love you.

She's Talking Behind Your Back:
Affirmations and Advice in Girls' Own Words

D ave, listen, I have something to tell you, but you can't tell Marion I told you. You'll blow both of our covers."

Marion was Dave's daughter, a junior in high school and one of my tutoring students. Dave had gone through a divorce and made the difficult decision to move for full custody due to concerns for his daughter's safety. Tensions were high in the house, with his daughter blaming him for ruining her life and constantly pouting and fighting him on his rules.

"Marion actually had some really nice things to say about you today," I said.

Dave was surprised. "Are you sure?"

"Yes," I said. "She told me that she understood completely why you wanted her to move in with you, that you have made a lot of efforts to make her feel comfortable, and that she has actually been having some fun with you. She said she knows and appreciates that you're trying."

Marion's sincere admission didn't surprise me. Yes, girls excel at critiquing and finding fault with their parents. You will mess up sometimes and other times your daughter will simply disagree with something you say or do. But though she may not share them with you, she'll also have clear moments of gratitude for some of your qualities and efforts. In my research for this book, I surveyed girls, asking them to share their thoughts about their dads. In their own words, here are some of the highlights:

What makes your dad a great dad?

- "He cares a lot, likes Marvel movies like I do, and he always compliments my art."

- "My dad makes the right decisions for me when I'm wrong, even when they may seem unfair in the moment."

- "I love how he tells me stories about his own adventures. And no matter how annoying I am he puts up with it."

- "He is very affectionate, which I am very grateful for because I know many people whose fathers are very distant from them emotionally, but I always feel very loved by my dad."

- "Even if he doesn't always have the right words to say or know exactly how to handle something, he is constantly trying, and I always feel very supported by him."

- "He helps me get better at the sports I play."

- "He always makes sure his family and friends are happy and will do anything to make sure we have what we need."

- "I love the fact that he loves my mom with his whole heart and demonstrates that sentiment."

What are some of your favorite activities to do with your dad?

- "I love to cook alongside him. He taught me the peace that can be found with making a dish and bringing people together with food."

- "Some of my favorite times with him are going to my meets, going to baseball games, or going to concerts, just the two of us."

- "I really like to work on essays with my dad because he brings a totally new point of view that is very helpful."

- "My favorite activity I do with my dad is when we go on our father-and-daughter date to IHOP. It is such a fun time because we just talk and eat delicious pancakes."

- "We love to sit and talk together early in the morning when no one else is up, enjoying our coffee and discussing big ideas."

- "A while back we went to go see a Chargers versus 49ers football game. He loves the Niners and I love the Chargers, so this was such a fun event! We spent all week surfing and laying out on the beach."

Any advice or words of encouragement for dads who want to be there for their daughters?

- "If you are a father who chooses to be present, please don't doubt yourself, just continue to be the person that you would want your daughter to marry. Tell her the truth, be honest, make her feel like she has a safe outlet when she needs advice."

- "Give her the logical advice along with giving the perspective of a male. Our genders (no matter how we identify) deal with emotions very differently."

- "It takes time and patience to develop that strong relationship with your daughter, but once it is there, it stays."

- "Don't worry if your kids are always on their phones. They will turn out just fine. And don't stress if your daughter gets a boyfriend or girlfriend that you don't approve of. It's important for them to experience heartbreak because it will make them stronger, and as long as you stay by their side they can get through anything."

- "Make sure you tell us when you're proud."

- "Send me handwritten notes or small treats since I'm far away in college!"

- "Dad, I love you even in times where I don't show it. I love you when I'm crying over friend or family issues. I love you when you make me laugh so hard I cannot breathe. You are my everything."

NOTES

Introduction: The Girls' Empowerment Movement Needs Its Dads

1. Jess Haines et al., "Family Functioning and Quality of Parent-Adolescent Relationship: Cross-sectional Associations with Adolescent Weight-Related Behaviors and Weight Status," *International Journal of Behavioral Nutrition and Physical Activity* 13, no. 1 (June 14, 2016): 68, doi:10.1186/s12966-016-0393-7.
2. Danielle J. DelPriore, Gabriel L. Schlomer, and Bruce J. Ellis, "Impact of Fathers on Parental Monitoring of Daughters and Their Affiliation with Sexually Promiscuous Peers: A Genetically and Environmentally Controlled Sibling Study," *Developmental Psychology* (July 2017): 1330-1343, doi:10.1037/dev0000327.
3. Alyssa Croft et al., "The Second Shift Reflected in the Second Generation: Do Parents' Gender Roles at Home Predict Children's Aspirations?," *Psychological Science* 25, no. 7 (July 2014): 1418–28, doi:10.1177/0956797614533968.

1. You Are Important, Even When You Feel Irrelevant

1. Brittany Allen and Katy Miller, "Physical Development in Girls: What to Expect During Puberty," HealthyChildren.org, accessed December 1, 2018, www.healthy children.org/English/ages-stages/gradeschool/puberty/Pages/Physical -Development-Girls-What-to-Expect.aspx; "Understanding Puberty," Kids Health, June 2015, accessed December 1, 2018, kidshealth.org/en/parents/understanding -puberty.html.
2. Deborah Schooler et al., "Cycles of Shame: Menstrual Shame, Body Shame, and Sexual Decision-making," *Journal of Sex Research* 42, no. 4 (November 2005): 324–34, doi:10.1080/00224490509552288.
3. Laurence Steinberg, telephone interview by author, November 21, 2019.
4. Steinberg, interview.
5. Steinberg, interview; Daniel Romer, "Adolescent Risk Taking, Impulsivity, and Brain Development: Implications for Prevention," *Developmental Psychobiology* 52, no. 3 (April 2010): 263–76, doi:10.1002/dev.20442.; Daniel Romer, Valerie F. Reyna, and Theodore D. Satterthwaite, "Beyond Stereotypes of Adolescent Risk Taking: Placing the Adolescent Brain in Developmental Context," *Developmental Cognitive Neuroscience* 27 (October 2017): 19–34, doi:10.1016/j.dcn.2017.07.007;

"The Teenage Brain: Under Construction," American College of Pediatricians, May 2016, accessed April 18, 2022, www.acpeds.org/position-statements/the -teenage-brain-under-construction; Dustin Wahlstrom et al., "Developmental Changes in Dopamine Neurotransmission in Adolescence: Behavioral Implications and Issues in Assessment," *Brain and Cognition* 72, no. 1 (February 2010): 146–59, doi:10.1016/j.bandc.2009.10.013.

6. Amy Ellis Nutt, "Why Kids and Teens May Face Far More Anxiety These Days," *Washington Post*, May 10, 2018, www.washingtonpost.com/news/to-your-health /wp/2018/05/10/why-kids-and-teens-may-face-far-more-anxiety-these-days/? noredirect=on&utm_term=.0a636a64ddd6.

7. "American Psychological Association Survey Shows Teen Stress Rivals That of Adults," American Psychological Association, 2014. Accessed February 17, 2020, www.apa.org/news/press/releases/2014/02/teen-stress; Norman B. Anderson et al., *Stress in America™: Are Teens Adopting Adults' Stress Habits?*, February 11, 2014, www.apa.org/news/press/releases/stress/2013/stress-report.pdf.

8. Melissa DeJonckheere, Andre Fisher, and Tammy Chang, "How Has the Presidential Election Affected Young Americans?," *Child and Adolescent Psychiatry and Mental Health* 12, no. 1 (February 2018), doi:10.1186/s13034-018-0214-7.

9. Danielle J. DelPriore, Gabriel L. Schlomer, and Bruce J. Ellis, "Impact of Fathers on Parental Monitoring of Daughters and Their Affiliation with Sexually Promiscuous Peers: A Genetically and Environmentally Controlled Sibling Study," *Developmental Psychology* 53, no. 7 (July 2017): 1330–343, doi:10.1037/dev0000327; Ali Serdar Sağkal, Yalçın Özdemir, and Nermin Koruklu, "Direct and Indirect Effects of Father-Daughter Relationship on Adolescent Girls' Psychological Outcomes: The Role of Basic Psychological Need Satisfaction," *Journal of Adolescence* 68 (October 2018): 32–39, doi:10.1016/j.adolescence.2018.07.001; Claire Vallotton et al., "Child Behavior Problems: Mothers' and Fathers' Mental Health Matters Today and Tomorrow," *Early Childhood Research Quarterly* 37 (2016): 81–93, doi:10.1016/j.ecresq.2016.02.006.

10. Bruce J. Ellis, telephone interview by author, December 4, 2019.

11. DelPriore et al., "Impact of Fathers"; Bruce J. Ellis et al., "Quality of Early Family Relationships and Individual Differences in the Timing of Pubertal Maturation in Girls: A Longitudinal Test of an Evolutionary Model," *Journal of Personality and Social Psychology* 77, no. 2 (1999): 387–401, doi:10.1037/0022-3514.77.2.387; Jess Haines et al., "Family Dinner and Disordered Eating Behaviors in a Large Cohort of Adolescents," *Eating Disorders* 18, no. 1 (January/February 2010): 10–24, doi:10.1080/10640260903439516.

12. Paul R. Amato, "Father-Child Relations, Mother-Child Relations, and Offspring Psychological Well-Being in Early Adulthood," *Journal of Marriage and the Family* 56, no. 4 (November 1994): 1031–42, doi:10.2307/353611; Seth J. Schwartz and Gordon E. Finley, "Father Involvement, Nurturant Fathering, and Young Adult Psychosocial Functioning," *Journal of Family Issues* 27, no. 5 (May 2006): 712–31, doi:10.1177/0192513x05284003.

13. William S. Aquilino, "The Noncustodial Father–Child Relationship from Adolescence into Young Adulthood," *Journal of Marriage and Family* 68, no. 4 (November 2006): 929–46, doi:10.1111/j.1741-3737.2006.00305.x; Daphne C. Hernandez,

Emily Pressler, and Cassandra Dorius, "The Role of Boomerang Fathers in Adolescent Female Depression," *Journal of Marriage and Family* 78, no. 5 (July 2016): 1285–299, doi:10.1111/jomf.12336; Leanne Lester et al., "The Association of Fly-in Fly-out Employment, Family Connectedness, Parental Presence, and Adolescent Well-being," *Journal of Child and Family Studies* 25, no. 12 (August 2016): 3619–626, doi:10.1007/s10826-016-0512-8.

14. Laurence Steinberg, *Authoritative Parenting and Adolescent Adjustment across Varied Ecological Niches*, report (Madison, WI: National Center on Effective Secondary Schools), https://eric.ed.gov/?id=ED324558.

15. Amato, "Father-Child Relations"; Jennifer Byrd-Craven et al., "The Father-Daughter Dance: The Relationship between Father-Daughter Relationship Quality and Daughters' Stress Response," *Journal of Family Psychology* 26, no. 1 (February 2012): 87–94, doi:10.1037/a0026588; Abdul Khaleque, "Perceived Parental Hostility and Aggression, and Children's Psychological Maladjustment, and Negative Personality Dispositions: A Meta-Analysis," *Journal of Child and Family Studies* 26, no. 4 (2017): 977–88, doi:10.1007/s10826-016-0637-9; Abdul Khaleque and Ronald P. Rohner, "Transnational Relations Between Perceived Parental Acceptance and Personality Dispositions of Children and Adults," *Personality and Social Psychology Review* 16, no. 2 (May 2012): 103–15, doi:10.1177/1088868311418986; Schwartz and Finley, "Father Involvement."

16. "A Father's Love Is One of the Greatest Influences on Personality Development," *ScienceDaily*, June 12, 2012, accessed July 6, 2020, www.sciencedaily.com/releases/2012/06/120612101338.htm#:~:text=06%2F120612101338.htm-,A%20fa ther's%20love%20contributes%20as%20much%20%2D%2D%20and%20some times%20more,as%20children%20and%20into%20adulthood; Khaleque and Rohner, "Transnational Relations."

17. Bruce J. Ellis et al., "Impact of Fathers on Risky Sexual Behavior in Daughters: A Genetically and Environmentally Controlled Sibling Study," *Development and Psychopathology* 24, no. 1 (February 2012): 317–332, https://doi.org/10.1017/S095457941100085X; Christine E. Stanik, Elizabeth M. Riina, and Susan M. McHale, "Parent-Adolescent Relationship Qualities and Adolescent Adjustment in Two-Parent African American Families," *Family Relations* 62, no. 4 (October 2013): 597–608, doi:10.1111/fare.12020; Marie-Anne Suizzo et al., "The Unique Effects of Fathers' Warmth on Adolescents' Positive Beliefs and Behaviors: Pathways to Resilience in Low-Income Families," *Sex Roles* 77, no. 1–2 (July 2017): 46–58, doi:10.1007/s11199-016-0696-9.

18. Elizabeth Dorrance Hall, Amanda Ruth-McSwain, and Merissa Ferrara, "Models of Health: Exploring Memorable Messages Received from Parents about Diet and Exercise," *Journal of Communication in Healthcare* 9, no. 4 (2016): 247–55, doi:10.1080/17538068.2016.1187892; Amanda Holman and Jody Koenig Kellas, "'Say Something Instead of Nothing': Adolescents' Perceptions of Memorable Conversations about Sex-Related Topics with Their Parents," *Communication Monographs* 85, no. 3 (January 2018): 357–79, doi:10.1080/03637751.2018.1426870.

19. Alyssa Croft et al., "The Second Shift Reflected in the Second Generation: Do Parents' Gender Roles at Home Predict Children's Aspirations?," *Psychological Science* 25, no. 7 (July 2014): 1418–28, doi:10.1177/0956797614533968.

20. Diann M. Ackard et al., "Parent–Child Connectedness and Behavioral and Emotional Health Among Adolescents," *American Journal of Preventive Medicine* 30, no. 1 (January 1, 2006): 59–66, doi:10.1016/j.amepre.2005.09.013; Khaleque, "Perceived Parental Hostility"; Khaleque and Rohner, "Transnational Relations."

21. Caroline Payne Purvis, Rosemary V. Barnett, and Larry Forthun, "Parental Involvement During Adolescence and Contraceptive Use in College," *Adolescent and Family Health* 6, no. 2 (November 2014): 1–17, https://scholar.utc.edu/cgi/viewcontent.cgi?article=1012&context=jafh.

22. Jess Haines et al., "Family Functioning and Quality of Parent-Adolescent Relationship: Cross-sectional Associations with Adolescent Weight-Related Behaviors and Weight Status," *International Journal of Behavioral Nutrition and Physical Activity* 13, no. 1 (June 14, 2016), doi:10.1186/s12966-016-0393-7; Michelle Miller-Day and Jennifer D. Marks, "Perceptions of Parental Communication Orientation, Perfectionism, and Disordered Eating Behaviors of Sons and Daughters," *Health Communication* 19, no. 2 (2006): 153–63, doi:10.1207/s15327027hc1902_7.

23. Ackard, et al., "Parent–Child Connectedness"; Leanne Lester et al., "The Association of Fly-in Fly-out Employment, Family Connectedness, Parental Presence and Adolescent Well-being," *Journal of Child and Family Studies* 25, no. 12 (August 2016): 3619–626, doi:10.1007/s10826-016-0512-8.

24. Chun Bun Lam, Susan M. Mchale, and Ann C. Crouter, "Parent-Child Shared Time from Middle Childhood to Late Adolescence: Developmental Course and Adjustment Correlates," *Child Development* 83, no. 6 (November 2012): 2089–103, doi:10.1111/j.1467-8624.2012.01826.x; Mengya Xia et al., "A Developmental Perspective on Young Adult Romantic Relationships: Examining Family and Individual Factors in Adolescence," *Journal of Youth and Adolescence* 47, no. 7 (July 2018): 1499–516, doi:10.1007/s10964-018-0815-8.

25. Xia et al., "Developmental Perspective."

2. "The Talk" Is Dead

1. Lisa Damour, "What Do Teenagers Want? Potted Plant Parents," *New York Times*, December 14, 2016, www.nytimes.com/2016/12/14/well/family/what-do-teenagers-want-potted-plant-parents.html.

2. Chun Bun Lam, Susan M. Mchale, and Ann C. Crouter, "Parent-Child Shared Time from Middle Childhood to Late Adolescence: Developmental Course and Adjustment Correlates," *Child Development* 83, no. 6 (November/December 2012): 2089–103, doi:10.1111/j.1467-8624.2012.01826.x.

3. Veronica Meredith, Penelope Rush, and Elly Robinson, "Fly-in Fly-out Workforce Practices in Australia: The Effects on Children and Family Relationships," CFCA Paper No. 19, Child Family Community Australia, February 2014, aifs.gov.au/cfca/publications/fly-fly-out-workforce-practices-australia-effects/introduction; Leanne Lester et al., "The Association of Fly-in Fly-out Employment, Family Connectedness, Parental Presence and Adolescent Well-being," *Journal of Child and Family Studies* 25, no. 12 (August 19, 2016): 3619–626, doi:10.1007/s10826-016-0512-8.

4. Mitch Prinstein, online interview by author, December 15, 2020.

5. S. C. Martino et al., "Beyond the 'Big Talk': The Roles of Breadth and Repetition in Parent-Adolescent Communication about Sexual Topics," *Pediatrics* 121, no. 3 (March 2008): e612–18, doi:10.1542/peds.2007–2156.

6. Joohong Min, Merril Silverstein, and Jessica P. Lendon. "Intergenerational Transmission of Values over the Family Life Course," *Advances in Life Course Research* 17, no. 3 (September 2012): 112–20. https://doi.org/10.1016/j.alcr.2012.05.001.

7. Jamie Howard, telephone interview by author, February 20, 2020.

8. Ming-Te Wang and Sarah Kenny, "Longitudinal Links Between Fathers' and Mothers' Harsh Verbal Discipline and Adolescents' Conduct Problems and Depressive Symptoms," *Child Development* 85, no. 3 (September 3, 2013): 908–23, doi:10.1111/cdev.12143.

9. Brian K. Barber et al., "Parental Support, Psychological Control, and Behavioral Control: Assessing Relevance across Time, Culture, and Method," *Monographs of the Society for Research in Child Development* 70, no. 4 (December 2005): 1–13, https://doi.org/10.1111/j.1540-5834.2005.00365.x.; Amador Calafat et al., "Which Parenting Style Is More Protective Against Adolescent Substance Use? Evidence Within the European Context," *Drug and Alcohol Dependence* 138 (May 1, 2014): 185–92, doi:10.1016/j.drugalcdep.2014.02.705; Barbara A. Oudekerk et al., "The Cascading Development of Autonomy and Relatedness From Adolescence to Adulthood," *Child Development* 86, no. 2 (October 23, 2014): 472–85. doi:10.1111/cdev.12313; "Teens Whose Parents Exert More Psychological Control Have Trouble With Closeness, Independence," *ScienceDaily*, October 23, 2014, www.sciencedaily.com/releases/2014/10/141023091944.htm; Rick Trinkner et al., "Don't Trust Anyone Over 30: Parental Legitimacy as a Mediator between Parenting Style and Changes in Delinquent Behavior over Time," *Journal of Adolescence* 35, no. 1 (February 2012): 119–32, doi:10.1016/j.adolescence.2011.05.003.

10. "Talking with Your Teen: Tips for Parents," American Academy of Pediatrics: Pediatric Parent Education, accessed June 20, 2020, https://patiented.solutions.aap.org/handout.aspx?gbosid=166251.

3. Maximizing Your Impact

1. Diane Carlson Jones, "Body Image Among Adolescent Girls and Boys: A Longitudinal Study," *Developmental Psychology* 40, no. 5 (September 2004): 823–35, doi:10.1037/0012-1649.40.5.823.

2. Jones, "Body Image."

3. Rachel Cohen, Toby Newton-John, and Amy Slater, "The Relationship Between Facebook and Instagram Appearance-Focused Activities and Body Image Concerns in Young Women," *Body Image* 23 (December 2017): 183–87, doi:10.1016/j.bodyim.2017.10.002.

4. Zoe Brown and Marika Tiggemann, "Attractive Celebrity and Peer Images on Instagram: Effect on Women's Mood and Body Image," *Body Image* 19 (December 2016): 37–43, https://doi.org/10.1016/j.bodyim.2016.08.007; Jasmine Fardouly, Rebecca T. Pinkus, and Lenny R. Vartanian, "The Impact of Appearance Comparisons Made Through Social Media, Traditional Media, and in Person in Women's Everyday Lives," *Body Image* 20 (March 2017): 31–39, doi:10.1016

/j.bodyim.2016.11.002; Lily Robinson et al., "Idealised Media Images: The Effect of Fitspiration Imagery on Body Satisfaction and Exercise Behaviour," *Body Image* 22 (September 2017): 65–71, doi:10.1016/j.bodyim.2017.06.001.

5. Lindsay M. Howard et al., "Is Use of Social Networking Sites Associated with Young Women's Body Dissatisfaction and Disordered Eating? A Look at Black–White Racial Differences," *Body Image* 23 (December 2017): 109–13, https://doi .org/10.1016/j.bodyim.2017.08.008; Jennifer S. Mills et a., "'Selfie' Harm: Effects on Mood and Body Image in Young Women," *Body Image* 27 (August 2018): 86–92, doi:10.1016/j.bodyim.2018.08.007; M. Masselink, E. Van Roekel, and A. J. Oldehinkel, "Self-esteem in Early Adolescence as Predictor of Depressive Symptoms in Late Adolescence and Early Adulthood: The Mediating Role of Motivational and Social Factors," *Journal of Youth and Adolescence* 47, no. 5 (August 7, 2017): 932–46, doi:10.1007/s10964-017-0727-z.

6. Kirsten Weir, "The Exercise Effect," *American Psychological Association Monitor* 42, no. 11 (December 2011): 48, www.apa.org/monitor/2011/12/exercise.

7. Mayo Clinic Staff, "Mindfulness Exercises: See How Mindfulness Helps You Live in the Moment," Mayo Clinic, accessed July 5, 2020, www.mayoclinic.org /healthy-lifestyle/consumer-health/in-depth/mindfulness-exercises/art-20046356.

8. "Mindful Eating 101," Harvard Health Publishing, January 2013, www.health .harvard.edu/staying-healthy/mindful-eating-101; Joseph B. Nelson, "Mindful Eating: The Art of Presence While You Eat," *Diabetes Spectrum* 30, no. 3 (August 2017): 171–74, doi:10.2337/ds17-0015.

9. Lawrence E. Armstrong et al., "Mild Dehydration Affects Mood in Healthy Young Women," *Journal of Nutrition* 142, no. 2 (December 21, 2011): 382–88, doi:10.3945/jn.111.142000; "The Importance of Hydration," Harvard T. H. Chan School of Public Health, accessed July 4, 2020, www.hsph.harvard.edu /news/hsph-in-the-news/the-importance-of-hydration.

10. Albert Bandura, *Social Learning Theory* (Englewood Cliffs, NJ: Prentice-Hall, 1977).

11. Molly Webster, "Can You Catch Up on Lost Sleep?," *Scientific American*, May 6, 2008, www.scientificamerican.com/article/fact-or-fiction-can-you-catch-up-on -sleep; Katherine Dudley, "Weekend Catch-Up Sleep Won't Fix the Effects of Sleep Deprivation On Your Waistline," *Harvard Health Blog*, September 24, 2019, www.health.harvard.edu/blog/weekend-catch-up-sleep-wont-fix-the-effects-of -sleep-deprivation-on-your-waistline-2019092417861; Rob Newsom, "Sleep Debt: Can You Catch up on Sleep?," Sleep Foundation, November 13, 2020, www.sleep foundation.org/how-sleep-works/sleep-debt-and-catch-up-sleep.

12. Dudley, "Weekend Catch-Up Sleep."

13. Sian Cotton et al., "Religion/Spirituality and Adolescent Health Outcomes: A Review," *Journal of Adolescent Health* 38, no. 4 (April 2006): 472–80, doi:10.1016/ j.jadohealth.2005.10.005; Timothy L. Davis, Barbara A. Kerr, and Sharon E. Robinson Kurpius, "Meaning, Purpose, and Religiosity in At-Risk Youth: The Relationship between Anxiety and Spirituality," *Journal of Psychology and Theology* 31, no. 4 (December 1, 2003): 356–65, doi:10.1177/009164710303100406; David R. Hodge, Paul Cardenas, and Harry Montoya, "Substance Use: Spirituality and Religious Participation as Protective Factors Among Rural Youths," *Social Work Research* 25, no. 3 (September 2001): 153–61, doi:10.1093/swr/25.3.153; David W.

Holder et al., "The Association Between Adolescent Spirituality and Voluntary Sexual Activity," *Journal of Adolescent Health* 26, no. 4 (April 2000): 295–302, doi:10.1016/s1054-139x(99)00092-0; Lisa Miller, Mark Davies, and Steven Greenwald, "Religiosity and Substance Use and Abuse Among Adolescents in the National Comorbidity Survey," *Journal of the American Academy of Child & Adolescent Psychiatry* 39, no. 9 (September 2000): 1190–197, doi:10.1097/00004583-200009000-00020; Michelle J. Pearce, Todd D. Little, and John E. Perez, "Religiousness and Depressive Symptoms Among Adolescents," *Journal of Clinical Child & Adolescent Psychology* 32, no. 2 (June 2003): 267–76, doi:10.1207/s15374424jccp3202_12; Anamara Ritt-Olson et al., "The Protective Influence of Spirituality and 'Health-as-a-Value' against Monthly Substance Use among Adolescents Varying in Risk," *Journal of Adolescent Health* 34, no. 3 (2004): 192–99, doi:10.1016/j.jadohealth.2003.07.009.

14. Sian Cotton et al., "Religion/Spirituality and Adolescent Health Outcomes: A Review," *Journal of Adolescent Health* 38, no. 4 (April 2006): 472–80, doi:10.1016/j.jadohealth.2005.10.005; Leilani Greening and Laura Stoppelbein, "Religiosity, Attributional Style, and Social Support as Psychosocial Buffers for African American and White Adolescents' Perceived Risk for Suicide," *Suicide and Life-Threatening Behavior* 32, no. 4 (Winter 2002): 404–17, doi:10.1521/suli.32.4.404.22333; Lynn Rew et al., "Correlates of Recent Suicide Attempts in a Triethnic Group of Adolescents," *Journal of Nursing Scholarship* 33, no. 4 (2001): 361–67, doi:10.1111/j.1547-5069.2001.00361.x; Rosanne M. Jocson et al., "Religion and Spirituality: Benefits for Latino Adolescents Exposed to Community Violence," *Youth & Society* 52, no. 3 (May 8, 2018): 349–76. https://doi.org/10.1177/0044118x18772714.

15. Joohong Min, Merril Silverstein, and Jessica P. Lendon, "Intergenerational Transmission of Values over the Family Life Course," *Advances in Life Course Research* 17, no. 3 (2012): 112–20, https://doi.org/10.1016/j.alcr.2012.05.001.

16. Mills et al., "'Selfie' Harm"; "Depression Linked to Social Media Twice as High Among Girls," University College London News, January 8, 2019, www.ucl.ac.uk/news/2019/jan/depression-linked-social-media-twice-high-among-girls-0; Denis Campbell, "Depression in Girls Linked to Higher Use of Social Media," *Guardian*, January 4, 2019, www.theguardian.com/society/2019/jan/04/depression-in-girls-linked-to-higher-use-of-social-media.

17. "Premenstrual Syndrome (PMS)," American College of Obstetricians and Gynecologists, accessed July 4, 2020, www.acog.org/patient-resources/faqs/gynecologic-problems/premenstrual-syndrome.

18. "Premenstrual Syndrome (PMS)."

19. "Premenstrual Syndrome (PMS)."

20. "Premenstrual Syndrome (PMS)."

21. Mitch Prinstein, online interview by author, December 15, 2020.

22. Shannon Palus and Nancy Redd, "The Best Period Underwear," *New York Times*, February 21, 2020, www.nytimes.com/wirecutter/reviews/thinx-period-panties.

23. Scott Faber, "On Cosmetics Safety, U.S. Trails More Than 40 Nations," Environmental Working Group, March 20, 2019, www.ewg.org/news-and-analysis/2019/03/cosmetics-safety-us-trails-more-40-nations.

24. Jamie Howard, email interview by author, January 28, 2021.

25. Lisa Damour, telephone interview by author, 2016.

26. Leoandra Onnie Rogers, telephone interview by author, March 3, 2020.

27. Nia Evans et al., *Dress Coded II: Protest, Progress and Power in D.C. Schools,* report (Washington, DC: National Women's Law Center, 2019), https://nwlc.org/wp-content/uploads/2019/09/final_nwlc_DressCodedII_Report.pdf.

28. Leoandra Onnie Rogers and Andrew N. Meltzoff, "Is Gender More Important and Meaningful Than Race? An Analysis of Racial and Gender Identity Among Black, White, and Mixed-Race Children," *Cultural Diversity and Ethnic Minority Psychology* 23, no. 3 (2017): 323–34, doi:10.1037/cdp0000125.

29. Kendra Cherry, "What Does the LGBTQ+ Acronym Mean?," Verywell Mind, November 30, 2020, accessed April 28, 2021, www.verywellmind.com/what-does-lgbtq-mean-5069804.

30. "A Guide to Being an Ally to Transgender and Nonbinary Youth," The Trevor Project, accessed April 18, 2022, www.thetrevorproject.org/resources/guide/a-guide-to-being-an-ally-to-transgender-and-nonbinary-youth; "Glossary," The Trevor Project, accessed June 18, 2020, www.thetrevorproject.org/trvr_support_center/glossary.

31. Melissa Locker, "Merriam Webster's Word of the Year 2019: 'They,'" *Time,* December 10, 2019, https://time.com/5746516/merriam-webster-word-of-the-year-2019; "Word of the Year 2019," Merriam-Webster, December 2019, accessed June 18, 2020, www.merriam-webster.com/words-at-play/word-of-the-year-2019-they/they.

32. Michael P. Dentato, "The Minority Stress Perspective," American Psychological Association, April 2012, www.apa.org/pi/aids/resources/exchange/2012/04/minority-stress; Dr. Tia Dole, telephone interview by author, December 13, 2019; Ilan H. Meyer, "Prejudice, Social Stress, and Mental Health in Lesbian, Gay, and Bisexual Populations: Conceptual Issues and Research Evidence," *Psychological Bulletin* 129, no. 5 (2003): 674–97, doi:10.1037/0033-2909.129.5.674.

33. *National Survey on LGBTQ Youth Mental Health 2019,* report (New York: The Trevor Project, 2019), www.thetrevorproject.org/wp-content/uploads/2019/06/The-Trevor-Project-National-Survey-Results-2019.pdf; "Trevor Project National Survey." The Trevor Project—Saving Young LGBTQ Lives. 2019, accessed June 18, 2020, www.thetrevorproject.org/survey-2019/?section=Introduction.

34. *National Survey on LGBTQ Youth Mental Health 2019.*

35. *National Survey on LGBTQ Youth Mental Health 2019.*

36. Dentato, "Minority Stress Perspective"; Dr. Tia Dole, telephone interview by author, December 13, 2019; Ilan H. Meyer, "Prejudice, Social Stress, and Mental Health in Lesbian, Gay, and Bisexual Populations: Conceptual Issues and Research Evidence," *Psychological Bulletin* 129, no. 5 (2003): 674–97, doi:10.1037/0033-2909.129.5.674.

37. *National Survey on LGBTQ Youth Mental Health 2019*; "Trevor Project National Survey."

38. Russell B. Toomey, Amy K. Syvertsen, and Maura Shramko, "Transgender Adolescent Suicide Behavior," *Pediatrics* 142, no. 4 (2018), doi:10.1542/peds.2017-4218.

39. Ritt-Olson et al., "Protective Influence."

40. PFLAG, *Cultivating Respect: Safe Schools for All—The Top 10 Ways to Make Schools Safer . . . for All Students*, report (Washington, DC: PFLAG, 2019), https://pflag.org/publication/toptenwaystomakeschoolssafe; Joseph G. Kosciw and Elizabeth Diaz, *Involved, Invisible, Ignored: The Experiences of Lesbian, Gay, Bisexual and Transgender Parents and Their Children in Our Nation's K-12 Schools*, report (New York: GLSEN, 2008).

41. Susan Nolen-Hoeksema and Joan S. Girgus, "The Emergence of Gender Differences in Depression During Adolescence," *Psychological Bulletin* 115, no. 3 (May 1994): 424–43, doi:10.1037/0033-2909.115.3.424; Ronald C. Kessler et al., "Lifetime Prevalence and Age-of-Onset Distributions of DSM-IV Disorders in the National Comorbidity Survey Replication," *Archives of General Psychiatry 62, no. 6* (June 2005): 593–602, doi:10.1001/archpsyc.62.6.593; Ron J. Steingard, "Mood Disorders and Teenage Girls," Child Mind Institute, accessed February 17, 2020, https://childmind.org/article/mood-disorders-and-teenage-girls.

42. "Eating Disorders," NAMI (National Alliance on Mental Illness), accessed June 11, 2020, www.nami.org/About-Mental-Illness/Mental-Health-Conditions/Eating-Disorders.

43. Robert Glatter, "Suicide Rates Sharply Increase Among Young Girls, Study Finds," *Forbes*, May 20, 2019, www.forbes.com/sites/robertglatter/2019/05/20/suicide-rates-sharply-increase-among-young-girls-study-finds/#27119c56b20c; Melonie Heron, *Deaths: Leading Causes for 2017. National Vital Statistics Reports*, report, vol. 68, 6th ed. (Hyattsville, MD: National Center for Health Statistics, 2019), www.cdc.gov/nchs/data/nvsr/nvsr68/nvsr68_06-508.pdf; Donna A. Ruch et al., "Trends in Suicide Among Youth Aged 10 to 19 Years in the United States, 1975 to 2016," *JAMA Network Open* 2, no. 5 (May 17, 2019), doi:10.1001/jamanetworkopen.2019.3886.

44. Benjamin L. Hankin, "Rumination and Depression in Adolescence: Investigating Symptom Specificity in a Multiwave Prospective Study," *Journal of Clinical Child & Adolescent Psychology* 37, no. 4 (2008): 701–13, doi:10.1080/15374410802359627; Daniel P. Johnson and Mark A. Whisman, "Gender Differences in Rumination: A Meta-Analysis," *Personality and Individual Differences* 55, no. 4 (August 2013): 367–7, doi:10.1016/j.paid.2013.03.019; Ron J. Steingard, "Mood Disorders and Teenage Girls," Child Mind Institute, accessed February 17, 2020, https://childmind.org/article/mood-disorders-and-teenage-girls.

45. Jamie Howard, telephone interview by author, February 20, 2020.

46. Howard, telephone interview.

47. Brittany Bokzam, "Mental Health Data Dhows Stark Difference Between Girls and Boys," *Guardian*, September 23, 2017, www.theguardian.com/society/2017/sep/23/mental-health-data-shows-stark-difference-between-girls-and-boys.

48. Howard, telephone interview.

49. Howard, telephone interview; "Identifying Signs of Stress in Your Children and Teens," American Psychological Association, accessed February 17, 2020, www.apa.org/topics/stress-children; Norman B. Anderson et al., *Stress in America™: Are Teens Adopting Adults' Stress Habits?*, report, February 11, 2014, www.apa.org/news/press/releases/stress/2013/stress-report.pdf; "Identifying Signs of Stress in Your

Children and Teens," American Psychological Association, accessed February 17, 2020, www.apa.org/topics/stress-children; "How Stress Affects Your Body and Behavior," Mayo Clinic, April 4, 2019, www.mayoclinic.org/healthy-lifestyle /stress-management/in-depth/stress-symptoms/art-20050987; "What Are Anxiety Disorders?," American Psychiatric Association, accessed February 18, 2020, www.psychiatry.org/patients-families/anxiety-disorders/what-are-anxiety -disorders; "Anxiety Basics," Child Mind Institute, January 28, 2019, https:// childmind.org/guide/anxiety-basics.

50. "Treatments," NAMI (National Alliance on Mental Illness), accessed October 28, 2020, www.nami.org/About-Mental-Illness/Treatments.

51. Juliana Menasce Horowitz and Nikki Graf, "Most U.S. Teens See Anxiety and Depression as a Major Problem Among Their Peers," Pew Research Center's Social & Demographic Trends Project, February 20, 2019, www.pewresearch.org /social-trends/2019/02/20/most-u-s-teens-see-anxiety-and-depression-as-a -major-problem-among-their-peers.

52. Mitch Prinstein, online interview by author, December 15, 2020.

53. US Department of Health and Human Services, *Facing Addiction in America: The Surgeon General's Report on Alcohol, Drugs, and Health*, report (Washington, DC: Office of the Surgeon General, 2016); "Underage Drinking," Centers for Disease Control and Prevention, accessed February 21, 2020, www.cdc.gov/alcohol/fact -sheets/underage-drinking.htm.

54. Géraldine Petit et al., "Why Is Adolescence a Key Period of Alcohol Initiation and Who Is Prone to Develop Long-Term Problem Use?: A Review of Current Available Data," *Socioaffective Neuroscience & Psychology* 3, no. 1 (2013): 21890, doi:10.3402 /snp.v3i0.21890.

55. "Teen Substance Use & Risks," Centers for Disease Control and Prevention, April 01, 2019, accessed February 21, 2020, www.cdc.gov/ncbddd/fasd/features/teen -substance-use.html; "The Partnership Attitude Tracking Study: Teens and Parents," report (New York: The Partnership to End Addiction, 2013), https://drug free.org/wp-content/uploads/2014/07/PATS-2013-FULL-REPORT.pdf.

56. "Teen Substance Use & Risks."

57. Jon-Patrick Allem et al., "Characterizing JUUL-related Posts on Twitter," *Drug and Alcohol Dependence* 190 (2018): 1–5, doi:10.1016/j.drugalcdep.2018.05.018.

58. Jon-Patrick Allem, telephone interview by author, November 20, 2019.

59. "FDA Finalizes Enforcement Policy on Unauthorized Flavored Cartridge-Based E-Cigarettes That Appeal to Children, Including Fruit and Mint," press release, HHS.gov: Office of Adolescent Health, January 2, 2020, www.hhs.gov/about /news/2020/01/02/fda-finalizes-enforcement-policy-unauthorized-flavored -cartridge-based-e-cigarettes.html.

60. "Trump Administration Combating Epidemic of Youth E-Cigarette Use with Plan to Clear Market of Unauthorized, Non-Tobacco-Flavored E-Cigarette Products," press release, US Food and Drug Administration, September 11, 2019, www.fda.gov/news-events/press-announcements/trump-administration -combating-epidemic-youth-e-cigarette-use-plan-clear-market-unauthorized-non.

61. "NIH-Funded Study Finds Teens Prefer Mint and Mango Vaping Flavors," National Institute on Drug Abuse (NIDA). November 5, 2019, www.drugabuse.gov

/news-events/news-releases/2019/11/nih-funded-study-finds-teens-prefer-mint
-mango-vaping-flavors.

62. Kar-Hai Chu et al., "JUUL: Spreading Online and Offline," *Journal of Adolescent Health* 63, no. 5 (2018): 582–86, doi:10.1016/j.jadohealth.2018.08.002.

63. Howard, telephone interview.

64. "'Vaping' Increases Odds of Asthma and COPD," Johns Hopkins Medicine Newsroom, January 7, 2020, www.hopkinsmedicine.org/news/newsroom/news-re leases/vaping-increases-odds-of-asthma-and-copd.

65. "How to Spot the Signs of Teen or Young Adult Substance Use," Partnership to End Addiction, accessed May 3, 2021, https://drugfree.org/article/spotting -drug-use.

66. Petit et al., "Why Is Adolescence a Key Period."

67. "Underage Drinking," Centers for Disease Control and Prevention: Alcohol and Public Health, accessed May 3, 2021, www.cdc.gov/alcohol/fact-sheets/underage -drinking.htm.

68. Antonia Abbey et al., "Sexual Assault and Alcohol Consumption: What Do We Know about Their Relationship and What Types of Research Are Still Needed?," *Aggression and Violent Behavior* 9, no. 3 (May 2004): 271–303, doi:10.1016/s1359-1789(03)00011-9.

69. Petit et al., "Why Is Adolescence a Key Period."

70. Howard, telephone interview.

71. Petit et al., "Why Is Adolescence a Key Period."

72. "Trump Administration Combating Epidemic."

73. Monica Anderson and Jingjing Jiang, *Teens, Social Media & Technology 2018*, report (Washington, DC: Pew Research Center, 2018).

74. Lauren DeLisa Coleman, "Here's Why Everyone Is Still Talking About Lady Gaga's Comment About Social Media Today," *Forbes*, March 3, 2019, www.forbes .com/sites/laurencoleman/2019/02/28/heres-why-everyone-is-still-talking -about-lady-gagas-comment-about-social-media-today/#4de4ed364dad.

75. Anderson and Jiang, *Teens, Social Media*.

76. Anderson and Jiang, *Teens, Social Media*.

77. "Depression Linked to Social Media Twice as High Among Girls," University College London News, January 8, 2019, www.ucl.ac.uk/news/2019/jan/depres sion-linked-social-media-twice-high-among-girls-0; Marika Tiggemann and Jessica Miller, "The Internet and Adolescent Girls' Weight Satisfaction and Drive for Thinness," *Sex Roles* 63, no. 1–2 (2010): 79–90, doi:10.1007/s11199-010-9789-z.

78. "Depression Linked to Social Media"; Campbell, "Depression in Girls."

79. Mills et al., "'Selfie' Harm."

80. Mills et al., "'Selfie' Harm."

81. Sarah Berger, "Tech-Free Dinners and No Smartphones Past 10 pm—How Steve Jobs, Bill Gates and Mark Cuban Limited Their Kids' Screen Time," CNBC, June 05, 2018, www.cnbc.com/2018/06/05/how-bill-gates-mark-cuban-and-oth ers-limit-their-kids-tech-use.html.

82. Niraj Chokshi, "Apple Investors Warn iPhones and Other Technology May Be Hurting Children," *New York Times*, January 08, 2018, www.nytimes.com/2018 /01/08/business/apple-investors-children.html.

83. Nick Hazelrigg, "Survey Shows Nearly Half of Students Distracted by Technology," *Inside Higher Ed*, July 10, 2019. www.insidehighered.com/digital-learning/article/2019/07/10/survey-shows-nearly-half-students-distracted-technology; Adrian Meier, Leonard Reinecke, and Christine E. Meltzer, "'Facebocrastination'? Predictors of Using Facebook for Procrastination and Its Effects on Students' Well-Being," *Computers in Human Behavior* 64 (2016): 65–76, doi:10.1016/j.chb.2016.06.011; Elena Neiterman and Christine Zaza, "A Mixed Blessing? Students' and Instructors' Perspectives about Off-Task Technology Use in the Academic Classroom," *Canadian Journal for the Scholarship of Teaching and Learning* 10, no. 1 (May 31, 2019), doi:10.5206/cjsotl-rcacea.2019.1.8002; "The Mere Presence of Your Smartphone Reduces Brain Power, Study Shows," *UT News*, November 8, 2018, https://news.utexas.edu/2017/06/26/the-mere-presence-of-your-smartphone-reduces-brain-power; Adrian F. Ward et al., "Brain Drain: The Mere Presence of One's Own Smartphone Reduces Available Cognitive Capacity," *Journal of the Association for Consumer Research* 2, no. 2 (April 3, 2017): 140–54, doi:10.1086/691462.

84. "Put the Phone Away! 3 Reasons Why Looking at It Before Bed Is a Bad Habit," Health Essentials from Cleveland Clinic, April 22, 2019, https://health.clevelandclinic.org/put-the-phone-away-3-reasons-why-looking-at-it-before-bed-is-a-bad-habit.

85. "Children and Media Tips from the American Academy of Pediatrics," American Academy of Pediatrics, May 01, 2018, www.aap.org/en-us/about-the-aap/aap-press-room/news-features-and-safety-tips/Pages/Children-and-Media-Tips.aspx.

86. "Family Media Agreement: Common Sense Media," Common Sense Media: Ratings, Reviews, and Advice, accessed March 4, 2020, www.commonsensemedia.org/family-media-agreement.

87. "American Academy of Pediatrics Announces New Recommendations for Children's Media Use," American Academy of Pediatrics, October 21, 2016, www.aap.org/en-us/about-the-aap/aap-press-room/Pages/American-Academy-of-Pediatrics-Announces-New-Recommendations-for-Childrens-Media-Use.aspx; "Family Media Use Plan," HealthyChildren.org. accessed March 4, 2020, www.healthychildren.org/English/media/Pages/default.aspx#wizard.

88. "Kids & Tech: Tips for Parents in the Digital Age." HealthyChildren.org, August 10, 2018, https://www.healthychildren.org/English/family-life/Media/Pages/Tips-for-Parents-Digital-Age.aspx.

89. A. R. Lauricella et al., *The Common Sense Census: Plugged-in Parents of Tweens and Teens*, report (San Francisco: Common Sense Media, 2016).

90. Jody J. Fiorini and Jodi A. Mullen, "Understanding Grief and Loss in Children," *Vistas Online*, www.counseling.org/docs/default-source/vistas/understanding-grief-and-loss-in-children.pdf?sfvrsn=8.

91. Jonathan Baxter, telephone interview by author, June 10, 2020.

92. Baxter, telephone interview.

93. "Helping Teens with Traumatic Grief: Tips for Caregivers," National Child Traumatic Stress Network. Accessed March 14, 2020. www.nctsn.org/sites/default/files/resources//helping_teens_with_traumatic_grief_caregivers.pdf.

94. Baxter, telephone interview.

95. "Past Trauma May Haunt Your Future Health," Harvard Health Publishing, February 2019, www.health.harvard.edu/diseases-and-conditions/past-trauma -may-haunt-your-future-health.

96. "Helping Teens with Traumatic Grief."

97. "Helping Teens with Traumatic Grief."

98. Michael I. Norton and Francesca Gino, "Rituals Alleviate Grieving for Loved Ones, Lovers, and Lotteries," *Journal of Experimental Psychology: General* 143, no. 1 (2014): 266–72, doi:10.1037/a0031772; Emily Esfahani Smith, "In Grief, Try Personal Rituals," *Atlantic*, June 4, 2018, www.theatlantic.com/health/archive/2014 /03/in-grief-try-personal-rituals/284397.

99. Robert Klemko (@RobertKlemko), "Last month was the first March without a school shooting in the United States since 2002," Twitter, April 13, 2020, https:// twitter.com/RobertKlemko/status/1249716012599083010; Sophie Lewis, "March 2020 Was the First March without a School Shooting in the U.S. since 2002," CBS News, April 14, 2020, https://www.cbsnews.com/news/coronavirus-first-march -without-school-shooting-since-2002-united-states/?ftag=CNM-00-10aab6a& linkId=86548834&fbclid=IwAR2Msl G-MU4c8G3fnZ07tU5yXPQ JN6lV9j3SL POoTje1O39AJYZ3DhJGthE.

100. Caroline Knorr, "How to Talk to Kids About School Shootings," Common Sense Media: Ratings, Reviews, and Advice, October 14, 2019, www.commonsenseme dia.org/blog/how-to-talk-to-kids-about-school-shootings.

101. Ralph Waldo Emerson, "Friendship," essay in *The Harvard Classics: Emerson, Ralph W. Essays and English Traits*, Charles William Eliot, ed. (New York: P. F. Collier & Son, 1909), 109–23.

102. David E. Szwedo et al., "Adolescent Support Seeking as a Path to Adult Functional Independence," *Developmental Psychology* 53, no. 5 (2017): 949–61, doi:10.1037 /dev0000277.

103. "Healthy Friendships in Adolescence," HHS.gov, March 25, 2019, www.hhs.gov /ash/oah/adolescent-development/healthy-relationships/healthy-friendships /index.html.

104. Jaana Juvonen, Guadalupe Espinoza, and Casey Knifsend, "The Role of Peer Relationships in Student Academic and Extracurricular Engagement," *Handbook of Research on Student Engagement*, 2012, 387–401, doi:10.1007/978-1-4614-2018-7 _18; "Healthy Friendships in Adolescence."

105. Rachel K., Narr et al., "Close Friendship Strength and Broader Peer Group Desirability as Differential Predictors of Adult Mental Health," *Child Development* 90, no. 1 (2017): 298–313, doi:10.1111/cdev.12905.

106. Grace M. Barnes and Michael P. Farrell, "Parental Support and Control as Predictors of Adolescent Drinking, Delinquency, and Related Problem Behaviors," *Journal of Marriage and the Family* 54, no. 4 (1992): 763, doi:10.2307/353159.

107. Mitch Prinstein, online interview by author, December 15, 2020.

108. Karina Schumann and Michael Ross, "Why Women Apologize More Than Men," *Psychological Science* 21, no. 11 (2010): 1649–655, doi:10.1177/0956797610384150.

109. Darlene Minnini, telephone interview by author, November 5, 2020.

110. Daniel T. Ragan, D. Wayne Osgood, and Mark E. Feinberg. "Friends as a Bridge to Parental Influence: Implications for Adolescent Alcohol Use," *Social Forces* 92, no. 3 (November 25, 2013): 1061–85, doi:10.1093/sf/sot117.

111. Laurence Steinberg, telephone interview by author, November 21, 2019.

112. Li-Hui Chen, "Carrying Passengers as a Risk Factor for Crashes Fatal to 16- and 17-Year-Old Drivers," *Jama* 283, no. 12 (2000): 1578, doi:10.1001/jama.283.12. 1578; A. H. Goodwin, R. D. Foss, and Natalie P. O'Brien. *The Effect of Passengers on Teen Driver Behavior*, report (Washington, DC: National Highway Traffic Safety Administration, 2012); Marie Claude Ouimet et al., "Young Drivers and Their Passengers: A Systematic Review of Epidemiological Studies on Crash Risk," *Journal of Adolescent Health* 57, no. 1 (July 2015), doi:10.1016/j.jadohealth.2015.03.010; "Teen Drivers: Get the Facts," Centers for Disease Control and Prevention, October 30, 2019, www.cdc.gov/motorvehiclesafety/teen_drivers/teendrivers_factsheet.html; "Teen Driving," National Highway Traffic Safety Administration (NHTSA), accessed March 9, 2020, www.nhtsa.gov/road-safety/teen-driving; "The Effect of Passengers on Teen Driving Behavior," United States Department of Transportation: National Highway Traffic Safety Administration (April 2012), accessed March 8, 2020, www.nhtsa.gov/sites/nhtsa.dot.gov/files/811613.pdf.

113. Laurence Steinberg, telephone interview by author, November 21, 2019.

114. R. M. Gladden et al., *Bullying Surveillance Among Youths: Uniform Definitions for Public Health and Recommended Data Elements, Version 1.0*, issue brief (Atlanta: National Center for Injury Prevention and Control, Centers for Disease Control and Prevention, and US Department of Education, 2014).

115. Gladden et al., *Bullying Surveillance*; "Preventing Bullying," Centers for Disease Control and Prevention, accessed February 19, 2020, www.cdc.gov/violenceprevention/youthviolence/bullyingresearch/fastfact.html?CDC_AA_refVal=https%3A%2F%2Fwww.cdc.gov%2Fviolenceprevention%2Fyouthviolence%2Fbullyingresearch%2Findex.html.

116. "Preventing Bullying."

117. "What Is Bullying?," StopBullying.gov, accessed February 24, 2020, www.stopbullying.gov/bullying/what-is-bullying#types.

118. "Indicators of School Crime and Safety, Indicator 10: Bullying at School and Electronic Bullying," National Center for Education Statistics, April 2019, https://nces.ed.gov/programs/crimeindicators/ind_10.asp.

119. "Effects of Bullying," StopBullying.gov, accessed February 24, 2020, www.stopbullying.gov/bullying/effects.

120. "Effects of Bullying."

121. "Effects of Bullying."

122. "Effects of Bullying."

123. *The Relationship Between Bullying and Suicide: What We Know and What It Means for Schools*, report (Chamblee, GA: Centers for Disease Control and Prevention National Center for Injury Prevention and Control Division of Violence Prevention, 2014), accessed April 18, 2022, https://stacks.cdc.gov/view/cdc/34163.

124. *Relationship Between Bullying and Suicide.*

125. Luna Centifanti et al., "Types of Relational Aggression in Girls Are Differentiated by Callous-Unemotional Traits, Peers and Parental Overcontrol," *Behavioral Sciences* 5, no. 4 (2015): 518–36, doi:10.3390/bs5040518.

126. Centifanti et al., "Types of Relational Aggression."

127. "What Bullying Is and Is Not," Anti-Defamation League, accessed February 19, 2020, www.adl.org/education/resources/tools-and-strategies/table-talk/what-bul lying-is-and-is-not.

128. Jennifer Lansford, telephone interview by author, December 11, 2019.

129. "Facts About Bullying," StopBullying.gov, December 18, 2019, www.stopbullying .gov/resources/facts#stats. This article refers to Maria M. Ttofi and David P. Farrington, "Effectiveness of School-Based Programs to Reduce Bullying: A Systematic and Meta-Analytic Review," *Journal of Experimental Criminology* 7, no. 1 (2010): 27–56, doi:10.1007/s11292-010-9109-1.

130. Nicola A. Conners-Burrow et al., "Adults Matter: Protecting Children from the Negative Impacts of Bullying," *Psychology in the Schools* 46, no. 7 (July 2, 2009): 593–604, doi:10.1002/pits.20400.

131. "Stages of Adolescence," HealthyChildren.org, 2012, accessed December 1, 2018, www.healthychildren.org/English/ages-stages/teen/Pages/Stages-of -Adolescence.aspx.

132. Ann Meier and Gina Allen, "Romantic Relationships from Adolescence to Young Adulthood: Evidence from the National Longitudinal Study of Adolescent Health," *Sociological Quarterly* 50, no. 2 (2009): 308–35, doi:10.1111/j.1533-8525 .2009.01142.x.

133. Amanda Lenhart, Aaron Smith, and Monica Anderson, *Teens, Technology, and Romantic Relationships*, report. (Washington, DC: Pew Research Center, 2017).

134. D. Exner-Cortens, J. Eckenrode, and E. Rothman, "Longitudinal Associations Between Teen Dating Violence Victimization and Adverse Health Outcomes," *Pediatrics* 131, no. 1 (2012): 71–78, doi:10.1542/peds.2012-1029; Benjamin R. Karney et al., *Adolescent Romantic Relationships as Precursors to Healthy Adult Marriages*, report (Santa Monica, CA: RAND Corporation, 2007); Meier and Allen, "Romantic Relationships."

135. Amanda Lenhart, Aaron Smith, and Monica Anderson, *Teens, Technology, and Romantic Relationships*, report (Washington, DC: Pew Research Center, 2015).

136. Richard Weissbourd et al., *The Talk: How Adults Can Promote Young Peoples' Healthy Relationships and Prevent Misogyny and Sexual Harassment*, report (Cambridge, MA: Harvard Graduate School of Education, 2017).

137. "Characteristics of Healthy & Unhealthy Relationships," Youth.gov, accessed May 6, 2021, https://youth.gov/youth-topics/teen-dating-violence/characteristics.

138. "Characteristics of Healthy & Unhealthy Relationships"; "What Should I Look for in a Partner?," Loveisrespect.org, accessed April 18, 2022, www.loveisrespect. org/resources/dating-basics-what-should-i-look-for.

139. "Characteristics of Healthy & Unhealthy Relationships."

140. "Adolescent Sexual and Reproductive Health in the United States," Guttmacher Institute, September 2019, www.guttmacher.org/fact-sheet/american-teens-sex ual-and-reproductive-health.

141. Jochen Peter and Patti M. Valkenburg, "Adolescents and Pornography: A Review of 20 Years of Research, " *The Journal of Sex Research* 53, no. 4–5 (2016): 509–531, https://doi.org/10.1080/00224499.2016.1143441; Paul J. Wright, Bryant Paul, and Debby Herbenick, "Preliminary Insights from a U.S. Probability Sample on Adolescents' Pornography Exposure, Media Psychology, and Sexual Aggression," *Journal of Health Communication* 26, no. 1 (2021): 39–46, https://doi.org/10.1080/1 0810730.2021.1887980.

142. S. C. Martino et al., "Beyond the 'Big Talk': The Roles of Breadth and Repetition in Parent-Adolescent Communication About Sexual Topics," *Pediatrics* 121, no. 3 (2008), doi:10.1542/peds.2007-2156; Amanda Holman and Jody Koenig Kellas, "'Say Something Instead of Nothing': Adolescents' Perceptions of Memorable Conversations about Sex-Related Topics with Their Parents," *Communication Monographs* 85, no. 3 (January 2018): 357–79, doi:10.1080/03637751.2018.1426870.

143. Paul Henry Gebhard, "Human Sexual Activity," *Encyclopædia Britannica*, April 17, 2019, www.britannica.com/topic/human-sexual-activity.

144. Jeremy E. Uecker, Nicole Angotti, and Mark D. Regnerus, "Going Most of the Way: 'Technical Virginity' Among American Adolescents," *Social Science Research* 37, no. 4 (2008): 1200–215, doi:10.1016/j.ssresearch.2007.09.006.

145. Lyndsey S. Benson et al., "Perceptions of Anal Intercourse Among Heterosexual Women: A Pilot Qualitative Study," *Sexual Medicine* 7, no. 2 (March 2, 2019): 198–206, doi:10.1016/j.esxm.2018.12.003; Renee M. Gindi, Khalil G. Ghanem, and Emily J. Erbelding, "Increases in Oral and Anal Sexual Exposure Among Youth Attending Sexually Transmitted Diseases Clinics in Baltimore, Maryland," *Journal of Adolescent Health* 42, no. 3 (March 2008): 307–08, doi:10.1016 /j.jadohealth.2007.09.015; Melissa A. Habel et al., "Heterosexual Anal and Oral Sex in Adolescents and Adults in the United States, 2011–2015," *Sexually Transmitted Diseases* 45, no. 12 (December 2018): 775–82, doi:10.1097/olq.0000000000000889.

146. Ann M. Meier, "Adolescent First Sex and Subsequent Mental Health," *American Journal of Sociology* 112, no. 6 (May 2007): 1811–847, doi:10.1086/512708.

147. "Adolescent Sexual and Reproductive Health."

148. Dean M. Busby, Jason S. Carroll, and Brian J. Willoughby, "Compatibility or Restraint? The Effects of Sexual Timing on Marriage Relationships," *Journal of Family Psychology* 24, no. 6 (December 2010): 766–74, doi:10.1037/a0021690; "Couples Who Delay Having Sex Get Benefits Later, Study Suggests," *ScienceDaily*, December 29, 2010, www.sciencedaily.com/releases/2010/12/101222112102.htm.

149. "What Consent Looks Like," RAINN, accessed October 27, 2020, www.rainn .org/articles/what-is-consent.

150. "What Consent Looks Like"; Zhana Vrangalova, "Everything You Need to Know About Consent That You Never Learned in Sex Ed," *Teen Vogue*, April 18, 2016, www.teenvogue.com/story/consent-how-to.

151. Megan Price et al., "Young Love: Romantic Concerns and Associated Mental Health Issues among Adolescent Help-Seekers," *Behavioral Sciences* 6, no. 2 (June 2016): 9, doi:10.3390/bs6020009.

152. Tiffany Field, "Romantic Breakups, Heartbreak and Bereavement—Romantic Breakups," *Psychology* 2, no. 04 (2011): 382–87, doi:10.4236/psych.2011.24060;

S. M. Monroe et al., "Life Events and Depression in Adolescence: Relationship Loss as a Prospective Risk Factor for First Onset of Major Depressive Disorder," *Journal of Abnormal Psychology* 108, no. 4 (November 1999): 606–14, doi:10.1037// 0021-843x.108.4.606.

153. "Anguish of Romantic Rejection May Be Linked to Stimulation of Areas of Brain Related to Motivation, Reward and Addiction," *Stony Brook University News*, July 21, 2010, https://news.stonybrook.edu/news/general/072110RomanticRejection; Helen E. Fisher et al., "Reward, Addiction, and Emotion Regulation Systems Associated with Rejection in Love," *Journal of Neurophysiology* 104, no. 1 (July 1, 2010): 51–60, doi:10.1152/jn.00784.2009.

154. D. Hollander, "Reconciliation After Breakup Is Common in Emerging Adulthood," *Perspectives on Sexual and Reproductive Health* 45, no. 2 (2013): 110, doi:10.1363 /4511013_1.

155. Charlene F. Belu, Brenda H. Lee, and Lucia F. O'Sullivan, "It Hurts to Let You Go: Characteristics of Romantic Relationships, Breakups and the Aftermath Among Emerging Adults," *Journal of Relationships Research* 7 (2016): article e11, doi:10.1017/jrr.2016.11.

156. Sarah Halpern-Meekin et al., "Relationship Churning, Physical Violence, and Verbal Abuse in Young Adult Relationships," *Journal of Marriage and Family* 75, no. 1 (2013): 2–12, doi:10.1111/j.1741-3737.2012.01029.x; Hollander, "Reconciliation After Breakup."

157. "Breakups Aren't All Bad: Coping Strategies to Promote Positive Outcomes," American Psychological Association. Accessed February 29, 2020, www.apa.org /research/action/romantic-relationships; Gary W. Lewandowski, "Promoting Positive Emotions Following Relationship Dissolution through Writing," *Journal of Positive Psychology* 4, no. 1 (January 28, 2009): 21–31, doi:10.1080/174397608020 68480.

158. "Definition of Sexual Misconduct," Davidson College, accessed April 18, 2022, www.davidson.edu/offices-and-services/dean-students/sexual-misconduct.

159. "FAQ: Understanding Sexual Violence and Sexual Assault," University of California, accessed May 6, 2020, https://sexualviolence.universityofcalifornia.edu /faq; "Sexual Harassment," RAINN, accessed February 26, 2020, www.rainn. org/articles/sexual-harassment; "Sexual Assault," Merriam-Webster.com, accessed February 26, 2020, www.merriam-webster.com/dictionary/sexual% 20assault; "Sexual Violence," Centers for Disease Control and Prevention, accessed February 26, 2020, www.cdc.gov/violenceprevention/sexualviolence/index .html.

160. "Intimate Partner Violence," Centers for Disease Control and Prevention, accessed February 26, 2020, www.cdc.gov/violenceprevention/intimatepartnervio lence/index.html.

161. "Sexual Consent," Planned Parenthood, accessed February 26, 2020, www .plannedparenthood.org/learn/relationships/sexual-consent.

162. "How to Avoid Victim Blaming," Harvard Law School HALT (Harassment Assault Law-Student Team), accessed February 26, 2020, https://orgs.law.har vard.edu/halt/how-to-avoid-victim-blaming.

163. "Facts About Sexual Harassment," US Equal Employment Opportunity Commission, January 15, 1997, www.eeoc.gov/fact-sheet/facts-about-sexual-harassment.

164. "Sexual Harassment," RAINN.

165. "Preventing Sexual Violence," Centers for Disease Control and Prevention, accessed February 26, 2020, www.cdc.gov/violenceprevention/sexualviolence/fast fact.html.

166. "Preventing Sexual Violence."

167. *Findings from the National Intimate Partner and Sexual Violence Survey 2010–2012 State Report* (Atlanta: National Center for Injury Prevention and Control Division of Violence Prevention, 2017).

168. *Findings from the National Intimate Partner and Sexual Violence Survey.*

169. "Preventing Sexual Violence," Centers for Disease Control and Prevention.

170. C. Krebs et al., *Campus Climate Survey Validation Study Final Technical Report,* report (Washington, DC: Bureau of Justice Statistics, 2016); "Sexual Assault on College Campuses Is Common," WomensHealth.gov, accessed February 27, 2020, www .womenshealth.gov/relationships-and-safety/sexual-assault-and-rape/college -sexual-assault#8.

171. David Cantor et al., *Report on the AAU Campus Climate Survey on Sexual Assault and Misconduct,* report (Washington, DC: Association of American Universities, 2020).

172. Sofi Sinozich and Lynn Langton. *Rape and Sexual Assault Victimization Among College-Age Females, 1995–2013,* report (Washington, DC,: US Department of Justice Office of Justice Programs Bureau of Justice Statistics, 2014).

173. *Why Don't They Tell? Teens and Sexual Assault Disclosure* (Los Angeles and Durham, NC: National Child Traumatic Stress Network, 2018).

174. "Reporting to Law Enforcement," RAINN, accessed February 27, 2020, www .rainn.org/articles/reporting-law-enforcement.

175. "Warning Signs for Teens," RAINN, accessed February 27, 2020, www.rainn .org/articles/warning-signs-teens.

176. "Reporting to Law Enforcement"; "Tips for Talking with Survivors of Sexual Assault," RAINN, accessed July 3, 2020, www.rainn.org/articles/tips-talking -survivors-sexual-assault.

177. "1.7.2 Consensual Sexual or Romantic Relationships In the Workplace and Educational Setting," Stanford University Administrative Guide, accessed October 27, 2020, https://adminguide.stanford.edu/chapter-1/subchapter-7/policy-1-7-2; "Definition of Sexual Misconduct," Davidson College; "Sexual Harassment," RAINN.

178. "Staying Safe on Campus," RAINN, accessed February 27, 2020, www.rainn.org /articles/staying-safe-campus.

179. "Staying Safe on Campus."

180. "How to Deal with Sexual Abuse," Crisis Text Line, accessed February 27, 2020, www.crisistextline.org/sexualabuse; "Steps You Can Take After Sexual Assault," RAINN, accessed February 27, 2020, www.rainn.org/articles/steps-you-can -take-after-sexual-assault.

181. "What Is a Sexual Assault Forensic Exam?," RAINN, accessed July 4, 2020, www .rainn.org/articles/rape-kit.

182. "Decades of Scientific Research That Started a Growth Mindset Revolution," MindsetWorks, accessed March 19, 2020, www.mindsetworks.com/science; Carol

S. Dweck, *Mindset: The New Psychology of Success* (New York: Ballantine Books, 2007), 7; "How Parents Can Instill a Growth Mindset at Home," MindsetWorks, accessed March 21, 2020, www.mindsetworks.com/parents/growth-mindset-parenting.

183. Rae Jacobson and Child Mind Institute, "Tips for Recognizing Learning Disorders in the Classroom," Child Mind Institute, accessed March 21, 2020, https://childmind.org/article/recognizing-learning-disorders-in-the-classroom.

184. Drew DeSilver, "A Majority of U.S. Colleges Admit Most Students Who Apply," Pew Research Center, April 9, 2019, www.pewresearch.org/fact-tank/2019/04/09/a-majority-of-u-s-colleges-admit-most-students-who-apply.

185. Elizabeth E. Lloyd-Richardson et al., "A Prospective Study of Weight Gain during the College Freshman and Sophomore Years," *Preventive Medicine* 48, no. 3 (2009): 256–61, doi:10.1016/j.ypmed.2008.12.009; Quentin Regestein et al., "Sleep Debt and Depression in Female College Students," *Psychiatry Research* 176, no. 1 (2010): 34–39, doi:10.1016/j.psychres.2008.11.006.

186. "Affordability," Harvard University, accessed May 3, 2021, https://college.harvard.edu/admissions/why-harvard/affordability.

187. Elaine Casap, telephone interview by author, June 26, 2020; Jaime Casap, telephone interview by author, June 25, 2020.

188. Mitra Toossi and Teresa L. Morisi, *Women in the Workforce Before, During, and After the Great Recession* (Washington, DC: Bureau of Labor Statistics, July 2017), www.bls.gov/spotlight/2017/women-in-the-workforce-before-during-and-after-the-great-recession/pdf/women-in-the-workforce-before-during-and-after-the-great-recession.pdf.

189. Benjamin Artz, Amanda H. Goodall, and Andrew J. Oswald, "Do Women Ask?," *Industrial Relations: A Journal of Economy and Society* 57, no. 4 (May 9, 2018): 611–36, doi:10.1111/irel.12214; Benjamin Artz, Amanda Goodall, and Andrew J. Oswald, "Research: Women Ask for Raises as Often as Men, but Are Less Likely to Get Them," *Harvard Business Review*, June 25, 2018, https://hbr.org/2018/06/research-women-ask-for-raises-as-often-as-men-but-are-less-likely-to-get-them#:~:text=The%20bottom%20line%20of%20our,don't%20"get."&text=Instead%2C%20we%20found%20that%20although,true%20of%20men%20and%20women; "Gender Wage Gap," OECD iLibrary, accessed June 23, 2020, www.oecd-ilibrary.org/employment/gender-wage-gap/indicator/english_7cee77aa-en; Nikki Graf, Anna Brown, and Eileen Patten, "The Narrowing, but Persistent, Gender Gap in Pay," Pew Research Center, March 22, 2019, www.pewresearch.org/fact-tank/2019/03/22/gender-pay-gap-facts; Tessa Holtzman, Ariane Hegewisch, and Cynthia Hess, "The Gender Wage Gap: 2018 Earnings Differences by Race and Ethnicity," Institute for Women's Policy Research, June 1, 2019, accessed June 22, 2020, https://iwpr.org/iwpr-general/the-gender-wage-gap-2018-earnings-differences-by-race-and-ethnicity; Labor Force Statistics from the Current Population Survey: Earnings," US Bureau of Labor Statistics, November 22, 2019, accessed June 22, 2020, www.bls.gov/cps/earnings.htm; "The Global Gender Gap Report 2018," World Economic Forum, December 17, 2018, https://www.weforum.org/reports/the-global-gender-gap-report-2018.

190. "Equal Pay Day: March 24, 2021," United States Census Bureau, March 24, 2021, accessed May 6, 2021, www.census.gov/newsroom/stories/equal-pay-day.html;

Courtney Connley, "Reminder: Today Isn't Equal Pay Day for All Women," CNBC, April 2, 2019, www.cnbc.com/2018/04/10/today-isnt-equal-pay-day-for-black-latina-or-native-american-women.html; "Women's Equal Pay Day," Equal Pay Today!, accessed May 2, 2021, www.equalpaytoday.org/equal-pay-day-2021.

191. Claire Cain Miller, Kevin Quealy, and Margot Sanger-Katz, "The Top Jobs Where Women Are Outnumbered by Men Named John," *New York Times*, April 24, 2018, www.nytimes.com/interactive/2018/04/24/upshot/women-and-men-named-john.html.

192. Shelley J. Correll, Stephen Benard, and In Paik, "Getting a Job: Is There a Motherhood Penalty?," *American Journal of Sociology* 112, no. 5 (2007): 1297–1339, doi:10.1086/511799; Graf et al., "Narrowing, but Persistent"; Julie Linn Teigland, "How Can More Women Become Architects of the Transformative Age?," EY, March 13, 2019, www.ey.com/en_gl/women-fast-forward/how-can-more-women-become-architects-of-the-transformative-age.

193. Marc J. Lerchenmueller, Olav Sorenson, and Anupam B Jena, "Gender Differences in How Scientists Present the Importance of Their Research: Observational Study," *BMJ* 367, no. I6573 (December 16, 2019), doi:10.1136/bmj.l6573; Marc J. Lerchenmueller, Olav Sorenson, and Anupam B. Jena, "Research: How Women Undersell Their Work," *Harvard Business Review*, December 20, 2019, https://hbr.org/2019/12/research-how-women-undersell-their-work; Tara Sophia Mohr, "Why Women Don't Apply for Jobs Unless They're 100% Qualified," *Harvard Business Review*, August 25, 2014, https://hbr.org/2014/08/why-women-dont-apply-for-jobs-unless-theyre-100-qualified.

194. Jaime Casap, telephone interview by author, August 11, 2017; Jaime Casap, telephone interview by author, June 25, 2020.

195. Hannah Riley Bowles, "Why Women Don't Negotiate Their Job Offers," *Harvard Business Review*, June 19, 2014, https://hbr.org/2014/06/why-women-dont-negotiate-their-job-offers; Olga Khazan, "Women Know When Negotiating Isn't Worth It," *Atlantic*, January 6, 2017, www.theatlantic.com/business/archive/2017/01/women-negotiating/512174.

196. Karina Schumann and Michael Ross, "Why Women Apologize More Than Men," *Psychological Science* 21, no. 11 (2010): 1649–655, doi:10.1177/0956797610384150.

197. Teigland, "How Can More Women Become Architects?"

198. "Breadwinner Moms," Pew Research Center's Social & Demographic Trends, May 29, 2013, www.pewsocialtrends.org/2013/05/29/breadwinner-moms; Anna Zakrzewski et al., *Managing the Next Decade of Women's Wealth*, report, accessed April 9, 2020, www.bcg.com/publications/2020/managing-next-decade-women-wealth.

199. Zakrzewski et al., *Managing the Next Decade*.

200. Pooneh Baghai et al., "Women As the Next Wave of Growth in US Wealth Management," McKinsey & Company, July 29, 2020, www.mckinsey.com/industries/financial-services/our-insights/women-as-the-next-wave-of-growth-in-us-wealth-management.

201. American Association of University Women (AAUW), "Women's Student Debt Crisis in the United States," AAUW, accessed February 9, 2020, www.aauw.org

/research/deeper-in-debt; Catherine Clifford, "Global Wealth Inequality Is 'Founded on Sexism,' Says Oxfam International," CNBC, January 19, 2020, www.cnbc.com/2020/01/17/global-wealth-inequality-is-founded-on-sexism-oxfam-international.html; Clare Coffey et al., *Time to Care: Unpaid and Underpaid Care Work and the Global Inequality Crisis*, report (Oxford, UK: Oxfam, 2020); "World's Billionaires Have More Wealth than 4.6 Billion People," Oxfam International, January 20, 2020, www.oxfam.org/en/press-releases/worlds-billionaires-have-more-wealth-46-billion-people.

202. Clifford, "Global Wealth Inequality"; Coffey et al., *Time to Care*; "World's Billionaires," Oxfam International.

203. Kim Parker, Juliana Menasce Horowitz, and Renee Stepler, "2. Americans See Different Expectations for Men and Women," Pew Research Center's Social & Demographic Trends, December 5, 2017, www.pewsocialtrends.org/2017/12/05/americans-see-different-expectations-for-men-and-women.

204. Carey Shuffman, telephone interview by author, March 11, 2020; Ashley B. Lebaron et al., "Can We Talk About Money? Financial Socialization Through Parent–Child Financial Discussion," *Emerging Adulthood* 8, no. 6 (February 2020):453–463, doi:10.1177/2167696820902673; "T. Rowe Price: Parents Are Likely to Pass Down Good and Bad Financial Habits to Their Kids," T. Rowe Price Investment Management, March 23, 2017, www.troweprice.com/corporate/us/en/press/t--rowe-price--parents-are-likely-to-pass-down-good-and-bad-fina0.html.

205. Martha C. White, "How Parents Fail Girls When They Talk About Money," *Time*, May 7, 2014, https://time.com/89657/girls-spending; Lynsey K. Romo and Anita L. Vangelisti, "Money Matters: Children's Perceptions of Parent-Child Financial Disclosure," *Communication Research Reports* 31, no. 2 (April–June 2014): 197–209, doi:10.1080/08824096.2014.907147; "T. Rowe Price."

206. "Women's Financial Security," Stanford Center on Longevity, accessed June 30, 2020, http://longevity.stanford.edu/spotlight-on-womens-financial-security.

207. UBS, *Own Your Worth: How Women Can Break the Cycle of Abdication and Take Control of Their Wealth* (2018), www.ubs.com/content/dam/WealthManagementAmericas/documents/2018-37666-UBS-Own-Your-Worth-report-R32.pdf; Lananh Nguyen and Michelle Kim, "Millennial Women Are Letting Men Take Care of the Money," *Bloomberg*, March 5, 2019, www.bloomberg.com/news/articles/2019-03-06/millennial-women-are-feminists-except-when-it-comes-to-money; Shuffman, telephone interview; UBS, *Own Your Worth*.

208. Alicia Adamczyk, "Gen Z Prioritizes Making Money and Having a Successful Career," CNBC, July 18, 2019, www.cnbc.com/2019/07/18/gen-z-prioritizes-making-money-and-having-a-successful-career.html.

209. Shuffman, telephone interview.

210. Uptin Saiidi, "Millennials Are Prioritizing 'Experiences' Over Stuff," CNBC, May 5, 2016, www.cnbc.com/2016/05/05/millennials-are-prioritizing-experiences-over-stuff.html.

211. Jennifer L. Aaker, Melanie Rudd, and Cassie Mogilner, "If Money Does Not Make You Happy, Consider Time," *Journal of Consumer Psychology* 21, no. 2 (April 2011): 126–30, doi:10.1016/j.jcps.2011.01.004; Ashley V. Whillans et al., "Buying

Time Promotes Happiness," *Proceedings of the National Academy of Sciences* 114, no. 32 (June 13, 2017): 8523–527, doi:10.1073/pnas.1706541114.

212. "Happy Couples: How to Avoid Money Arguments," American Psychological Association, 2015, www.apa.org/topics/money-conflict; Kelley Holland, "Fighting with Your Spouse? It's Probably About This," CNBC, February 4, 2015, www .cnbc.com/2015/02/04/money-is-the-leading-cause-of-stress-in-relationships .html; *Stress in America: Paying with Our Health*, report (Washington, DC: American Psychological Association, 2015).

213. Soyoung Q. Park et al., "A Neural Link between Generosity and Happiness," *Natural Communications* 8 (2017): 15964, doi:10.1038/ncomms15964; Lalin Anik et al., "Feeling Good about Giving: The Benefits (and Costs) of Self-Interested Charitable Behavior," Harvard Business School Working Paper 10-012, 2009, www .hbs.edu/faculty/Publication%20Files/10-012_0350a55d-585b-419d-89e7 -91833a612fb5.pdf.

214. Maya Salam, "Money Is Not Just for Men," *New York Times*, June 14, 2019, www.nytimes.com/2019/06/14/business/sallie-krawcheck-gender-gaps.html; "T. Rowe Price."

215. Carey Shuffman, telephone interview.

216. Beth Braverman, "Men Spend More on Impulse Buys than Women. Here Are 6 Ways to Break the Habit," CNBC, July 1, 2019, www.cnbc.com/2019/06/28/men -spend-more-on-impulse-buys-than-women-how-to-break-the-habit.html; Laura Wronski, "CNBC | SurveyMonkey Poll: 'Invest in You' July 2019," SurveyMonkey, July 2019, www.surveymonkey.com/curiosity/cnbc-invest-in-you-july-2019.

217. Tammy Tibbetts, telephone interview by author, February 6, 2020.

218. "What Is Global Citizenship?," Oxfam GB, accessed February 15, 2020, www .oxfam.org.uk/education/who-we-are/what-is-global-citizenship.

219. Kim Parker and Ruth Igielnik. "On the Cusp of Adulthood and Facing an Uncertain Future: What We Know About Gen Z So Far," Pew Research Center's Social & Demographic Trends, May 14, 2020, www.pewsocialtrends.org/essay/on-the -cusp-of-adulthood-and-facing-an-uncertain-future-what-we-know-about -gen-z-so-far.

220. "Racial and Social Justice: Introduction," National Education Association, accessed May 6, 2021, www.nea.org/advocating-for-change/racial-social-justice.

5. FAQs

1. Leanne Lester et al., "The Association of Fly-in Fly-out Employment, Family Connectedness, Parental Presence and Adolescent Well-being," *Journal of Child and Family Studies* 25, no. 12 (2016): 3619–626, doi:10.1007/s10826-016-0512-8.

2. Elizabeth C. Hair et al., "Parent Marital Quality and the Parent–Adolescent Relationship: Effects on Adolescent and Young Adult Health Outcomes," *Marriage & Family Review* 45, no. 2–3 (2009): 218–48, doi:10.1080/01494920902733567.

6. You've Got This

1. Albert Bandura, *Social Learning Theory* (Englewood Cliffs, NJ: Prentice-Hall, 1977); Erik H. Erikson, *Identity and the Life Cycle* (New York: W. W. Norton, 1994); Jutta

Heckhausen, Carsten Wrosch, and Richard Schulz, "A Motivational Theory of Life-Span Development," *Psychological Review* 117, no. 1 (January 2010): 32–60, doi:10.1037/a0017668.

2. Richard W. Robins and Kali H. Trzesniewski, "Self-Esteem Development Across the Lifespan," *Current Directions in Psychological Science* 14, no. 3 (2005): 158–62, doi:10.1111/j.0963-7214.2005.00353.x.

3. William S. Aquilino, "From Adolescent to Young Adult: A Prospective Study of Parent–Child Relations during the Transition to Adulthood," *Journal of Marriage and the Family* 59, no. 3 (1997): 670, doi:10.2307/353953; William S. Aquilino, "The Noncustodial Father? Child Relationship from Adolescence into Young Adulthood," *Journal of Marriage and Family* 68, no. 4 (2006): 929–46, doi:10.1111/j.1741-3737.2006.00305.x.

4. Shawn D. Whiteman, Susan M. McHale, and Ann C. Crouter, "Family Relationships from Adolescence to Early Adulthood: Changes in the Family System Following Firstborns' Leaving Home," *Journal of Research on Adolescence* 21, no. 2 (2010): 461–74, doi:10.1111/j.1532-7795.2010.00683.x.

READING AND RESOURCES

General Girls Health and Wellness

Center for Young Women's Health (from Boston Children's Hospital)—
youngwomenshealth.org
HealthyChildren.org (from the American Academy of Pediatrics)—
healthychildren.org
Mayo Clinic—mayoclinic.org

Gender and Sexual Identity

Human Rights Watch—hrc.org
PFLAG—pflag.org
The Trevor Project—thetrevorproject.org

Mental Health

Anxiety & Depression Association of America (ADAA)—adaa.org
Child Mind Institute—childmind.org
Crisis Text Line—crisistextline.org or text HOME to 741741
National Alliance on Mental Illness (NAMI)—nami.org
National Eating Disorders Association (NEDA)—neda.org
National Suicide Prevention Lifeline—800-273-8255

Substance Use

Partnership for Drug Free Kids—drugfree.org

Substance Abuse and Mental Health Services Administration (SAMHSA)—www.samhsa.gov

Social or Academic Support

The Child Mind Institute—childmind.org
Learning Disabilities Association of America—ldaamerica.org
StopBullying.gov—stopbullying.gov

Technology and Social Media

Common Sense Media—commonsense.org

Love and Sexual Health

SexEtc.org (from Rutgers University)—sexetc.org
Go Ask Alice (from Columbia University)—goaskalice.org
Scarleteen—scarleteen.com

Sexual Misconduct

Rape, Abuse & Incest National Network (RAINN)—rainn.org or call 800.656.HOPE

College Admissions

Kahn Academy College Admissions—khanacademy.org

Financial Literacy

FDIC Money Smart for Young People—FDIC.gov

Global Citizenship

DoSomething—DoSomething.org
Teaching Tolerance—tolerance.org

INDEX